HELPLESSNESS

A series of books in psychology

Editors:

Richard C. Atkinson
Gardner Lindzey
Richard F. Thompson

HELPLESSNESS

ON DEPRESSION, DEVELOPMENT, AND DEATH

with a new introduction by the author

MARTIN E. P. SELIGMAN
University of Pennsylvania

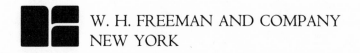

W. H. FREEMAN AND COMPANY
NEW YORK

Library of Congress Cataloging in Publication Data
Seligman, Martin E   P
    Helplessness.

    Bibliography: p.
    Includes indexes.
    1. Helplessness (Psychology) 2. Depression,
Mental. I. Title.
BF575.H4S44   616.8'528   74-23125
ISBN 0-7167-0752-7
ISBN 0-7167-2328-X

Printed in the United States of America

Excerpt from "When the Watchman Saw the Light," p. 96, translated
by Edmund Keeley and George Savidis in *C. P. Cavafy, Passions and
Ancient Days.* Copyright 1971 by the Dial Press.

Excerpt from "Do Not Go Gentle into That Good Night," p. 188, copyright
1952 by Dylan Thomas. Reprinted by permission of New Directions
Publishing Corporation and J. M. Dent & Sons Ltd.

1 2 3 4 5 6 7 8 9 0   VB   9 9 8 7 6 5 4 3 2

Dedicated to my father, Adrian Seligman (1906–1972), who knew well the struggle against helplessness.

CONTENTS

PREFACE

People become involved in psychology for various reasons. Some people are fascinated by the elegance of a simple system, some by the habits of a particular species, and some by the awesome possibility of controlling what other men shall do. I have made psychology my life's work in order to better understand one species—man.

This is an unfashionable thing for a learning theorist and comparative psychologist to admit; nevertheless it is true. Although I have spent much of my time working with species other than man and thinking about simple processes, I am also a clinical psychologist who has observed other human beings and interacted with them, both in experimental and in therapeutic settings. These two faces of my work—the experimental and the clinical—are intimately related, for I believe that an understanding of other species and of simple processes is relevant to the understanding of complex processes in man. More than relevant—essential. That is one way of saying what this book is about. It is an attempt to analyze human helplessness, in its many aspects, by applying theory and relevant knowledge from the laboratory.

For seventy-five years experimental psychologists, from the isolation of their laboratories, have written many promissory notes. These promissory notes claimed that an understanding of simple processes, lower species, and highly controlled experimental situations would shed light on real problems, in particular, human psychopathology. What follows is my attempt to begin to pay off what is owed.

Since much of the subject matter of this book derives from experimentation, I must say a few words about ethics. Many of the experiments I shall describe may seem cruel, particularly to the non-scientist: pigeons are deprived of food, dogs are shocked, rats are plunged into cold water, infant monkeys are deprived of their mothers, and all experimental animals are deprived of their freedom by confinement to cages. Are such manipulations ethically justifiable? To my mind they are by and large not only justifiable, but, for scientists whose basic commitment is to the alleviation of human misery, not to do them would be unjustifiable. In my opinion, each scientist must ask himself one question before doing any experiment on an animal: is it likely that the pain and deprivation that this animal is about to endure will be greatly outweighed by the resulting alleviation of human pain and deprivation? If the answer is yes, the experiment is justified.

Anyone who has spent time with severely depressed patients or with schizophrenic adults can appreciate the degree of their misery; to argue, as some do, that people should not do experiments on animals, is to ignore the misery of their fellow human beings. Not to do such research is to consign millions of humans to continued misery. Most human beings, as well as household pets, are alive today because animal experiments with medical ends were carried out; without such studies, polio would still be rampant, smallpox widespread and almost always fatal, and phobias incurable. As for the studies discussed in this book, I believe that what we have learned about depression, anxiety, sudden death, and their cure and prevention justifies the animal experiments that have led us to these insights.

This book has been ten years in the making. A large number of people have contributed to it by collaborating with me in experiments, by brainstorming sessions, by teaching and advice, and by general sustenance. The easiest way to thank them is in chronological order.

From 1964 to 1967 I was a National Science Foundation graduate fellow in the Department of Psychology at the University of Pennsylvania. Richard L. Solomon and J. Bruce Overmier first interested me in the phenomenon of helplessness; Bruce collaborated with Russell Leaf on the first experiments and worked with me in my first year, and his last, of graduate school. During that year Steven F. Maier and I began three years of working together on helplessness; we performed our first studies that were self-consciously about helplessness and formulated the rudiments of the theory presented in this book. James Geer collaborated with Steve and me on therapy for helplessness. During those three years so many people taught us, read our manuscripts, and gave us advice that I fear I have forgotten some. Among them were Francis Irwin, Robert Rescorla, J. Brooks Carder, Henry Gleitman, Vincent LoLordo, Frank Norman, Joseph Wolpe, Arnold Lazarus, Jack Catlin, Lynn Hammond, David Williams, Morris Viteles, Nicholas MacKintosh, Elijah Lovejoy, Phillip Teitelbaum, Larry Stein, J. Paul Brady, Julius Wishner, Martin Orne, Peter Madison, Joseph Bernheim, Lucy Turner, Jay Weiss, Vivian Paskal, Paul Rozin, Justin Aronfreed, Albert Pepitone, and, above all, Richard Solomon, who sponsored my candidacy for the Ph.D.

From 1967 to 1969 I taught at Cornell University and continued experiments on helplessness. During that period students were my main source of collaboration and intellectual stimulation; among them were Robert Radford, Dennis Groves, Suzanne Johnson Taffel, Bruce Taffel, James C. Johnston, Susan Mineka, Charles Ives, Dorothy Brown, Irving Faust, Leslie Schneider, Anne Roebuck, Bruce Meyer, Joanne Hager, Chris Risley, Charles Thomas, Marjorie Brandriss, Ron Hermann, Richard Rosinski, and Martha Zaslow. Others who brainstormed, gave advice, or read manuscripts were Steve Jones, Ulric Neisser, Harry Levin, Fred Stollnitz, Bruce Halpern, Carl Sagan, Steve Emlen, Randy Gallistel, Jerome Bruner, David Thomas, Henry Alker, Abe Black, F. Robert Brush, Russel Church, Byron Campbell, Eric Lenneberg, and Neal Miller. Many of the ideas in this book had their beginning in conversations with these people or in work done with them. Until 1970, my studies were supported by grant MH 16546 from the Public Health Service.

My students persuaded me that our experiments were highly relevant to clinical problems, particularly depression and anxiety, and urged that I learn something firsthand about patients and psychopathology. Consequently, in 1970 I took a leave of absence from Cornell to work at the Department of Psychiatry at the University of Pennsylvania. Aaron T. Beck and Albert J. Stunkard were my main sponsors, as well as being teachers and sources of stimulation. I learned a great deal about psychopathology that year; it was then that I actually began to write this book. Among my teachers and advice-givers were Dean Schuyler, James Stinnet, Igor Grant,

Ellen Berman, J. Paul Brady, Burton Rosner, Reuben Krone, Joseph Mendels, Alan Fraser, Lester Luborsky, Tom Todd, Henry Bachrach, Rochel Gelman, Peter Brill, and Stephanie and Jim Cavanaugh. Since 1970, my research has been supported by grant MH 19604 from the Public Health Service. I am also grateful for the financial support of Louise Harper in 1970–1971.

In 1971 I happily rejoined the Department of Psychology at the University of Pennsylvania on a permanent basis. Intellectual stimulation is so continual here that there is virtually no member of the department from whom I haven't benefited. My students and collaborators during the last four years have been a blessing: William Miller, Yitzchak Binik, David Klein, Donald Hiroto, Robert Rosellini, Lyn Abramson, Linda Cook, Gwynneth Beagley, Robert Hannum, Peter Rapaport, James C. Johnston, Susan Mineka, Lisa Rosenthal, Michael Gurtman, Larry Clayton, Diana Strange, Michael Kozak, Harold Kurlander, Ellen Fencil, Martha Stout, and Sherry Fine.

Others who gave useful advice and help in the formulation of ideas for this book are Alan Kors, Judy Rodin, Jerre Levy, T. George Harris, Joyce Fleming, Ed Banfield, Robert Nozick, Mark Adams, Gerald Davison, Maj. F. Harold Kushner, Barry Schwartz, Elkan Gamzu, Michael Parrish, Kayla Friedman, Kate O'Hare, Janet Greenberg, David Rosenhan, Mike D'Amato, Perrin Cohen, Alan Teger, and Debby Kemler.

W. Hayward Rogers, of W. H. Freeman and Company, and Lawrence Erlbaum, of Lawrence Erlbaum Associates, are the men in the publishing profession who encouraged me to write the manuscript in its present form. I received very useful comments on the entire manuscript from Barry Schwartz, Phil Zimbardo, Jonathan Freedman, and Edward Banfield; I am most grateful to them. I owe special thanks to Andrew Kudlacik of W. H. Freeman and Company, who edited the manuscript. Over the last few years patient and careful secretarial work on the book has been carried out by Victoria Raybourne, Dorothy Lynn, Marguerite Wagner, Nancy Sawnhey, Lynn Brehm, Carolyn Suplee, and Deborah Muller.

One person—my wife, Kerry—has read every word of this book several times and rewritten many of them. Her support, inspiration, and trust over the decade in which this book was written are more deeply appreciated than I can say. The love provided by my mother, Irene, and my children, Amy and David, while sometimes distracting, made the whole process much sweeter.

August 1974   Martin E. P. Seligman

INTRODUCTION*

Learned helplessness refers to three interlocked things: First, an environment in which some important outcome is beyond control; second, the response of giving up; and third, the accompanying cognition: the expectation that no voluntary action can control the outcome. This volume explores the original experiments—in animals and people—which discovered learned helplessness. It presents the theory of helplessness and then four applications of helplessness: to human depression, to anxiety, to child development, and to sudden death. It suggests how helplessness might be overcome.

*Much of the material in this introduction is taken from, and expanded upon, in my recent book *Learned Optimism* (Knopf, 1991, with permission).

When *Helplessness: On Depression, Development, and Death* was first published, I thought it was an end, or at least a resting point. I was wrong. It was a beginning. In the seventeen years since its publication, the volume of work in the field of personal control has increased tenfold. In this new introduction to the book, I want to lay out the major new findings that stand out in my mind.

First I will present an overview of fashions in social science to set *Helplessness* in context. Then I will discuss an important change in the theory of helplessness, which I call the "reformulation" that we constructed three years after the book's publication to take into account criticisms of the initial theory. Then I will summarize the new work on helplessness and "explanatory style" in three domains: depression, achievement, and physical health. Finally, I will speculate about what the coming seventeen years might hold for the psychology of personal control.

FASHIONS IN SOCIAL SCIENCE

There has been a sea change in recent decades in what counts as a respectable explanation of human action. When I was a graduate student in psychology, twenty-five years ago, human action was explained as a product of the environment. The prevailing explanation of human action was that people were "pushed" by their internal drives or "pulled" by external events. Though the details of the pushing and pulling depended on the particular theory you happened to hold, in outline all the fashionable theories agreed on this proposition. The Freudians held that unresolved childhood conflicts drove adult behavior. The followers of B. F. Skinner held that behavior was repeated only when it was reinforced externally. The ethologists held that behavior resulted from fixed action patterns determined by our genes, and the behaviorist follow-ers of Clark Hull held that we were goaded into action by the need to reduce drives and satisfy biological needs.

Starting about 1965, the favored explanation began to change. The environment became less and less important as a cause. Four different lines of thought converged on the propo-sition that self-direction, rather than outside forces, were primary in explaining human action.

- In 1959 Noam Chomsky wrote his devastating critique of B. F. Skinner's seminal book *Verbal Behavior.* Chomsky argued that language specifically, and human action generally, was not the result of strengthening past verbal habits by reinforcement. The essence of language, he said, is that it is generative: Sentences never spoken or heard before (such as, "There's a purple gila monster sitting on your lap") could nevertheless be understood immediately.[1]

- Jean Piaget, the great Swiss investigator of how children de-velop, had persuaded most of the world—the Americans last—that the developing mind of the individual child could be studied scientifically.

- By 1967 the field of cognitive psychology, led by Ulric Neisser and George Miller, had begun to capture the imagination of the young experimental psychologists fleeing the dogmas of behaviorism. Cognitive psychologists argued that the workings of the human mind could be measured and their consequences studied by using the information-processing activities of com-puters as a model.

- Behavioral psychologists found that animal and human behav-ior was inadequately explained by drives and needs and began to invoke the cognitions—the thoughts—of the individual to explain complex behavior. The first edition of *Helplessness* em-bodied and summarized this trend.

So by the late 1970's the dominant theories in psychology had shifted focus from the power of the environment to individual expectation, preference, choice, control, and helplessness.

This fundamental change in the field of psychology is intimately related to a fundamental change that has taken place in our own psychology. The development of technology, mass production, and mass distribution has enabled large numbers of people to have a significant measure of choice, and therefore of personal control, over their lives. Not the least of these choices concerns our own habits of thinking. By and large, people have welcomed that control. We belong to a society that grants to its members powers that the individual has never had before, a society that takes the pleasures and pains of the individual very seriously. It is a society that exalts the self and deems the personal fulfillment of its individual members a legitimate goal, an almost sacred right.

The most important change in the theory of helplessness moves the self, and its explanations for the bad and good events that befall it, to center stage.

EXPLANATORY STYLE

When is learned helplessness momentary and when is it life-long? When is helplessness global, subverting all one's endeavors, and when is it local? When do we blame ourselves for our helplessness and when do we blame the world?

Such questions nagged me and my colleagues twenty years ago. In 1978 the *Journal of Abnormal Psychology* devoted an entire issue to the controversies generated by the ideas set forth in *Helplessness*. The attempts to answer them generated significant change in the theory of helplessness, which we dubbed the "reformulation".[2,5]

How do you think about the causes of the tragedies, small and large, that befall you? Some people, the ones who give up so easily, habitually say of their tragedies, "It's my fault, it's going to last forever, it's going to undermine everything I do." Others, those who resist giving in to tragedy, say, "It was caused by circumstances, it will fade quickly anyway, and besides, there's much more to life."

Your way of explaining good and bad events, your "explanatory style," is more than just the words you mouth when you succeed or fail. It is a habit, learned in childhood and adolescence. Your explanatory style stems directly from your view of your place in the world—whether you think you are valuable and deserving or worthless and hopeless. It is the mediator of whether you suffer greatly from helplessness or not at all.

There are three crucial dimensions to one's explanatory style: permanence, pervasiveness, and personalization.

Permanence: Permanent versus Temporary

People who give up easily believe the causes of the bad events that happen to them are permanent—the bad events will persist, are always going to be there to affect their lives. People who resist helplessness believe the causes of bad events are temporary.

PERMANENT (PESSIMISTIC)	TEMPORARY (OPTIMISTIC)
"I'm all washed up."	"I'm exhausted."
"Diets never work."	"Diets don't work if I eat out."
"You always nag."	"You nag when I don't clean my room."
"My boss is a bastard."	"My boss is in a bad mood."
"You never talk to me."	"You haven't talked to me lately."

If you think about bad things in terms of "always" and "never" and abiding traits, you have a permanent, pessimistic style. If you think in terms of "sometimes" and "lately," if you use qualifiers and blame bad events on ephemera, you have an optimistic style.

Here's why the permanence dimension matters so much. When we fail, everyone becomes at least momentarily help-less. It's like a punch in the stomach. It hurts, but the hurt goes away, for some people almost instantly. These are the people who see bad events as temporary. Others dwell on the hurt; it seethes, it roils, it congeals into a grudge. These people remain helpless for days or perhaps months, even after only small setbacks. After major defeats they may never rebound.

Pervasiveness: Universal versus Specific

Permanence is about time. Pervasiveness is about space.

Consider this example: In a large retailing firm, half the accounting department was fired. Two of the fired accountants, Nora and Kevin, both became depressed. Neither could bear to look for another job for several months, and both avoided doing their income tax or anything else that reminded them of accounting. Nora, however, remained a loving and active wife. She maintained her normal social life, her health stayed robust, and she continued to work out three times a week. Kevin, in contrast, fell apart. He ignored his wife and baby son, spending all his evenings in sullen brooding. He refused to go to parties, saying he couldn't bear to see people. He never laughed at jokes. He caught a cold which lasted all winter, and he gave up jogging.

Some people can put their troubles neatly in a box and go about their lives even when one important aspect of it—their job, for example, or their love life—is crumbling. For others, when one thread of their lives breaks, the whole fabric unravels.

It comes down to this: People who make *universal* explanations for their failures give up on everything when a failure strikes in one area. People who make *specific* explanations may become helpless in that part of their lives yet march stalwartly on in the others.

Here are some universal and some specific explanations of bad events:

UNIVERSAL (PESSIMISM)	SPECIFIC (OPTIMISM)
"All teachers are unfair."	"Professor Seligman is unfair."
"I'm repulsive."	"I'm repulsive to him."
"Books are useless."	"This book is useless."

Nora and Kevin both made highly permanent explanations of their troubles. They were both pessimists in this respect. When they were fired, they both remained depressed *for a long time.* But on the pervasiveness dimension, their explanations were strikingly different. When Kevin was fired, he thought he was no good *at anything.* Nora believed bad events have very specific causes. When she was fired, she thought she was no good *at accounting.*

Here then are the three basic predictions about who becomes helpless and who doesn't that result from our reformulation:

♦ The first concerns *permanence,* for how long a person gives up: permanent explanations for bad events produce long-lasting helplessness and temporary explanations produce resilience.

♦ The second prediction is about *pervasiveness*—with universal explanations producing helplessness across many situations and specific explanations producing helplessness only in the original arena.

Personalization: Internal versus External

The third prediction is about personalization.

When bad things happen, we can blame ourselves (internal) or we can blame other people or circumstances (external). People who blame themselves when they fail suffer from low self-esteem as a consequence; they think they are worthless, unlovable, and without talent. People who blame external events do not lose self-esteem when bad events strike; on the whole, they respect themselves more.

Low self-esteem usually comes from an internal style of explaining bad events.

INTERNAL (LOW SELF-ESTEEM)	EXTERNAL (HIGH SELF-ESTEEM)
"I'm stupid."	"You're stupid."
"I have no talent at poker."	"I have no luck at poker."
"I'm insecure."	"I grew up in poverty."

DEPRESSION

Put these dimensions together and you can see there is one particularly self-defeating way to think about experiences of helplessness: that it is personal, permanent, and pervasive. People who have this most pessimistic of all styles are likely, once they fail, to have the symptoms of learned helplessness for a long time, across many endeavors, and to lose self-esteem. Such protracted learned helplessness amounts to depression. This is a central prediction from the reformulation: People who have a pessimistic explanatory style and who suffer bad events will probably become depressed, whereas people who have the opposite "optimistic" explanatory style and suffer bad events will tend to resist depression.[3,4,5]

If this is so, then pessimism is a risk factor for depression in just the same sense as smoking is a risk factor for lung cancer or being a hostile, hard-driving person is a risk factor for a heart attack.

I have spent much of the last ten years testing this prediction. The first thing my colleagues and I did was the simplest. We gave questionnaires to depressed people, thousands of them, people with all kinds and degrees of depression. We found consistently that when people are depressed they are also pessimistic. The finding was so consistent and was repeated so often that, according to one metanalysis, it would take over ten thousand negative studies to cast doubt on it.[3]

This finding does not show that pessimism causes depression, only that depressed people happen to be pessimistic at the same time they are depressed. You'd get this same coincidence of pessimism and depression if (to reverse the causal chain) it is depression which causes pessimism, or if something else (like brain chemistry) causes both conditions. Finally, part of the way we diagnose depression is to listen to what pessimistic people say. If a patient tells us he is worthless, this pessimistic explanation is part of the reason we diagnose him as depressed. So, the association between pessimistic explanatory style and depression could simply be circular.

To demonstrate that pessimism causes depression, we needed to take a group of people who were not depressed and show that, after some catastrophe, the pessimistic ones became depressed more easily than the optimistic ones. The ideal way to do this would have been something like this: to test everyone in a small town on the Gulf coast of Mississippi for depression and explanatory style and then wait for a hurricane to hit. After the hurricane passed, we'd go see who lay there passively and who got up and rebuilt the town. There were both ethical and funding problems involved in conducting this "experiment of nature." So we had to find other ways of testing the causal chain.

One of my sophomores, Amy Semmel, solved the dilemma by pointing out that there were natural disasters which hit much closer to home—ones that hit my own classes, in fact, twice a semester. Exams. When my classes began in September, we tested all the students both for depression and for their explanatory style. In October, as the midterm approached, we asked them all what would count as a "failure" for them. On average, they said getting a B+ would constitute failure. This was fine for the experiment since the average grade on my exams was a C, which meant most of my students would be subjects. One week later, they took the midterm, and the next week they got their midterm grades back—along with a copy of a Depression Inventory.

Thirty percent of the people who (by their own definition of failure) failed the midterm became very depressed. And 30 percent of the people who were pessimists in September did too. But 70 percent of the people who were both pessimists in September and failed the exam got depressed. So a recipe for depression is pre-existing pessimism encountering failure. In fact, those of this group who made the most permanent and pervasive explanations for why they failed were the people who were still depressed when we tested them again in December.

A much grimmer setting for an experiment of nature was a prison. We measured the depression level and explanatory style of male prisoners before and after incarceration. Because suicide in prison is so prevalent, we wanted to try to predict who was at most risk for becoming depressed. To our surprise, no one was seriously depressed upon entering prison. To our dismay, almost everyone was depressed on leaving. Some might say this means the prisons are doing their job, but it seems to me as if something deeply demoralizing is happening during imprisonment. At any rate, we once again correctly predicted who became most depressed: those who entered as pessimists. This means pessimism is fertile soil in which depression grows, particularly when the environment is hostile.

These various findings all pointed to pessimism as a cause of depression. We knew we could take a group of normal people and predict, far in advance, who among them were most likely to succumb to depression when bad events struck.

Another way of finding out if pessimism causes depression was to look at a group of people across time, in the course of their natural lives, a "longitudinal" study. We followed a group of 400 third graders through the seventh grade, twice a year measuring their explanatory style, their depression level, their school achievement, and their popularity. We found, statistically, that on average the children who started out as pessimists were the ones most likely, over the next four years, to become depressed and stay depressed. Those children who started out as optimists remained free of depression, if they did get depressed, they recovered rapidly. When major bad events occurred, like parents separating or getting divorced, the pessimists went under most readily. We also studied young adults and found the same pattern.

ACHIEVEMENT

The theory of helplessness—a state in which our initiation of voluntary responses is crucially undermined—is essentially an achievement theory. A central claim is that people who become helpless easily—pessimists—will achieve less than they are expected to—in school, at sports, and at work. In the last decade these predictions have been tested.

School

In 1983 we tested the explanatory style of three hundred entering freshmen at the University of Pennsylvania. And then we just waited. We waited for them to suffer through their first midterms and the grueling two weeks of final exams. We waited for them—many of whom were academic all-stars in high school—to find out what the competition at a major university was like. We waited for some to go under and some to rise to the challenge.

At the end of the first semester, fully one-third of the students had done either much better or much worse than their SATs, high school grades, and achievement tests predicted. Of these three hundred freshman about twenty did much worse and about eighty did much better than expected. The other two hundred did about as well as predicted. Those freshmen who rose to the occasion and did much better than their predicted level of grades—were on the average optimists when they entered. The ones who did much worse than they should have were the ones who entered as pessimists.[8]

Sports

In October 1988, before the Berkeley swimming season began, all fifty of the men's and women's varsity swimmers were tested for explanatory style. The coaches rated each of the swimmers on how they thought the swimmers were likely to do over the season, particularly under pressure.

We found right away that we knew something the coaches didn't. The optimism scores were totally unrelated to the coaches' ratings of how the swimmers would do under pressure. But did these scores predict actual swimming?

To find this out the coaches rated each swim for each swimmer for the entire season on whether it was "worse than expected" or "better than expected." We merely totalled up the number of "worse than expected" swims for the season. The pessimists had about twice as many unexpectedly poor swims as the optimists. The optimists lived up to their swimming potential, and the pessimists fell below their potential.

Did explanatory style work its effect in how the swimmers responded to helplessness, to defeat?

To test this, we simulated defeat under controlled conditions. At the end of the season, we had each swimmer swim one of their best events all out. The coaches then told the swimmer that his or her time was between 1.5 and 5 seconds (depending on the distance) worse than it actually was. We chose this amount because we knew it would be very disappointing (one swimmer sat and rocked liked a baby in a corner for twenty minutes afterwards), but undetectable as false. Each swimmer then rested and swam the event again as fast as he or she could. As we expected, the pessimists got worse. Two of the stars, who were also pessimists, deteriorated in their hundred yard events by a full two seconds, the difference typically between winning their event and finishing poorly. The optimists either held on to their previous pace or improved on it. Several of the optimists got faster by between two and five seconds, again enough to be the difference between a poor finish and a win.[9]

Work

We picked a profession in which there is plenty of helplessness in order to test our theory: selling life insurance. As an agent, nine out of ten of your prospects say "no," most rudely and abruptly. In early 1985, fifteen thousand applicants to Met Life nationwide took both a test of explanatory style and the "Career Profile" inventory, the standard industry predictor of success.

Met Life had two goals. The first was to hire one thousand agents by the usual criterion, passing the Career Profile. For these thousand agents, the explanatory style score did not enter into the hiring decision. We wanted only to see if the half who were the optimists on this "Regular Force" would go on to outsell the pessimists.

The second goal was much riskier for Met Life. We decided to create a "Special Force" of optimistic agents— applicants who had failed the Career Profile marginally (scoring 9 to 11) but who had scored in the top half of explanatory style. Over one hundred agents whom no one else would hire, because they failed the industry test, would be taken on. They would not know they were Special Agents. If this group failed utterly, Met Life stood to lose about three million dollars in training costs.

Over the next two years the new agents were monitored, and this is how they did:

In the first year, the optimists in the Regular Force outsold the pessimists, but only by 8 percent. In the second year, the optimists sold 31 percent more insurance.

As for the Special Force, it did beautifully. They outsold the pessimists in the Regular Force by 21 percent during the first year, and by 57 percent in the second year. They even outsold the average of the Regular Force over the first *two* years, by 27 percent. In fact, they sold at least as much as the optimists in the Regular Force.

We also saw that the optimists kept on improving over the pessimists. Why? Helplessness theory claims that optimism matters because it produces persistence. At first, we expected, talent and motivation for selling should be at least as important as persistence. But as time goes on and the mountain of no's accumulates, persistence should become decisive. This proved to be exactly the pattern.[7]

HEALTH

The final domain in which there has been a burgeoning of work on helplessness and explanatory style is physical health. The prediction is the same as for depression and achievement. People who are pessimists and experience helplessness will get sicker and perhaps die earlier than optimists.

Here is a description of one of several important studies: In the mid 1930s, the William T. Grant Foundation decided to study healthy people across the adult span of their lives. The originators of the study wanted to follow a group of exceptionally gifted men to learn about the determinants of success and good health, and so they winnowed five Harvard freshmen classes, looking for men who were physically very fit and intellectually and socially gifted. On the basis of extensive testing they picked out 200 men—about 5 percent of the classes of 1939 to 1944—and have followed them ever since. These men, who are now nearing seventy, have for fifty years cooperated fully with this demanding study. They receive extensive physical check-ups every five years, are interviewed periodically, and endlessly fill out questionnaires. They have produced a gold mine of information about what makes a person healthy and successful.

Would the optimists among them lead healthier lives than the pessimists? Would they live longer?

In order to find out we decided to use the "sealed envelope" technique. We worked in complete ignorance of who the men were and which ones had remained healthy. George Vaillant, the custodian of the Grant study, picked, by random sample, half of the men (99) and gave us essays they had written when they returned from the Second World War in 1945–6. These were rich documents—full of explanations, pessimistic and optimistic:

"The ship went down because the admiral was so stupid."

"I could never get along with the men because they resented my privileged Harvard background."

We compiled an explanatory style portrait of each of the men at the end of their youth. We found that health at age sixty was strongly related to optimism at age twenty-five. The pessimistic men had started to come down with the diseases of middle age earlier and more severely than the optimistic men, and the differences in health by age forty-five were already large. Before age forty-five optimism has no effect on health. Until that age the men remained in the same state of health as at age twenty-five. But at age forty-five the male body starts its decline. How fast and how severely is well predicted by pessimism twenty-five years earlier. What's more, when we fed several other factors into the equation—the ego defenses and physical and mental health at age twenty-five—optimism still stood out as a primary determinant of health, beginning at age forty-five and continuing for the next twenty years. These men are just entering the time of mortality, and so in the next decade we will be able to find out if optimism predicts a longer life—as well as a healthier one.[10]

THE FUTURE OF THE PSYCHOLOGY OF PERSONAL CONTROL

Helplessness, one of the central constructs of personal control, is a useful predictor of depression, of low achievement, and of poor physical health. We can expect more such studies in the future. We can also expect that the techniques of preventing helplessness—as discovered by cognitive therapy—may be applied to prevent depression, raise achievement, and better health.

But there is a downside to the field of personal control, and I want to end this introduction with a yellow light.

Americans have lived in the age of personal control for quite a while. Eastern Europe is likely to join Western Europe and America in this state of rampant individualism. The self is glorified. The individual is a frantic trading floor of options. Decision, choice, expectation, preference—all properties of a self—are the crucial variables. A flourishing psychology of personal control rides this wave, and the new developments in the concept of helplessness, with its emphasis on the self, is but one example of this approach to the human condition.

What is the future of personal control as a fact and of the psychological field that seeks to understand it? I believe it is limited. I believe unbridled individualism of the sort we have and Eastern Europe is probably about to have has such negative consequences that it may destroy itself.

For one thing, a society that exalts the individual to the extent ours now does will be ridden with depression. We have experienced a tenfold increase in depression in the last two generations, and one of the possible culprits is the fact that depression is a disorder of individual helplessness. If individualism sets us up for depression, individualism will become a less appealing creed to live by.

A second and perhaps more important factor is meaninglessness. I am not going to be foolish enough to attempt to define "meaning," but one necessary condition for meaning is the attachment to something larger than you are. To the extent that it is now difficult for people to take seriously their relationship to God, to care about their duties to the country, or to be part of a large and abiding family, meaning in life will be very difficult to find. The self alone, to put it another way, is a very poor site for meaning.

If individualism contributes to depression and meaninglessness on a massive scale, then something has to give. What? One possibility is that exaggerated individualism will fade away. Another, frightening possibility is that, in order to shed depression and attain meaning, we will rashly surrender the newly won freedoms that individualism brings, giving up personal control and concern for the individual. The twentieth century is riddled with disastrous examples of societies that have done just this to cure their ills. The current yearning for fundamentalist religion throughout the world appears to be such a response.

There is another, more hopeful, possibility. It exploits a strength of individualism. The glorified self reflected in revised concepts of helplessness and of personal control generally, is self-improving. Perhaps, through the very process of improvement, our modern self will come to see that its inordinate preoccupation with itself, while gratifying in the short run, is destructive of its well-being in the long run. Selfishly, as a tactic of self-improvement, it might actually choose to scale down its own importance, in the knowledge that depression and meaninglessness follow from self-preoccupation. Perhaps we could retain our belief in the importance of the individual but diminish our preoccupation with our own comfort and discomfort. This would allow room for a new attachment to larger things.

The future might, if we are lucky, hold a balance between the psychology of personal control and what is called "social" psychology.

Wynnewood, Pennsylvania
March 9, 1992

NOTES TO THE INTRODUCTION

1. Chomsky, N. Review of *Verbal Behavior*. *Language*, 1959, 35, 26–58.
2. Abramson, L. Y., Seligman, M. E. P., and Teasdale, J. D. Learned Helpless-

ness in Humans: Critique and Reformulation. *Journal of Abnormal Psychology,* 1978, 37, 49–74.

3. Sweeney, P., Anderson, K., and Bailey, S. Attributional Style in Depression: A Meta-analytic Review. *Journal of Personality and Social Psychology,* 1986, 50, 974–991.

4. Robins, C. Attributions and Depression: Why Is the Literature So Inconsistent?. *Journal of Personality and Social Psychology,* 1988, 54, 880–889.

5. Peterson, C. and Seligman, M. E. P. Causal Explanations as a Risk Factor for Depression: Theory and Evidence. *Psychological Review,* 1984, 91, 347–374.

6. Abramson, L. Y., Metalsky, G. I., and Alloy, L. B. Hopelessness Depression: A Theory-Based Process-Oriented Sub-type of Depression. *Psychological Review,* 1989, 96, 357–372.

7. Seligman, M. E. P. and Schulman, P. Explanatory Style as a Predictor of Performance as a Life Insurance Agent. *Journal of Personality and Social Psychology,* 1986, 50, 832–838.

8. Kamen, L. and Seligman, M. E. P. Explanatory Style Predicts College Grade Point Average. Unpublished manuscript, University of Pennsylvania.

9. Seligman, M. E. P., Nolen-Hoeksema, S., Thornton, N., and Thornton, K. M. Explanatory Style as a Mechanism of Disappointing Athletic Performance. *Psychological Science,* 1990, 1, 143–146.

10. Peterson, C., Seligman, M. E. P., and Vaillant, G. Pessimistic Explanatory Style as a Risk Factor for Physical Illness: A Thirty-five-year Longitudinal Study. *Journal of Personality and Social Psychology,* 1988, 55, 23–27.

11. Seligman, M. E. P. *Learned Optimism.* New York: Knopf, 1991.

HELPLESSNESS

CHAPTER ONE

OVERVIEW

Depression

Recently a middle-aged woman presented herself to me for psychotherapy. Every day, she says, is a struggle just to keep going. On her bad days she cannot even bring herself to get out of bed, and her husband comes home at night to find her still in her pajamas, with dinner unprepared. She cries a great deal; even her lighter moods are continually interrupted with thoughts of failure and worthlessness. Small chores such as shopping or dressing seem very difficult and every minor obstacle seems like an impassable barrier. When I reminded her that she is a good-looking woman and suggested that she go out and buy a new dress, she replied, "That's just too hard for me. I'd have to take the bus across town and I'd probably get lost. Even if I got to the store, I couldn't find a dress that would fit.

What would be the use anyway, since I'm really so unattractive?"

Her gait and speech are slow and her face looks very sad. Up until last fall she had been vivacious and active, the president of her suburban PTA, a charming social hostess, a tennis player, and a spare-time poet. Then two things happened: her twin boys went away to college for the first time, and her husband was promoted to a position of much greater responsibility in his company, a position that took him away from home more often. She now broods about whether her life is worth living, and has toyed with the idea of taking the whole bottle of her antidepressant pills at once.

Golden Girl

Nancy entered the university with a superb high-school record. She had been president and salutatorian of her class, and a popular and pretty cheerleader. Everything she wanted had always fallen into her lap; good grades came easily and boys fell over themselves competing for her attentions. She was an only child, and her parents doted on her, rushing to fulfill her every whim; her successes were their triumphs, her failures their agony. Her friends nicknamed her Golden Girl.

When I met her in her sophomore year, she was no longer a Golden Girl. She said that she felt empty, that nothing touched her any more; her classes were boring and the whole academic system seemed an oppressive conspiracy to stifle her creativity. The previous semester she had received two F's. She had "made it" with a succession of young men, and was currently living with a dropout. She felt exploited and worthless after each sexual adventure; her current relationship was on the rocks, and she felt little but contempt for him and for herself. She had used soft drugs extensively and had once enjoyed being carried away on them. But now even drugs had little appeal.

She was majoring in philosophy, and had a marked emotional attraction to Existentialism: like the existentialists, she believed that life is absurd and that people must create their own meaning. This belief filled her with despair. Her despair increased when she perceived her own attempts to create meaning—participation in the movements for women's liberation and against the war in Vietnam—as fruitless. When I reminded her that she had been a talented student and was still an attractive and valuable human being, she burst into tears: "I fooled you, too."

Anxiety and unpredictability

As I write, a debate is proceeding in the letters column of the travel section of the Sunday *New York Times*.[1] Although the debate might seem a tempest in a teapot, it happens to be of considerable theoretical and practical import. Mrs. Samuels had been a passenger on a Boeing 747 flying from Los Angeles to New York; she wrote to the *Times* with a complaint. Over the Rockies, as she was waiting for lunch to be served, it was announced that they would be making an unscheduled stop in Chicago for "operational reasons." A few minutes later the pilot spoke again: "Some of the passengers want clarification of what 'operational reasons' really means. One of the engines has conked out, so an intermediate landing will be necessary for safety reasons. Of course, the plane could fly on to New York even if it had only two engines left."

Mrs. Samuels reported that the alarm was considerable, and complained that, since the passengers were paying to leave decisions to the pilot, they should have been kept in the dark about their plight; they couldn't do anything about it anyway, except get high blood pressure. She concluded by asking, "How many readers feel as I do about the gratuitous confidence of the pilot—if the plane was truly in no trouble, as assured? On the other hand, how many feel that their civil rights are being violated if they know nothing at all?" It is interesting that most of those responding say they want to hear all about it when something goes wrong.

Childhood failure

Victor is a nine-year-old of unusual intelligence—at least his mother and his friends think so. His teacher in the third grade of an all-black Philadelphia public school wholeheartedly disagrees. At home Victor is lively, quick to respond, highly verbal, and outgoing. With his playmates out on the streets he is the acknowledged leader; even though he is a bit smaller than his peers, his charm and imagination more than make up for his size. But inside a classroom, he is a problem.

Victor was a slow starter when reading instruction began in kindergarten and first grade. He was eager, but just wasn't ready to make the connection between words on paper and speech. He tried hard at first, but made no progress; his answers, readily volunteered, were consistently wrong. The more he failed, the more reluctant to try he became; he said less and less in class. By second grade, although he participated eagerly in music and art, when reading came around he became sullen. His teacher gave him special drilling for a while, but they both soon gave up. By this time he might have been ready to read, but simply seeing a word card or a spelling book would set off a tantrum of sullenness or of defiant aggression. This attitude began to spread to the rest of his school day. He vacillated between being despondent and being a hellion.

An astonishing thing happened last summer. Two psychologists from a nearby university came to the school to teach reading to some "unteachable" children; Victor, of course, was included. As usual, he made no progress. Just seeing a sentence written on the blackboard would send him into one of his moods. Then the researchers tried something different: they wrote a Chinese character on the blackboard and said it stood for "knife." Victor learned it immediately. Then another one standing for "sharp." He learned this one, too. Within a few hours, Victor was reading English sentences and paragraphs disguised as Chinese characters. The summer is now over and the researchers have gone back to the university. Victor has a 150-character vocabulary but can't read or write any English. He is presenting more of a disciplinary problem, and his new teacher thinks he is mentally retarded.

Sudden psychosomatic death

In 1967 a distraught woman, pleading for help, entered the Baltimore City Hospital a few days before her twenty-third birthday. She and two other girls, it seems, had been born, of different mothers assisted by the same midwife, in the Okefenokee Swamp on a Friday the thirteenth. The midwife cursed all three babies, saying that one would die before her sixteenth birthday, another before her twenty-first birthday, and the third before her twenty-third birthday. The first had died in a car crash during her fifteenth year; the second was accidentally shot to death in a night-club fight on the evening of her twenty-first birthday. Now she, the third, waited in terror for her own death. The hospital somewhat skeptically admitted her for observation. The next morning, two days before her twenty-third birthday, she was found dead in her hospital bed—physical cause unknown.[2]

What do all these examples have in common? They all present aspects of human helplessness. To the extent that the reader understands them better by the end of this book, I shall have succeeded in my purpose. What follows is a summary of the intent and conclusion of each chapter, revealing the overall plan of the book.

In order to deal with such problems as sudden death, depression, anxiety and predictability of danger, and childhood failure and motivational development, the reader must first master those concepts necessary for an understanding of helplessness. In the next chapter, the concepts of helplessness and uncontrollability are defined, analyzed, and set in the context of learning theory. Once the subject matter is defined, the reader will go on in Chapter Three to the paradigmatic experiments on helplessness. Laboratory experiments on helplessness produce three deficits: they undermine the motivation to respond, they retard the ability to learn that responding works, and they result in emotional disturbance, primarily depression and anxiety.

In Chapter Four, I propose a unified theory integrating the motivational, cognitive, and emotional disturbances seen in the basic helplessness experiments. In addition, the theory suggests ways of curing and preventing helplessness. The reader will explore the ways in which this theory has been tested and examine alternative psychological theories of helplessness as well as some physiological approaches. This chapter completes the conceptual and experimental groundwork that allows the reader, in the second half of the book, to closely examine depression, anxiety, motivational development, and sudden psychosomatic death.

The fifth chapter deals with depression in man and discusses compelling parallels, both observational and experimental, between human depression in the real world and helplessness in the laboratory. This chapter offers a theory of depression, and suggests ways of curing and preventing it. Using this theory of depression, I shall speculate on depression among our "golden" young people and suggest that a childhood of receiving the good things in life independently of responding can lead to a depressed adulthood, in which one is largely incapable of coping with stress.

Anxiety caused by unpredictability and uncontrollability is the topic of Chapter Six. Unpredictability is a first cousin of uncontrollability; it is defined and related to the previous discussions of helplessness. Predictability is preferred to unpredictability; stress and anxiety are considerably greater when events occur unpredictably than when they occur predictably, and the behavior of animals and men can be seriously disrupted. More stomach ulcers occur, along with terror and panic. A theory relates the need for safety to the effects of unpredictability, and this theory is compared to alternatives. The reader will then be able to apply the theory, along with his knowledge about helplessness and anxiety, to the question of what goes on in therapy for anxiety. Systematic desensitization is a highly effective mode of dealing with anxiety in neuroses; I propose a "safety signal–helplessness" explanation of this mode of behavior therapy.

In Chapters Five and Six, the *states* of depression and anxiety are related to uncontrollability and unpredictability. But what are the long term, or *trait*, effects of helplessness? The infant begins life in a state of helplessness and learns to control the important events in his world. Chapter Seven explores the effects of uncontrollability and unpredictability on the motivational and emotional development of children. From the point of view of the theory of helplessness the reader will look at hospitalism, at monkeys deprived of mothers, at kittens deprived of synchrony between responding and feedback, at the development of self-esteem, at the effects of overcrowding, and at failure in the classroom. The notions of *ego strength* and *competence* are related to mastery over events; I shall suggest that synchrony between responding and its consequences is crucial to healthy development. I shall explore the role of helplessness in poverty, and I shall speculate on the relation of the perception of personal control to the perception of freedom.

Helplessness is not only involved in failure of motivation early in life, but has some of its most dramatic effects at the end of life. Sudden psychosomatic death produced by helplessness is the topic of the eighth, and final, chapter. I shall propose helplessness as a frequent cause of sudden, unexpected death in animals and man. The reader will look at Voodoo death in the Caribbean, at the death of cockroaches from submission, at death caused by the old-age home as it is now organized, at anaclitic depression and death of infants from hospitalism, at sudden drowning of wild rats, and at the high rate of mortality among zoo animals. Uncontrollability, as defined in Chapter Two, may be at the heart of these bizarre, but real, phenomena.

Laboratory research on animals has produced the theory that is used to explain, first, the experimental research and, then, real-life phenomena. This book is organized in the same way. The last half of the book applies the concepts and experiments developed in the first half to the real-life problems of depression, anxiety, motivational failure, and sudden death.

CHAPTER TWO

CONTROLLABILITY

Helplessness is the psychological state that frequently results when events are uncontrollable. What does it mean for an event to be uncontrollable? What is the place of control in the lives of organisms? Our intuitions are a good starting point: an event is uncontrollable when we can't do anything about it, when nothing we do matters. Let's explore our intuitions with a few examples. I shall then be in a position to define rigorously what uncontrollability is and so to identify a wide range of phenomena—some surprising—as instances of helplessness.

Your five-year-old daughter comes into the house from the back yard; she is screaming, and blood is running down her leg. Being a competent parent with a smattering of first aid, you quiet her screams with a few reassuring words and a hug. You then wash the dirt off her knee, uncovering a medium-size gash; you clean the cut, and stem the flow of blood with a compress. While you are doing this she begins to whimper again, so to quiet her fears you tell her about the time you cut your arm when you were six. Her whimpering soon stops. You put on some antiseptic and a bandage. Your little girl is happy again, and the bleeding has stopped.

In this simple example, notice all the times that you exerted active control over your child's problem. By your own actions, you quieted her screaming; by cleaning the cut and bandaging it, you helped the wound to begin healing properly. In the midst of this, you skillfully stilled her fears and relieved some pain by telling her a story. Without your intervention, things would have been much worse.

Now consider the following sequel to the example. That night you wake up to the squalls of your daughter—she is running a high fever and her leg is swollen, and red streaks extend from the cut. You rush her to the emergency room of a hospital, where you wait for three hours while nurses, orderlies, and doctors walk by, ignoring you. Your little girl continues to whine and perspire. In frustration, you buttonhole a passing intern and begin to tell him the problem; he doesn't listen, but rushes off, telling you to be patient. You go up to the admitting desk; it happens that the forms you filled out when you came in have been misplaced, so you fill out new ones. Finally, at 7:00 A.M., a doctor takes your little girl off to an examination room; half an hour later, she is returned. The doctor tells you he's given her a shot, and without explanation rushes off to his next patient. Within a few hours, your child recovers.

In this sequel, most of your actions were to no avail. The hospital staff paid no attention to your plight, lost your forms, and ignored your request for an explanation; your child recovered without your having brought it about. The course of events was uncontrollable—the outcome was independent of each of your voluntary responses. In this last sentence lies a rigorous definition of uncontrollability. The two crucial concepts are *voluntary response* and *response-outcome independence*; these two concepts are intimately related.

VOLUNTARY RESPONDING

Plants and most lower animals cannot control events in their environment; they merely react to them. The roots of a tulip react by growing away from light; the stem grows toward light. An amoeba reacts to a morsel of food by embracing it with its pseudopods and flowing around it. Why do I call such movements mere reactions and not voluntary responses? What's wrong with saying that such movements control certain events in the organism's environment? What these movements do not have is plasticity—they do not change when the *contingency*, the relationship between the movement and its outcome, is changed, for they are locked to the stimuli they produce. If an experimenter reversed the contingencies for an amoeba, by feeding it only when it *failed* to flow around the food, the amoeba could not change its behavior despite repeated failures to be fed. Similarly, an experimenter could never train a tulip's roots to grow upward by giving them water only for growing toward the sun. In short, I shall call only those responses that can be modified by reward and punishment *voluntary responses*.[1]

The hallmark of these responses is the fact that we will do them more frequently if we are rewarded for doing them, and refrain from doing them if we are punished. The responses we make that are not sensitive to reward and punishment are called reflexes, blind reactions, instincts, or tropisms. My writing the word "pickle" in the next sentence is voluntary: if you give me a million dollars for writing "pickle" I will surely do it—I might even put in two or three for good measure; if you give me a strong electric shock for writing "pickle," "pickle" shall not appear. On the other hand, the contraction of the pupil of my eye when light is shined on it is not voluntary; if you promise me a million dollars for not contracting my pupil when light is shined on it, I shall still contract my pupil.[2]

Voluntary responses are the sole concern of one important approach to psychological learning theory—*operant conditioning*, founded by E. L. Thorndike and developed and popularized by B. F. Skinner. While the ins and outs of this field may seem mysterious to the student, the basic, covert premise of the operant tradition is a simple one: by studying the laws of those responses—called instrumental or "operant" responses because they "operate" on the environment—that can be modified by reward and punishment, operant conditioners believe they will discover the laws of voluntary behavior in general. The notion of the operant response is important for my definition, not because rats pressing bars for food or pigeons pecking at keys for grain inherently fascinate me, but because this notion corresponds so well to what I mean by voluntary responding. When an organism can make no operant response that controls an outcome, I will say the outcome is *uncontrollable*.

While operant conditioning studies voluntary responses, the other major approach to learning theory—Pavlovian or classical conditioning—is concerned only with responses that are not voluntary. In a typical Pavlovian conditioning experiment a person hears a tone that is followed by a brief, painful electric shock. The tone is called a conditioned stimulus (CS) and the shock an unconditioned stimulus (US); the pain reaction caused by the shock is the unconditioned response (UR). Once the person comes to anticipate the shock, he will sweat and his heart rate will go up when he hears the tone. These anticipatory responses are called conditioned responses (CR). It is crucial to appreciate that conditioned responses do not control the shock; the person will get shocked regardless of whether he sweats or not. What defines a Pavlovian experiment and distinguishes it from an operant experiment is precisely helplessness. No response, conditioned or otherwise, is allowed to change the CS or US in classical conditioning; whereas in an operant study, there must be some response that obtains reward or alleviates punishment. Put another way, in instrumental learning the subject has a voluntary response that controls outcomes, but in Pavlovian conditioning he is helpless.

RESPONSE INDEPENDENCE AND RESPONSE CONTINGENCY

A voluntary response is a response that will increase in probability when rewarded and decrease when punished. When a response is explicitly rewarded or punished, it is obvious that the outcome is dependent on the response. But precisely what *response dependence* and *response independence* mean is one of the deepest issues in modern learning theory.

Learning theory began, naturally enough, with the simplest premises about learning. What kinds of relationships between actions and outcomes can animals and men learn about? The earliest answer was stark: learning occurs only when an organism makes a response that is immediately followed by a reward or punishment. For example, once each day at 9:00 A.M. you walk into the lobby of your office building; within thirty seconds of arriving you push the elevator button, and the elevator arrives at the end of the thirty seconds. This happens faithfully every day.

Such simple pairing of response and outcome, called *continuous reinforcement*, does not exhaust the contingencies that are learned about; learning can also occur if you make a response and nothing at all happens. For example, one day you push the elevator button and the elevator doesn't arrive (perhaps the electricity is off). Obviously, you don't stand there pushing the button forever; after a while you give up and climb the stairs. This kind of learning is called *extinction*: a response that once produced an outcome now produces nothing. So learning theorists allowed that organisms that respond can learn about two kinds of "magic moments": explicit pairing of response and outcome, and explicit unpairing. I call these contingencies magic moments to highlight their instantaneous aspect; their major claim to be fundamental contingencies is that they happen almost photographically—no complex integration over time is necessary for memory of them to be encoded and stored.

But this scheme is not close to describing what can be learned. In the late 1930's L. J. Humphreys and B. F. Skinner independently discovered *partial* or *intermittent reinforcement*, complicating matters somewhat more.[3] For example, on Monday and Tuesday morning you push the elevator button and the elevator arrives, on Wednesday and Thursday you push the button but the elevator doesn't come, and on Friday it's working again. If the elevator finally gives up the ghost, how many days will you go on pushing the button before you give up entirely and go directly up the stairs? If you've had partial reinforcement first, you'll push for a few weeks before giving up; but if you've had only continuous reinforcement, you'll give up in a few days.

People and animals learn readily that their responses are followed only intermittently by the outcome. Moreover, once they learn this, their responses become highly resistant to extinction. To accommodate these facts, a slightly more complicated organism is required: one that can put together the two kinds of moments—explicit unpairing and explicit pairing—and come up with an average. In other words, organisms can learn "sometimes" or "maybe," as well as "always" and "never." Figure 2-1 illustrates this relationship generally.

What happens when the outcome occurs even though you haven't responded? In the partial-reinforcement design and in the simpler cases, it never happened that reinforcement occurred

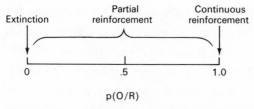

Figure 2-1
Probability of outcome (O) when the response (R) is made

when the response was *not* made. Yet organisms that learn are complicated enough to learn that outcomes occur even when they don't make a specified response. In operant language, such a contingency is called DRO—*differential reinforcement of other behavior* (see Figure 2-2).[4] To return to our example, one morning you merely stand by the elevator for thirty seconds[5] without pushing the button, but the elevator arrives anyway. It might take you a while, but you will learn to refrain from pushing the button if the elevator is rigged to arrive only when the button

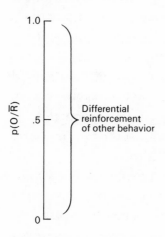

Figure 2-2
Probability of outcome (O) when the response (R) is not made. The absence of R is designated $\overline{R}$.

isn't pressed. Here are two more kinds of magic moment besides explicit pairing and unpairing of a response with an outcome: you can fail to respond, but be reinforced anyway; or you can fail to respond, and not be reinforced. Just as with explicit pairing and unpairing, these two can come in an intermittent sequence. For example, on each of the next ten days, you fail to push the button; on seven days the elevator arrives, but on the other three it doesn't.

This kind of learning still implies a fairly simple learning apparatus if the organism learns separately about the consequences of responding and the consequences of failing to respond; yet organisms that can learn at all can learn about both of these dimensions at the same time. Consider a final complication of our example: sometimes the elevator comes within thirty seconds if you press the button, but it is just as likely to come within thirty seconds if you don't press the button. All four magic moments occur with the same elevator on various days: button-push/elevator, button-push/no-elevator, no-button-push/elevator, no-button-push/no-elevator. What do you learn about the relationship between your responses and the elevator's arriving? You learn that the elevator is just as likely to come whether or not you push the button. This is at the heart of what response independence means.

For any given response and outcome, the probabilities of all four magic moments can be represented by a single point in the *response contingency space* (Figure 2-3). The horizontal or *x*-axis measures $p(O/R)$, while the vertical or *y*-axis measures $p(O/\bar{R})$ (see Figures 2-1 and 2-2).

Consider the 45° line of a response contingency space. At any point on this line, the probability of the outcome is the same whether or not the response occurs. When the probability of an outcome is the same whether or not a given response occurs, the outcome is *independent* of that response. When this is true of all voluntary responses, the outcome is *uncontrollable*.

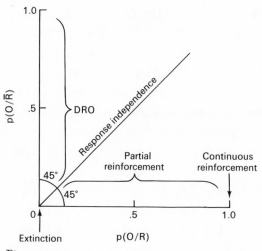

Figure 2-3
The response contingency space

Conversely, if the probability of an outcome when some response occurs is different from the probability of the outcome when that response doesn't occur, then that outcome is *dependent* on that response: the outcome is *controllable*. Any point off the 45° line implies some controllability. For example, if I slap your hand every time you reach into the cookie jar, you can control getting slapped on the hand: the probability of getting slapped when you reach is 1, but if you refrain from reaching you won't get slapped. However, if I slap your hand whether or not you reach into the cookie jar, getting slapped is uncontrollable and you are helpless.

We have now—almost painlessly, I hope—given a rigorous definition of the objective circumstances under which helplessness occurs: a person or animal is *helpless* with respect to some outcome when the outcome occurs independently of all his voluntary responses.

In the process of spelling out the definition I have moved to a view of learning more complicated than those that early theorists held. Not only can an organism learn that its responding produces an outcome with a certain probability, and that refraining from responding produces an outcome with a certain probability; it can also put these two together. This implies the ability to integrate the occurrence of the four kinds of magic moments over time and to come up with an overall estimate of the contingency.

While contingency learning is more complicated to express formally than magic-moment learning, this does not mean that it must be psychologically more complex. There need be no correspondence between formal complexity and psychological complexity. Learning that events are independent of responding has a basic, simple, and indispensable place in the real life of men and animals. It need not be a conscious or even a cognitive process: when I was two and a half years old, I knew that whether or not it rained next Sunday was independent of my wishes. I knew this full-blown, even though it would be twenty years before I came to understand the abstract concept of response independence. When a rat learns to press a bar for food, he must also learn that tail wriggling is independent of food. To learn that some response controls an outcome implies that he has also learned that other responses do not control the outcome. It would be a woefully maladaptive animal that could not learn this.

The superstition experiments

An underlying premise of the theory and research I shall describe is that an organism can learn when outcomes are uncontrollable. There is a body of literature that suggests otherwise. Experimenting in 1948, B. F. Skinner dropped grain at brief, regular intervals near hungry pigeons. What the pigeons actually did had no influence on the dropping of grain; grain was uncontrollable. Skinner observed that his pigeons were each reliably doing *something* by the end of training: one bird was pecking, another hopping in the center of the cage. He claimed that this was superstitious behavior—akin to walking around ladders, rather than under them.

Skinner argued that whatever the pigeon happened to be doing when grain arrived would be reinforced, and would therefore increase in frequency. This, in turn, would make it more likely that the bird would be doing that when grain arrived again. Here we have the extreme of magic-moment theorizing: only those moments count in which reinforcement follows a response; occurrences of the reinforcer without the preceding response do not weaken the response. Implicit in this view is the belief that animals (as well as people) cannot learn that any response they make is independent of reinforcement.

I shall present many examples in which it appears that the learning of response independence not only can occur, but does occur reliably and with disastrous consequences. But how are we to account for Skinner's results? While true superstitious behavior undoubtedly occurs in men, I believe that the pigeon results are of low generality, that they are artifacts of the species and the particular schedule of reinforcement Skinner chose. His experiment is probably an instance of classical conditioning rather than instrumental learning based on reinforcement. It has been shown that certain nonarbitrary responses emerge in the pigeon when food is presented at short, regular intervals; these responses are biologically highly prepared and prewired.[6] J. E. R. Staddon and V. L. Simmelhag have reanalyzed the pigeon superstition data, and they find that the pigeon is performing those responses that pigeons typically perform when hungry and expecting food.[7] These responses are not superstitious; they did not get stamped in by happy coincidences between them and food. Rather they are involuntary *species-specific responses*, exactly akin to a dog's licking his chops when anticipating supper.

I conclude that under limited circumstances response-independent presentation of outcomes may lead to the classical conditioning of species-specific responses that have evolved appropriately to that outcome. These can easily be mistaken for "superstitious" instrumental responses. Usually, however, as we shall see, the result is helplessness; helpless animals and people do not appear to have learned any superstitious connection between their responses and reinforcers—on the contrary, they appear to have learned to be exceedingly passive.

We have defined the objective circumstances under which an event is uncontrollable. There is a wide variety of disruption to behavior, cognition, and emotion that is a consequence of uncontrollability: dogs, rats, and men become passive in the face of trauma, they cannot solve easy discrimination problems, and they form stomach ulcers; cats have trouble learning to coordinate their movements; and college sophomores become less competitive. In the next chapter we shall look carefully at the paradigmatic studies of uncontrollability that led to my formulations of helplessness.

CHAPTER THREE

EXPERIMENTAL STUDIES

About ten years ago Steven F. Maier, J. Bruce Overmier, and I discovered an unexpected and striking phenomenon while we were doing experiments on the relationship of fear conditioning to instrumental learning.[1] We had restrained mongrel dogs in a Pavlovian hammock, and given them classical conditioning with tones followed by shocks. The shocks were moderately painful, but not physically damaging. What my colleagues and I had forgotten about, but were soon reminded of, was the defining feature of Pavlovian conditioning: the shock US's were inescapable. No voluntary response the animal made—tail wagging, struggling in the hammock, barking—could influence the shocks. Their onset, offset, duration, and intensity were determined only by the experimenter. (These conditions meet the definition of uncontrollability.) After this experience the dogs were placed in a shuttle box, a two-sided chamber in which a dog jumping over a barrier from one side to the other side turns off or *escapes* shock. Jumping can also prevent or *avoid* shock altogether if the jump occurs before the shock begins. We intended to teach the dogs to become expert shock avoiders so that we could test the effects of the classically conditioned tones on their avoidance behavior. But what we saw was bizarre, and can best be appreciated if I first describe the behavior of a typical dog that has not been given uncontrollable shock.

When placed in a shuttle box, an experimentally naive dog, at the onset of the first electric shock, runs frantically about until it accidentally scrambles over the barrier and escapes the shock. On the next trial, the dog, running frantically, crosses the barrier more quickly than on the preceding trial; within a few trials it becomes very efficient at escaping, and soon learns to avoid shock altogether. After about fifty trials the dog becomes nonchalant and stands in front of the barrier; at the onset of the signal for shock it leaps gracefully across and never gets shocked again.

A dog that had first been given inescapable shock showed a strikingly different pattern. This dog's first reactions to shock in the shuttle box were much the same as those of a naive dog: it ran around frantically for about thirty seconds. But then it stopped moving; to our surprise, it lay down and quietly whined. After one minute of this we turned the shock off; the dog had failed to cross the barrier and had not escaped from shock. On the next trial, the dog did it again; at first it struggled a bit, and then, after a few seconds, it seemed to give up and to accept the shock passively. On all succeeding trials, the dog failed to escape. This is the paradigmatic learned-helplessness finding.

Laboratory evidence shows that when an organism has experienced trauma it cannot control, its motivation to respond in the face of later trauma wanes. Moreover, even if it does respond, and the response succeeds in producing relief, it has trouble learning, perceiving, and believing that the response worked. Finally, its emotional balance is disturbed: depression and anxiety, measured in various ways, predominate. The motivational deficits produced by helplessness are in many ways the most striking, so I turn to them first for a careful analysis.

HELPLESSNESS SAPS THE MOTIVATION TO INITIATE RESPONSES

Learned helplessness in the dog

What helpless dogs do typifies what many species do when they are faced with uncontrollability. Here is the typical procedure that we used to produce and detect learned helplessness in dogs:[2] On the first day, the subject was strapped into the hammock and given 64 inescapable electric shocks, each 5.0 seconds long and of 6.0 milliamperes (moderately painful) intensity. The shocks were not preceded by any signal and they occurred randomly in time. Twenty-four hours later, the subject was given 10 trials of signalled escape-avoidance training in a two-way shuttle box: the dog had to jump over the barrier from one compartment into the other to escape or avoid shock. Shocks could occur in either compartment, so there was no *place* that was always safe, but the *response* of shuttling or jumping always led to safety. The onset of a signal (light dimming) began each trial, and the signal stayed on until the trial ended. The interval between the start of the signal and the shock was 10 seconds; if the dog jumped the shoulder-high barrier during this interval, the signal terminated and shock was prevented. Failure to jump during the signal-shock interval led to a 4.5 milliampere shock, which continued until the dog jumped the barrier. If the dog failed to jump the barrier within 60 seconds after signal onset, the trial automatically ended.

From 1965 through 1969 we studied the behavior of about 150 dogs who had received inescapable shock. Of these, two-thirds (about 100) were helpless. These animals went through the striking giving-up sequence that I have described. The other one-third were completely normal; like naive dogs, they escaped efficiently, and readily learned to avoid shock by jumping the barrier before the shock came on. There was no intermediate outcome. Occasionally, helpless dogs jumped the barrier between trials. Further, if a dog had been sitting and taking shock after shock on the left side of the box, and the door on the right side was opened at the end of the session, the dog often came bounding across to escape from the box altogether. Since helpless dogs were physically capable of jumping the barrier, their problem must have been psychological.

It is interesting that, of the several hundred naive dogs who were given shuttle-box training, about 5 percent were helpless even without prior exposure to inescapable shock. I believe that the history of these dogs before they arrived at the laboratory may account for whether a naive dog became helpless and whether a dog given inescapable shock was immune from helplessness. When I discuss ways of preventing helplessness in the next chapter, I shall be more explicit about how to immunize against it.

Helplessness in the dog occurs under a variety of circumstances and is easily produced. It does not depend on any particular shock parameters; we have varied the frequency, intensity, density, duration, and temporal pattern of shocks, and still produced the effect. Furthermore, it does not matter at all whether the inescapable shock is preceded by a signal. Finally, it does not matter what apparatus the inescapable shocks are given in or where the escape-avoidance training takes place; the shuttle box and hammock are interchangeable. If the dog is first given inescapable shock in the shuttle box and then asked to press panels with its head to escape shock in the hammock, he is still helpless. Further, after uncontrollable shock, dogs are not only unable to escape the shock itself, but they also seem to be unable to prevent or avoid it. Overmier (1968) gave dogs inescapable shock in the hammock and then brought them to the shuttle box; then if the dog jumped after the signal went on, but before the shock came on, it could avoid the shock. But no escape was allowed, for if the dog failed to jump in the signal-shock interval, the barrier was closed and inescapable shock occurred. The helpless dogs failed to avoid, just as they had failed to escape. So helpless dogs cope with signals for shock as poorly as with shock itself.

Outside the shuttle box, too, helpless dogs act differently from nonhelpless dogs. When an experimenter goes to the home cage and attempts to remove a nonhelpless dog, it does not comply eagerly: it barks, runs to the back of the cage, and resists handling. In contrast, helpless dogs seem to wilt; they passively sink to the bottom of the cage, occasionally even rolling over and adopting a submissive posture; they do not resist.

The triadic design

How can we tell that learned helplessness results from being unable to control a physical trauma, and not merely from experiencing physical trauma. To put it another way, how can we tell whether helplessness is a psychological phenomenon and not merely the result of a physical deficit?

There is a simple and elegant experimental design that isolates the effects of controllability from the effects of the stimulus being controlled. In this *triadic design*, three groups of subjects are used: One group receives as its pretreatment an outcome that it can control by some response. A second group is *yoked*—a subject in this group receives exactly the same physical outcomes as its counterpart in the first group, but there is no response the yoked subject can make that modifies these outcomes. A third group receives no pretreatment. Later, all groups are tested on a new task.

The triadic design provides a direct test of the hypothesis that it is not shock itself, but learning that shock is uncontrollable, that causes helplessness.[3] Two examples of the triadic design follow. In the first, three groups of eight dogs were used.[4] Dogs in an escape group were trained in the hammock to turn off shock by pressing a panel with their noses. A yoked group received shocks identical in number, duration and pattern to the shocks delivered to the escape group. The yoked group differed from the escape group only with respect to the instrumental control that it had over the shock: pressing the panel did not affect the shock programmed to the yoked group. A naive control group received no shock in the hammock.

Twenty-four hours after the hammock treatment, all three groups received escape-avoidance training in the shuttle box. The escape group and the naive control group performed well in the shuttle box; they jumped the barrier readily. In contrast, the yoked group was significantly slower to respond than the escape group and the naive control group. Six of the eight subjects in the yoked group failed completely to escape shock. So it was not the shock itself, but inability to control the shock, that produced failure to escape.

Maier (1970) provided more striking confirmation of this hypothesis. When the dogs in the escape group were in the hammock, instead of being trained to make an active response, like panel pressing, they were trained to make a *passive* response to turn off shock. The dogs of this group (passive-escape) were tied down in the hammock and had panels placed at a distance of 1/4 inch from the sides and tops of their heads. Only by *not* moving their heads, by remaining still, could these dogs turn off the shock. Another group of ten received the same shock in the hammock, but the shock was independent of any response and therefore uncontrollable. A third group received no shock. When they were later put in the shuttle box, the dogs in the yoked group were predominantly helpless, and the naive controls escaped normally. The passive-escape group at first did not move around much; they appeared to be looking for some passive way to minimize shock in the shuttle box. Failing to find one, they all began to escape and avoid vigorously. So it is not trauma in itself that is sufficient to produce failure to escape but learning that no response at all—neither active *nor passive*—can control trauma.

Motivational deficits in several species

Students beginning an introductory psychology course—or better yet, students who avoid this course—have a common reaction: "Rats! What do rats have to do with people?" This reaction is not nearly as naive as it sounds to the jaded ear of the professional psychologist. Too often, laboratory experimenters have glibly assumed that laws found true of one species are generally true of other species, particularly man. The history of comparative psychology is littered with invalidated experiments and discredited theories that made this assumption without warrant. Recent developments have taught us to be very careful about generalizing without evidence from one species to another.[5] The way a quail will learn to cope with trauma is very different from what a rat or a man will learn: if a quail is poisoned by water that is blue in color and sour in taste, it will later avoid blue, but not sour water; a rat or man, on the other hand, will avoid sour, but not blue water. Even within the same species, what a rat will learn to cope with shock is very different from what it will learn to cope with poison: if a rat is shocked after blue, sour water, it will avoid blue water; but if poisoned, it will avoid sour. If we are to use learned helplessness as a basis for explaining such important human phenomena as depression and psychosomatic death, it is mandatory to find out if it occurs in a wide variety of species, including man. Otherwise, we can dismiss it as a species-specific behavior, akin to the peculiar ritual a male stickleback fish performs while courting the female.

Debilitation of response initiation as a consequence of uncontrollable outcomes has been found in cats, rats, mice, birds, primates, fish, cockroaches, and man. Learned helplessness seems general among species that learn, so it can be used with some confidence as an explanation of a variety of phenomena.

Cats. Earl Thomas has reported an effect in cats that seems identical to helplessness in dogs.[6] He designed a hammock for cats and gave them inescapable shock in it. When later placed in a cat shuttle box, these cats failed to escape; like dogs, they sat and took the shock. Thomas has been pursuing the physiological basis of helplessness; he believes that the septum, a brain structure beneath the cortex, may be responsible, because blocking the activity of the septum counteracts helplessness. He also reports that, with direct electrical stimulation of the septum, his cats became helpless. I shall return to this physiological correlation in the next chapter, when I discuss the theory of helplessness and its therapy.

Fish. Following inescapable shock, fish also show poor escape and avoidance responding. A. M. Padilla and his colleagues gave inescapable shock to goldfish, then tested them in an aquatic shuttle box. These fish were slower to avoid than naive controls. It is interesting that helplessness lifted with the same time course in the goldfish as in the dog.[7]

Primates other than man. To my knowledge as of 1974, no one has carried out an explicit helplessness experiment using the triadic design with monkeys or apes. There is, however, a substantial literature describing the effects of other uncontrollable events on primates. Experimenters have applied three kinds of uncontrollable conditions to primates: social helplessness in infancy, separation from mother, and rearing in isolation. Since their striking results have not previously been interpreted using the concept of helplessness, I will defer discussion of them until Chapter Seven.

Rats. The white rat and the college sophomore are the most widely used subjects of psychological experiments. This is less due to any conceptual reason than to the convenient fact that so much is known about their behavior and physiology; even so, some experimenters will not believe that a phenomenon is real until it has been demonstrated in the white rat. Until recently, the rat proved a difficult creature to produce helplessness in. A large number of experiments were done using inescapable shock; by and large, these showed rather small effects, if any, on later response initiation.[8] Unlike dogs, rats given prior inescapable shock were typically only a bit slower to escape shock on the first few trials, or slower to acquire avoidance—they did not sit and take shock passively.

After intensive experimentation, however, several investigators have now independently produced substantial helplessness in rats.[9] In these experiments, one crucial factor emerged—the response tested for must be difficult, not something the rat does very readily. For example, if rats are first exposed to inescapable shock, then tested on a simple escape response like pressing a bar once or fleeing to the other side of a shuttle box, no deficits are found. If, however, the response requirement is increased—so the bar must be pressed three times in order for shock to end, or the rat has to run across and back—then the rat that has experienced inescapable shock responds very slowly. In contrast, rats who had prior escapable shock or no shock perform the more difficult responses without giving up.

To the degree that a response is very natural or automatic in the rat, uncontrollable shock will not interfere. If the response is somewhat unnatural and therefore must be performed "deliberately," the rat shows helplessness following the experience of uncontrollable shock.

Man. What are the laboratory effects of inescapable trauma in *Homo sapiens?* Like the dog, cat, rat, fish, and non-human primates, when a man is faced with noxious events that he cannot control, his motivation to respond is drastically undermined.

Donald Hiroto replicated our findings on dogs, quite exactly, in college students.[10] His escape group received loud noise, which they learned to turn off by pushing a button; the yoked group received the same noise, but independently of any response; a third group received no noise. Each subject was then taken to a finger shuttle box: in order to escape noise the individual had only to move his hand from one side to the other. Both the no-noise group and the escape group learned readily to shuttle with their hands. As with other species, however, the human yoked group failed to escape and avoid; most sat passively and accepted the aversive noise.

Hiroto's design was actually more complicated and had two other important factors. Half the subjects in each of the three groups were told that their performance in the shuttle box was a test of skill; the other half was told that their score was governed by chance. Those who received chance instructions tended to respond more helplessly in all groups. Finally, the personality dimension of "external vs. internal locus of control of reinforcement" was also varied in his design, with half of all the students in each group being "externals," and half "internals."[11] An external is a person who believes, as shown by his answers on a personality inventory, that reinforcements occur in his life by chance or luck, and are beyond his control. An internal believes that *he* controls his own reinforcers, and that skill will out. Hiroto found that externals became helpless in his experiment more easily than internals. So three independent factors produced learned helplessness: the laboratory experience of uncontrollability, the cognitive set induced by chance instructions, and the external personality. Given this convergence, Hiroto concluded that these three factors all erode the motivation to escape by contributing to the expectation that responding and relief are independent.

D. C. Glass and J. E. Singer (1972), in studies attempting to simulate urban stress, found that uncontrollable loud noise resulted in subjects who did poorly at proofreading, found the noise highly irritating, and gave up at problem solving. The mere belief that they could turn the noise off if they so desired, as well as actually having control over the melange of urban sound, abolished these deficits. Furthermore, merely believing that they had access to someone who could provide relief produced beneficial effects. The relationship of the perception of control to actual control, as we have defined it, is important and complex; I shall discuss it more fully in the next chapter.

This concludes the survey of motivational deficits produced by learned helplessness in different species. It seems to be generally true that uncontrollability produces deterioration of the readiness of dogs, cats, rats, fish, monkeys, and men to respond adaptively to trauma.

Generality of helplessness across situations

When a freshman objects to introductory psychology, saying that he doesn't care about rats, he is not only objecting to the limitation of many psychological phenomena to one species, but also to the limited circumstances under which those phenomena can be produced. Helplessness is a general characteristic of several species, including man, but if we are to take helplessness seriously as an explanatory principle for real-life depressions, anxiety, and sudden death, it must not be peculiar to shock, shuttle boxes, or even just to trauma. Does uncontrollability produce a habit limited to circumstances like the ones under which helplessness is learned, or does it produce a more general trait? To put it another way, is helplessness just an isolated set of habits or does it involve a more basic change in "personality"? I believe that what gets learned when the environment is uncontrollable has profound consequences for the entire repertoire of behavior.

At the lowest level of generality, we already know that helplessness transfers from one apparatus to another, as long as shock occurs in both: dogs given inescapable shock in a hammock fail to escape later in a shuttle box. But does what is learned transfer to traumatic experiences not involving shock? Braud and his co-workers used a triadic design with mice.[12] One group could escape shock by climbing up a pole, a second group was yoked, and a third group received no shock; all groups were then placed in an alley flooded with water and had to swim out in order to escape. The yoked group was poorest at escaping from water. In a different experiment in which shock helplessness may have transferred to a different aversive event, three groups of rats received escapable shock, inescapable shock, or no shock.[13] They had first of all been deprived of food and taught to run down an alleyway in order to get food in a goal box, where food was present in every trial. Once they had learned, food was no longer placed in the goal box; during this extinction procedure, the rats ran down the alleyway into the goal box, where they expected food but found none. This has been shown to be a frustrating and aversive experience for a rat.[14] The rats were then given an opportunity to jump out of the goal box and escape frustration. Rats who had received escapable shock or no shock escaped frustration readily; rats who had received inescapable shock sat passively without escaping from the frustrating goal box. So helplessness with respect to one aversive experience—shock—generalizes to another—frustration.[15]

Another instance of transfer of helplessness is related to a phenomenon called *shock-elicited aggression*. Anyone who has bumped his head on a car door and become furious, yelling at the passengers, is familiar with the phenomenon. At the animal level, if a rat is shocked while another rat is nearby, the shocked rat will attack the other rat furiously. In a triadic design, rats received escapable shock, inescapable shock, or no shock, and then were provoked to shock-elicited aggression against another rat.[16] The rats who had been able to escape attacked the most when shocked, the control group was intermediate, and the helpless group attacked the least. In a related study in our laboratory, we found that dogs who had received inescapable shock as puppies lost in competition for food (only one nose fits into a coffee cup full of Alpo) with dogs who had received no shock or escapable shock. Helplessness retards the initiation of aggressive as well as defensive responses.

Does helplessness acquired under traumatic circumstances have effects on the nontraumatic aspects of life? Recently, Don Hiroto and I systematically explored the transfer of helplessness from instrumental tasks to cognitive tasks.[17] Three groups of college students received escapable, inescapable, or no loud noise; they then switched to a nonaversive anagram test, and their time to solve anagrams like "IATOP" was recorded. Students who had received inescapable loud noise found the solutions less often than the group that had received escapable noise and the no-noise group. Aversive helplessness retards solution of nonaversive cognitive problems.

Are the debilitating effects of uncontrollability produced only by uncontrollable trauma? What happens to response initiation when it is preceded by a history of uncontrollable outcomes that are not traumatic? Don Hiroto and I tried to produce helplessness by using unsolvable discrimination problems instead of inescapable noise.[18]

In a typical discrimination-learning problem, a person or animal confronts two stimulus cards, one white and one black. Behind one of these cards, say the black one, reward is to be found consistently: some bran mash for a rat, an M&M for a child, a dime or "correct" for an adult. On some trials, black is on the left side, white on the right; on other trials this is reversed. The problem is solvable, since picking the black card will produce reward. Reward is controllable since the probability of reward for picking black is 1.0, and for picking white is 0. Children, adults, rats, and even earthworms learn to solve such problems. An unsolvable discrimination problem is uncontrollable in the same sense that an inescapable shock is uncontrollable. Consider what happens when there is no solution to a discrimination problem. Procedurally, this requires baiting the white card and the black card randomly: on half the trials, chosen at random, black is rewarded; on the other half, white is correct. It also requires that on half the trials the left side be correct, and on the other half the right side. Such a design characterizes an experiment on helplessness: the probability of getting reward by choosing left is 0.5, choosing black 0.5, choosing white 0.5. Reward is independent of response; by definition, it is uncontrollable.[19]

With the formal similarity of unsolvability and inescapability in mind, Don Hiroto and I gave three groups of college students solvable or unsolvable sets of discrimination problems, or no problems at all.[20] Then all groups were tested on the finger shuttle box, with loud noise to be escaped. Individuals who had solvable discrimination problems or no prior problems escaped noise with alacrity; the group that had been given unsolvable problems took the noise passively. Initiation of responses that control noxious events may be impaired by experience with uncontrollable reward.

We have also found that uncontrollable reward impairs responding for reward. Different groups of hungry rats had pellets of food dropped "from the sky" through a hole in the roof of their cage, independently of their responses; then they had to learn to get food by pressing a bar. The more free food they had received in pretraining, the worse they did at learning instrumental responses for food. Some of the rats just sat around for days, waiting for more food to drop in; they never pressed the bar.[21]

The crucial manipulation in this study was a "spoiled brat" design—no matter what the subject did, he was rewarded. A related and controversial paper entitled "The pigeon in a welfare state" was recently read at a meeting of the Psychonomic Society.[22] One group of hungry pigeons learned to jump on a pedal for grain. A second, "welfare state," group received the same grain, but regardless of what it did; food and responding were independent. A third group received no grain. All the pigeons were then set to an *autoshaping* task, in which they learned to get grain by pecking a lighted key. The group that had controlled grain by pedal pressing autoshaped fastest, the control group next, and the "welfare state" group slowest. Once all three groups had learned, they were shifted to a schedule in which they had to learn to refrain from pecking. Again, the pedal-pressing pigeons learned fastest, the control group next, and the helpless or "learned-laziness" group, as the authors called it, slowest. These results are controversial and can only with caution be interpreted as appetitive helplessness: the pigeons' autoshaped key peck is no longer believed to be a voluntary instrumental response. B. Schwartz and D. R. Williams (1972) found it to be of short duration, and therefore *elicited* or involuntary. If autoshaping should actually result in an elicited conditioned response, I would not predict that appetitive helplessness retards it, since I believe that helplessness undermines only voluntary responses.

Uncontrollable reward has similar debilitating effects on the competitiveness of people later placed in laboratory games. Harold Kurlander, William Miller, and I gave college students solvable, unsolvable, or no discrimination problems.[23] Then each person played the "prisoner's dilemma" game. In this game the object is to win more points than a competitor. On any trial there are three responses a player can make: he can compete, cooperate, or withdraw with minimal losses. If he chooses to compete, and his opponent cooperates, the player wins heavily and his opponent loses heavily; if his opponent also competes, however, they both lose heavily. If he chooses to cooperate and his opponent competes, the player loses heavily and his opponent wins; while if they both choose to cooperate, they both win moderately. The final alternative is withdrawal: any time either player chooses withdrawal, both players lose a small amount.

If, prior to the game, the player had solvable problems or no discrimination problems, he competed frequently and withdrew infrequently. In contrast, if he had unsolvable discrimination problems first, he withdrew more frequently and competed less. So helplessness produced by uncontrollable reward undermines competitive responding.

I believe that the psychological state of helplessness produced by uncontrollability undermines response initiation quite generally. After receiving uncontrollable shock, dogs, rats, cats, fish, and people make fewer responses to escape shock. Furthermore, these motivational deficits are not limited to shock or even noxious events generally. Aggressive action, escape from frustration, and even the ability to solve anagrams are undermined by inescapable aversive events. Conversely, uncontrollable reward disrupts escape from loud noise, learning to procure food, and competitiveness.

Men and animals are born generalizers. I believe that only in the rarest circumstances is a specific, punctate response or association learned. The learning of helplessness is no exception: when an organism learns that it is helpless in one situation, much of its adaptive behavioral repertoire may be undermined. On the other hand, the organism must also discriminate those situations in which it is helpless from those in which it is not, if it is to continue to behave adaptively. If we failed to keep our helplessness within bounds and went to pieces every time we flew on an airplane, life would be a madhouse. Those factors that provide limits to generalization of helplessness—immunization, discriminative control, and significance of the uncontrollable event—will be discussed in the next chapter.

HELPLESSNESS DISRUPTS THE ABILITY TO LEARN

We have seen that a major consequence of experience with uncontrollable events is *motivational:* uncontrollable events undermine the motivation to initiate voluntary responses that control other events. A second major consequence is *cognitive:* once a man or an animal has had experience with uncontrollability, he has difficulty *learning* that his response has succeeded, even when it is actually successful. Uncontrollability distorts the perception of control.

This phenomenon appears in helpless dogs, rats, and men. Occasionally, a naive dog sits and takes shock on the first three or four trials in the shuttle box; then on the next trial jumps the barrier and escapes shock successfully for the first time. Once a naive dog makes one response that produces relief, he catches on; on all further trials he responds vigorously and learns to avoid shock altogether. But dogs who first received inescapable shock are different in this respect also. About one-third of them go through a similar pattern—sitting through shock on the first three or four trials, then escaping successfully on the next. These dogs, however, then revert to taking the shock, and they fail to escape on future trials. It looks as if one success is just not enough to make a helpless dog learn that his responding now works.

William Miller and I found that such a negative cognitive set results from learned helplessness in man.[24] Three groups of students received escapable, inescapable, or no loud noise. Then they confronted two new tasks, a task of skill and a task of chance. In the skill task, on each of ten trials they sorted 15 cards into ten categories of shape, attempting to finish within

15 seconds. Unknown to them, the experimenter arranged to have them succeed or fail on any given trial by saying that time was up before they had finished or after, so that they went through a prearranged run of successes and failures. At the end of each trial, the subject rated (on a 0–10 scale) what he thought his chances of succeeding on the next trial were. Subjects who were previously helpless in loud noise showed very little change in their expectancy for success after each new success and failure. They had difficulty perceiving that responses could affect success or failure. Control subjects and subjects who had escaped noise showed large expectancy changes following each success and failure. This showed that they believed outcomes to be dependent on their actions. The three groups did not differ in expectancy changes following success and failure in a "chance" task that they perceived as a guessing game. Learned helplessness produces a cognitive set in which people believe that success and failure is independent of their own skilled actions, and they therefore have difficulty learning that responses work.

Don Hiroto and I have also reported negative cognitive set in another form.[25] As the reader will recall, students had to solve anagrams after experiencing escapable noise, inescapable noise, or no noise. Two kinds of cognitive deficits emerged: Inescapable noise interfered with their ability to solve any given anagram. In addition, there was a pattern to the 20 anagrams to be solved—each was arranged with its letters in the order 34251 (e.g., ISOEN, OCHKS, OURPG, etc.); students who had received inescapable noise had great difficulty discovering the pattern. Unsolvable discrimination problems produced the same disruption of anagram solution.

The existence of a negative cognitive set produced by independence between response and outcome bears on a deep issue in learning theory. When two events are presented independently of each other, for example, a tone and a shock presented at random, does the subject learn anything at all about the tone or does the tone merely come to be ignored? From our point of view, men and animals can actively learn that responses and outcomes are independent of each other, and one way the learning is manifested is by the difficulty they later have in learning when the response *does* produce the outcome. This suggests that organisms should also actively learn when a tone and shock are independent, and show this by having trouble later learning when the tone *is* followed by the shock. R. A. Rescorla (1967) has held the contrary view: independence between a tone and shock is a neutral condition in which nothing is learned; in fact, it is the ideal *control* group for classical conditioning. I have argued (1969) that this "ideal control group" shows powerful learning in its own right, and therefore is not the appropriate control. As we will see in the chapter on anxiety, the group develops ulcers and chronic fear. Furthermore, recent investigation has shown that active learning does indeed occur when CS's and US's are independently presented. R. L. Mellgren and J. W. P. Ost (1971) reported on a group of rats to which CS's had been presented independently of food; they later took longer than naive rats (or even rats for whom the CS's had predicted the *absence* of food) to learn that the CS's were associated with the food. D. Kemler and B. Shepp (1971) showed that children learned most slowly about stimuli relevant to the solution of a discrimination problem when those stimuli had previously been presented as irrelevant. D. R. Thomas and co-workers showed that pigeons that had two colors presented independently of food tended not to discriminate later between two line tilts, one of which predicted food and the other did not.[26] N. J. MacKintosh (1973) also reported that conditioning was retarded by prior CS-US independence.

Independence between two stimuli produces active learning, and this learning retards the ability of rats, pigeons, and men to learn later that the stimuli depend on one another. The evidence for this is consistent with the effects of response-outcome independence on cognition, and reinforces our conclusion that response-outcome independence distorts the perception that responding has contingent consequences.

HELPLESSNESS PRODUCES EMOTIONAL DISTURBANCE

Our first hint that helplessness has emotional, as well as motivational and cognitive, consequences came when we found that the motivational effects dissipated in time. Trauma often produces disturbances in animals and man that have surprising time courses, and are readily seen as emotional changes. When catastrophe strikes a group of men, a time-limited phenomenon called the *disaster syndrome* ensues:

> One winter's day in 1659, a band of warriors from the Petun Indian village of St. Jean, south of Georgian Bay, went out to intercept an invading war party of Iroquois. They did not find the enemy. When they returned to the village, four days later, they saw only the ashes of their homes and the charred and mutilated bodies of many of their wives, children, and old men. Not one living soul had been spared from the flames. The Petun warriors sat down in the snow, mute and motionless, and no one moved or spoke for half a day, no one even stirred to pursue the Iroquois in order to save the captives or gain revenge.[27]

This is not a culturally determined reaction, since it occurs generally following a disaster. When a tornado strikes a town, people function well during the tornado, but soon thereafter, the victims become nearly stuporous for about 24 hours. After another day or so, people begin to pick up the pieces and go about their business (see p. 88).

We have observed a similar time course of learned helplessness in dogs.[28] If a dog is placed in the shuttle box within 24 hours after uncontrollable shock in the harness, he will be helpless. If, however, we wait 72 hours or a week after the single session of inescapable shock in the harness, the dog will escape normally in the shuttle box. One experience with un-controllable trauma produces an effect that dissipates in time.

But what happens if many experiences of uncontrollability occur before the dog is given an opportunity to escape? If a dog is given four sessions, spread out over a week, of inescapable shock in the harness, then he will remain helpless weeks later. Repeated uncontrollability produces an interference with re-sponse initiation that is chronic. On the other hand, it should be mentioned that helplessness produced in the rat, even by only one session of inescapable shock, does not dissipate in time.[29]

In the next chapter, when I give a theoretical account of helplessness, I shall discuss a cognitive, as well as an emotional, interpretation of this time course. On the face of it, however, it appears that uncontrollability sets up some emotional state that—if not reinforced—will dissipate in time.

One common measure of emotionality is stomach ulcers. In 1958 the famous "executive monkey" study appeared.[30] This study is intimately related to uncontrollability and help-lessness, but the results appeared to show less emotionality with uncontrollability. Two groups of four monkeys were given shocks; one group—the "executives"—had control over the shocks and could avoid by pressing a bar. The other four were yoked, or helpless, since they could not modify shock. The executives formed stomach ulcers and died, while the helpless monkeys did not develop ulcers. These results were widely noted in the press and have found their way into most intro-ductory psychology textbooks. Unfortunately, they are an artifact of the way the monkeys were assigned to the two groups: all eight monkeys were placed on the executive sched-ule originally, and the first four to start pressing the bar be-came the executives; the last four became the yoked subjects.

It has been shown since then that the more emotional a monkey is, the sooner it begins to press the bar when it is shocked;[31] so that the four most emotional animals became the executives, and the four most phlegmatic became the yoked subjects.

J. M. Weiss has recently repeated the study correctly.[32] Three groups of rats were assigned randomly to the triadic design. The executive animals got fewer and less severe ulcers than the yoked animals, who lost more weight, defecated more, and drank less than the executives. Helpless rats show more anxiety, when measured by ulcers, than rats who can control shock.

There is still further evidence that uncontrollable shock produces more anxiety in rats than controllable shock. O. H. Mowrer and P. Viek (1948) shocked two groups of rats while they were eating. One group could control the shock by jumping into the air, while the other group received uncontrollable shock. The rats getting uncontrollable shock subsequently ate less than those controlling shock.[33] In an analogous study, J. E. Hokanson and co-workers had people perform a symbol-matching task while being shocked. The schedules were individually arranged so that each subject received an average of one shock every forty-five seconds. One group was allowed to take as many time-outs from shock as they wished, when they wished. A yoked group received the same number of time-outs at the yoked times. Measures of blood pressure taken at thirty-second intervals indicated that yoked group showed consistently higher blood pressure.[34]

Using rats, E. Hearst (1965) found that the presentation of uncontrollable shocks resulted in the breakdown of a well-trained appetitive discrimination. During uncontrollable shock his rats no longer discriminated between two stimuli, one of which signalled the presence, and the other the absence, of food. During controllable shock the appetitive discrimination was maintained.

Such a breakdown of appetitive discrimination is reminiscent of the famous work on "experimental neuroses." The concept of experimental neurosis is not a homogeneous one, nor is it well defined. Controllability has not been manipulated explicitly to produce it; yet, looking at the experimental procedures, we can speculate that the lack of control or loss of it is important in the etiology of the neurosis. Typically, an animal is restrained in some type of harness that seriously limits what it can do. Often the procedure is classical conditioning, where by definition the organism has no control over the onset or the offset of the stimuli presented. In Shenger-Krestnikova's classic experiment, an appetitive discrimination deteriorated and signs of distress were noted when the dog could no longer tell the difference between the rewarded and nonrewarded stimulus.[35] In the work of H. S. Liddell and others, sheep developed a range of maladaptive behaviors following uncontrollable electric shock.[36] J. H. Masserman (1943) trained monkeys to feed in response to a signal, then made them neurotic by presenting a fear-arousing stimulus during feeding. Without therapy these monkeys remained disturbed almost indefinitely. According to Masserman:

Markedly different, however, was the case of animals that had been taught to manipulate various devices that actuated the signals and feeder because in this way they could exert at least partial control over their environment. This stood them in good stead even after they were made neurotic in as much as when their hunger increased they gradually made hesitant, but spontaneous, attempts to reexplore the operation of the switches, signals and food boxes, and were bolder and more successful as food began to reappear.

In a striking primate study, C. F. Stroebel (1969) trained a group of rhesus monkeys to press a lever that air-conditioned their overheated chamber and also controlled loud noise, annoying light, and mild shocks. He then retracted the lever so that it could still be seen, but could no longer be pressed. No further physical stressors were presented. Initial responding was frantic, but then gave way to other disturbances:

> As [circadian] rhythm disturbance developed, members of this . . . group of subjects began to show lassitude and weakness; their fur became knotted, mottled and poorly groomed; behaviorally they performed unpredictably if at all on the right hand lever problems, pausing often for naps and rest. The behaviors exhibited by these animals were clearly nonadaptive in nature; for example, two subjects spent hours in catching "imaginary" flying insects, one subject masturbated almost continuously, three subjects became almost compulsive hair pullers, and all tended to show movement stereotypy alternating with an almost total lack of interest in their external environment.

It is not clear whether there can be any one theory that can account for experimental neuroses, nor is it clear that all these phenomena are essentially the same. But uncontrollability is prominently present and emotional disruption is the universal result.

In summary, helplessness is a disaster for organisms capable of learning that they are helpless. Three types of disruption are caused by uncontrollability in the laboratory: the motivation to respond is sapped, the ability to perceive success is undermined, and emotionality is heightened. These effects hold across a wide variety of circumstances and species, and are prominent in *Homo sapiens*. In the next chapter, I shall propose a unified theory to account for these facts.

CHAPTER FOUR

THEORY: CURE AND IMMUNIZATION

What must an adequate theory of helplessness accomplish? It must account for the three facets of the disorder: disturbances of motivation, cognition, and emotion. It must be testable: there should be experiments that can be performed that will confirm it if it is true, or disconfirm it if it is false. Finally, it must be applicable outside the laboratory: it must be useful in explaining helplessness as found in the real world.

The groundwork has been prepared by the way I laid out the data in the last chapter. The theory I shall now present accounts directly for the motivational deficit and the cognitive distortion and, with an additional premise, for the emotional disturbance. It has been tested in several ways, some of which have suggested methods of curing helplessness and of preventing it. Furthermore, I shall set out the boundary conditions of helplessness in order to answer the question: Since everyone occasionally faces uncontrollable events, why isn't everyone always helpless? Finally, I shall review some alternative theories that seem less adequate. The later chapters on depression, child development, and sudden death are attempts to apply the theory to helplessness in the real world.

THE STATEMENT OF THE THEORY

When an animal or a person is faced with an outcome that is independent of his responses, he learns that the outcome is independent of his responses. This is the cornerstone of the theory and probably seems so obvious, to all but the most sophisticated learning theorist, as not even to need stating. But you will recall our lengthy discussion of the response contingency space (Figure 2-3); learning theorists would much prefer that the kinds of contingencies that can be learned about be as simple as possible. First they believed that the most that could be learned was a simple pairing of a response and an outcome, or pairing of the response with the absence of the outcome. But this had to be broadened to include partial reinforcement, with the subject integrating both kinds of pairings to come up with a "maybe"; what could be learned about was broadened to the *probability* of an outcome, given a response. Then it was shown that an organism could also learn about the probability of an outcome given that it didn't make that response. The new step that our theory makes is that an organism can learn about both these probabilities conjointly, that variation of experience corresponding to different points in the response contingency space will produce systematic changes in behavior and cognition.[1] In particular, I claim that when organisms experience events corresponding to the 45° line, in which the probability of the outcome is the same whether or not the response of interest occurs, learning takes place. Behaviorally, this will tend to diminish the initiation of responding to control the outcome; cognitively, it will produce a belief in the inefficacy of responding, and difficulty at learning that responding succeeds; and emotionally, when the outcome is traumatic, it will produce heightened anxiety, followed by depression.

The basic triadic design employed in all the helplessness studies reviewed in the last chapter is, of course, directly pertinent to the premise that men and animals learn about independence between outcome and response, and form expectations concerning it. For example, in the study by Seligman and Maier (1967), only the yoked dogs were helpless, while the dogs who could escape by panel pressing and the dogs who were not shocked did not become helpless. Clearly something different happened to the dogs who received shock independently of their responses. I believe they learned that responding was futile and therefore expected future responding to shock to be futile. In the studies by Weiss (1968, 1971a, b, c), only the yoked rats formed massive stomach ulcers; it is clear that these rats learned something different from those who had been able to escape shock and those who had received no shock. Here, too, I believe they learned that responding was futile.

The theory I am proposing has three basic components:

| Information about the contingency | $\longrightarrow$ | Cognitive representation of the contingency (learning, expectation, perception, belief) | $\longrightarrow$ | Behavior |

A man or an animal must begin with information about the contingency of outcome upon response. This information is a property of the organism's environment, not a property of the perceiver. I have carefully defined what can be called objective information that a response and an outcome are independent.

The second component in the sequence is crucial, yet is easily overlooked, especially in the zealous concern common to many learning theorists for operational definitions and objective contingencies. The information about the contingency must be processed and transformed into a cognitive representation of the contingency.[2] Such a representation has been variously called "learning," "perceiving," or "believing" that response and outcome are independent. I prefer to call the representation the *expectation* that responding and an outcome are independent.

This expectation is the causal condition for the motivational, cognitive, and emotional debilitation that accompanies helplessness. Mere exposure to the information is insufficient; a person or animal can be exposed to the contingency in which an outcome and response are independent, yet not form such an expectation. Immunization, as we shall see later in this chapter, is an example. Conversely, a person can become helpless without being exposed to the contingency as such: he can merely be told that he is helpless.

In 1972, D. C. Glass and J. E. Singer reported an extensive series of studies on the role of controllability in reducing stress; they found that merely telling a human subject about controllability duplicates the effects of actual controllability. They attempted to duplicate the stress of the urban environment, by having their subjects—college students—listen to a very loud melange of sound: two people speaking Spanish, one person speaking Armenian, a mimeograph machine, a calculator, and a typewriter. When subjects could *actually* turn off the noise by pushing a button, they were more persistent at problem solving, they found the noise less irritating, and they did better at proofreading than yoked subjects. Actual control had beneficial effects of the sort we saw in the previous chapter.

Another group of subjects was presented with the same noise, but this time it was uncontrollable. However, this group had a panic button and was told, "You can terminate the noise by pressing the button. But we'd prefer you not do it." None of the subjects in fact tried to turn off the noise. All they had was the false belief that they could control the noise if they had to.[3] These people performed just as well as the people who actually controlled the noise. So actual controllability and actual uncontrollability can produce identical expectations. This experiment, in which the expectation was invalid, highlights the fact that it is the expectation, not the objective conditions of controllability, that is the crucial determinant of helplessness. How does this expectation of response-outcome independence produce the motivational, cognitive, and emotional disturbances associated with helplessness?

Motivational disturbance

The incentive to initiate voluntary responses in a traumatic situation has one primary source: the expectation that responding will produce relief.[4] In the absence of this incentive, voluntary responding will decrease in likelihood. When a person or animal has learned that relief is independent of responding, the expectation that responding will produce relief is negated, and therefore response initiation wanes. Most generally put, the incentive to initiate voluntary responses to control *any* outcome (e.g., food, sex, shock termination) comes from the expectation that responding will produce that outcome. When a person or animal has learned that the outcome is independent of responding, the expectation that responding will produce the outcome wanes; therefore response initiation diminishes.

Some theorists might think that this is a pretty big "therefore." Exactly why should a person or an animal who believes that responding is futile cease responding? This question plunges us into a fundamental controversy of learning theory, which is best illustrated by analogy: "Why does a heavenly body move?" is a question that concerned physicists from Aristotle to Galileo. Aristotle believed that the natural state of bodies was rest, and that an outside agent, or mover, was needed to get them moving. Galileo, in contrast, made the radical and useful assumption that the natural state of bodies was motion, and that they would always move unless some outside force, like friction, slowed them down.

There are parallel, and usually covert, assumptions buried in learning theories about why organisms make voluntary responses. The Galilean assumption is that the natural state of animals is voluntary responding, that they are always making some voluntary response. There is no such state as not responding: an apparently passive animal is voluntarily being passive. It has "chosen" passivity, "decided" on it, or been reinforced for it. On this view, an animal who expects that responding is futile becomes passive because passivity costs less, because doing it is more reinforcing. However, there is very little reason to believe that animals will choose low-effort over high-effort responding.[5]

I incline toward the opposite, Aristotelian, view: that voluntary responding requires incentive, and in the absence of incentive voluntary responding does not occur. On this view, people and animals can be in either of two states: engaged in voluntary responding, or not doing anything at all. For voluntary responding to occur, an incentive must be present in the form of an expectation that responding may succeed. In the absence of such an expectation, that is, when an organism believes responding is futile, voluntary responding will not occur.

It follows from this that animals who experience uncontrollable outcomes will later tend not to make responses to control that outcome. This deduction of the motivational deficit does not need much more elaboration. Except for the cognitive language in which it is cast, most learning theorists would accept it; and even the notions of expectation and incentive can be translated into more operational language for the benefit of theorists more behavioristically inclined.[6]

This undermining of motivation has been seen with crystal clarity in a human helplessness study using shock.[7] Following inescapable shock, college students sat and took escapable shock; when asked why they did not respond appropriately, 60 percent of the subjects reported that they had no control over shock, "So why try?" These subjective reports strongly suggest that a belief in uncontrollability undermines the incentive to initiate responses. More direct evidence would be hard to imagine.

Cognitive disturbance

Learning that an outcome is independent of a response makes it more difficult to learn, later on, that responses produce that outcome. Response-outcome independence is learned actively and, like any other active form of learning, interferes with learning about contingencies that contradict it. Here is an example of how such *proactive interference* works with verbal learning: My wife's married name is Kerry Seligman, but her maiden name was Kerry Mueller. People who first met her as "Mueller" had trouble learning to call her "Seligman"; years after our wedding, they would occasionally slip. Because they tended to call her Kerry Mueller, this interfered with remembering that she was now Kerry Seligman. They had more trouble learning to call her Kerry Seligman than someone who met her for the first time after her wedding, who had to learn her name *de novo*.

Parallel to this is the case of a dog who made a number of responses in the hammock and found that each of them was unrelated to shock going off. The dog would, for example, turn his head and shock might happen to go off that time, but just as often he would turn his head and shock would not go off; shock would also go off when he hadn't turned his head. When he goes to the shuttle box and jumps the barrier, in reality causing shock termination, the dog has trouble learning this. This is because, as for head turning, he still expects that shock will be just as likely to go off if he fails to jump the barrier. Such a dog will revert to taking shock passively even after he makes one or two successful jumps. In contrast, a naive dog has no interfering expectation that shock termination is independent of responding, so one jump over the barrier resulting in shock termination is sufficient for him to catch on.

Maier and Testa (1974) have reported three experiments

that point to the cognitive deficit as crucial for learned help-lessness in the rat. The reader will recall that rats who had received inescapable shock were not helpless when they had to shuttle once to escape (Fixed Ratio 1—FR1), but became helpless if they had to go across and then back (FR2) (p. 29). In order to test whether the deficit depended on difficulty in *seeing* the relationship between responding and shock termination, or on the difficulty of *performing* an FR2, Maier and Testa did a clever thing. They had the rats learn an FR1 to escape, but with a slight delay of shock termination: when a rat ran across, shock went off, not immediately, but one second after it crossed. In this experiment the effortfulness of the response was identical to the easy FR1; what differed was that the contingency was hard to see. To the extent that helplessness produces difficulty in seeing response-outcome contingencies, the FR1 with a delay should be interfered with; any view of helplessness that merely postulates difficulty in responding will not predict a deficit here. As Maier and Testa expected, rats that had received inescapable shock failed to learn the FR1 with the delay, while rats who received no shock learned well. Similar results occurred when the contingency was obscured by partial reinforcement (50 percent shock termination) of the FR1. Finally, the experimenters tried to make the FR2 contingency clearer for helpless rats, while holding response effort constant: after a rat crossed the shuttlebox once, shock was very briefly turned off, but immediately went back on, only to terminate when the second response was made. Here the contingency was clearer, but the response requirement was the difficult one. As expected, the rats who had received inescapable shock were not helpless. So interference with responding is not sufficient to explain rat helplessness. In addition, a cognitive deficit—difficulty in seeing that responding works—is needed.

I believe that learning about response-outcome independence is just a special case of learning that any two events are independent. D. Kemler and B. Shepp (1971) have performed the most elegant study I know on learning that events are independent. Recall for a moment what must be learned in a solvable discrimination problem with black-white as the relevant dimension and left-right as the irrelevant dimension. White correlates perfectly with the presence and black with the absence of reward: on half the trials, randomly arranged, the black card is on the left and the white card on the right, while on the other trials the white card is on the left and black on the right. Left-right is independent of, or irrelevant to, reward: the probability of reward if you respond consistently to left is the same as if you respond consistently to right—0.5. When a dimension, like left-right, is independent of reward, what is learned? Does a person actively learn what is irrelevant, or does he passively ignore the irrelevant cues? It is crucial to the cognitive premise of my theory of helplessness that a person can actively learn independence between left-right and outcome.

In a discrimination learning experiment like the one described, Kemler and Shepp gave problems in which left-right was the relevant dimension to children who had had left-right irrelevant on earlier problems. Their ability to learn that a previously irrelevant dimension was now the relevant dimension was compared to an elaborate set of control groups. These children were the slowest to learn that left-right was correct, even slower than groups that had not previously been exposed to the dimension. This elegantly designed study showed that children actively learn that responding to the irrelevant dimension doesn't matter, and that they then have trouble finding out that this is the relevant dimension when the rules change.

Little more need be said except to remind the reader of the other evidence, reviewed in the last chapter, that showed that independence interferes with the future learning of dependence.[8]

Emotional disturbance

When a traumatic event first occurs, it causes a heightened state of emotionality that can loosely be called fear. This state continues until one of two things happens: if the subject learns that he can control the trauma, fear is reduced and may disappear altogether; or if the subject finally learns he cannot control the trauma, fear will decrease and be replaced with depression.

For example, when a rat, a dog, or a man experiences inescapable trauma he first struggles frantically. Fear, I believe, is the dominant emotion accompanying this state. If he learns to control the trauma, frenetic activity gives way to an efficient and nonchalant response. If the trauma is uncontrollable, however, struggling eventually gives way to the helpless state I have described. The emotion that accompanies this state is, I believe, depression. Similarly, when an infant monkey is separated from its mother, great distress is produced by the traumatic experience.[9] The monkey runs around frantically, making distress calls. Two things can happen: if the mother returns, the infant can now control her again, and distress will cease; or if the mother does not return, the infant eventually learns that it cannot bring mother back, and depression ensues, displacing the fear. The infant curls up in a ball and whines. Such a sequence is in fact what happens in all primate species that have been observed.

A recent human helplessness experiment by S. Roth and R. R. Bootzin (1974) also suggests such a sequence. College students received solvable or unsolvable problems, then were taken to a second room in which a new set of problems, which were all solvable, appeared on a TV screen. On every tenth trial, the screen blurred. The students who first had unsolvable problems were the first to go get the experimenter to fix the screen; it seemed that this group was made anxious and frustrated, rather than helpless, by unsolvability, at least as measured by their readiness to seek help. However, these students tended to be poorer at actually solving the problems on the screen. The authors hypothesized that uncontrollability first produces frustration, which gives way to helplessness as more uncontrollability occurs. Confirming this, Roth and Kubal (1974) observed helplessness, not facilitation, when they gave more uncontrollability, or when the subject perceived the failure as more significant.

Fear and frustration can be viewed as motivators that have evolved in order to fuel coping and that are set off by trauma. The initial responses to control a trauma are elicited by this fear. Once trauma is under control, fear has little use, and it decreases. As long as the subject is uncertain whether or not he can control trauma, fear is still useful, since it maintains the search for a response that will work. Once the subject is certain that trauma is uncontrollable, fear decreases—it is worse than useless since it costs the subject great energy in a hopeless situation. Depression then ensues.[10]

Many theorists have talked about the need or drive to master events in the environment. In a classic exposition, R. W. White (1959) proposed the concept of *competence*. He argued that the basic drive for control had been overlooked by learning theorists and psychoanalytic thinkers alike. The need to master could be more pervasive than sex, hunger, and thirst in the lives of animals and men. Play in young children, for example, is motivated not by "biological" drives, but by a competence drive. Similarly, J. L. Kavanau (1967) has postulated that the drive to resist compulsion is more important to wild animals than sex, food, or water. He found that captive white-footed mice spent inordinate time and energy just resisting experimental manipulation. If the experimenters turned the lights up, the mouse spent his time setting them down. If the experimenters turned the lights down, the mouse turned them up.

A drive for competence or to resist compulsion is, from my point of view, a drive to avoid helplessness. The existence of such a drive follows directly from the emotional premise of our theory. Since being helpless arouses fear and depression, activity that avoids helplessness thereby avoids these aversive emotional states. Competence may be a drive to avoid the fear and depression induced by helplessness.[11]

This, then, is our theory of helplessness: the expectation

that an outcome is independent of responding (1) reduces the motivation to control the outcome; (2) interferes with learning that responding controls the outcome; and, if the outcome is traumatic, (3) produces fear for as long as the subject is uncertain of the uncontrollability of the outcome, and then produces depression.

CURE AND PREVENTION

The theory suggests a way to cure helplessness, once it has set in, and a way to prevent it from occurring. If the central problem in lack of response initiation is the expectation that responding will not work, cure should occur when the expectation is reversed. My colleagues and I worked for a long time without success on this problem: first, we took the barrier out of the shuttle box, so the dog could lick the safe side if he chose, but he just lay there. Then I got into the other side of the shuttle box and called to the dog, but he just lay there. We made the dogs hungry and dropped Hebrew National salami[12] onto the safe side, but still the dog just lay there. We were trying, by all these procedures, to seduce the dog into responding during shock, and thus into seeing that its response had turned off shock. Finally, we showed one of our helpless dogs to James Geer, a behavior therapist, who said, "If I had a patient like that I would give him a swift kick to get him going." Geer was right: this therapy always works on helpless dogs and rats.[13] What it meant to us was that we should *force* the dog to respond—over and over, if necessary—and so have it come to see that changing compartments turns off shock. To this end we put long leashes around the necks of the dogs and began to drag them back and forth across the shuttle box during the CS and shock, with the barrier removed. Getting to the other side turned off the shock.

After from 25 to 200 draggings all dogs began to respond on their own. Once responding began, we gradually built up the barrier, and the dogs continued to escape and avoid. The recovery from helplessness was complete and lasting, and we have replicated the procedure in about 25 dogs and as many helpless rats. The behavior during leash pulling was noteworthy. At the beginning of the procedure, we had to exert a good deal of force to pull the dog across the center of the shuttle box. Usually the whole dead weight of the dog had to be dragged; in some cases the dog resisted. Less and less force was needed as training progressed. Typically, we reached a stage in which a slight nudge of the leash would drive the dog into action. Finally, each dog initiated its own response, and thereafter never failed to escape.

Once the correct response had occurred repeatedly, the dog caught on to the response-relief contingency. It is significant that so much "directive therapy" was required before the dogs would respond on their own. This observation supports the cognitive-motivational interpretation of the effects of inescapable shock: uncontrollability lowers the motivation to initiate responses during shock, and it impairs the ability to associate responses with relief.

Striking successes in medicine have come more frequently from prevention than from treatment, and I would hazard a guess that inoculation and immunization have saved many more lives than cure. In psychotherapy, procedures are almost exclusively curative, and prevention rarely plays an explicit role. In our studies of dogs and rats we found that *behavioral immunization*, as suggested by our theory, was an easy and effective means of preventing learned helplessness.

Initial experience with control over trauma should interfere with forming the expectation that responding and shock termination are independent, just as not being able to control shock interferes with learning that responding produces relief. To test this, we gave one group of dogs ten escape trials in the shuttle box before they received inescapable shocks in the hammock.[14] This eliminated interference with subsequent escape-avoidance behavior. That is, immunized dogs responded normally when placed in the shuttle box 24 hours after inescapable shock treatment in the hammock. Another interesting finding emerged: the dogs that began by learning to escape shock by jumping in the shuttle box pressed the panels in the hammock four times as often during the inescapable shocks as did naive dogs, even though pressing panels had no effect on shock. Such panel pressing probably measures the attempts of the dogs to control shock. David Marques, Robert Radford, and I extended these findings by first letting the dogs escape shock by pressing panels in the hammock. This was followed by inescapable shock in the same place. The experience with control over shock termination prevented the dogs from becoming helpless when they were later tested in the shuttle box. To my knowledge, no parametric study of immunization has been done. How much immunization does it take to overcome a given amount of uncontrollability? Is there an amount of immunization that makes an organism invulnerable to helplessness? Is there an amount of uncontrollability that nullifies all immunization?

Other findings from our laboratory support the idea that the experience of controlling trauma may protect organisms from the helplessness caused by inescapable trauma. Recall that, among dogs of unknown history, helplessness is a statistical effect: approximately two-thirds of dogs given inescapable shock become helpless, while one-third respond normally. About 5 percent of naive dogs are helpless in the shuttle box without any prior experience with inescapable shock. Why do some dogs become helpless while others do not? Could it be possible that those dogs who do not become helpless, even after inescapable shock, have had a history of controllable trauma before arriving at the laboratory—for example, leading a pack, cowing little children? We tested this hypothesis by raising dogs singly in laboratory cages.[15] Compared to dogs of unknown history, these dogs had very limited experience controlling anything, since food and water was provided for them and their contact with other dogs and humans was very limited. Cage-reared dogs proved to be more susceptible to helplessness: while it took four sessions of inescapable shock to produce helplessness, one week later, in dogs of unknown history, only two sessions of inescapable shock in the hammock were needed to cause helplessness in the cage-reared dogs. It has also been reported that dogs reared in isolation tend to fail to escape shock.[16] It seems that dogs who, in their developmental history, have been deprived of natural opportunities to master reinforcers may be more vulnerable to helplessness than naturally immunized dogs.

In this regard, we should mention C. P. Richter's (1957) striking findings on the sudden death of wild rats. Richter discovered that after he had squeezed wild rats in his hand until they stopped struggling, they drowned within 30 minutes of being placed in a water tank from which there was no escape, unlike nonsqueezed rats, who swam for 60 hours before drowning. Richter could prevent sudden death by a technique that resembled our immunization procedure: if he held the rat, then released it, held it again, and released it again, sudden death did not occur. Further, if, after holding it, he put the rat in the water, took it out, put it in again, and rescued it again, sudden death was prevented. These procedures, like our own with dogs, may provide the rat with a sense of control over trauma, and thereby immunize him against sudden death caused by inescapable trauma. Richter speculated that the critical variable in sudden death was "hopelessness": being held and squeezed in the hands of a predator is, for a wild animal, an overpowering experience of loss of control over its environment. The phenomenon of death from helplessness is so important that I will devote the entire final chapter to it.

Limits on helplessness

Since we all experience some uncontrollability, why aren't we always helpless?

Suppose I take a train to work one morning. I sit helplessly in a vehicle whose workings I do not really understand, driven by an engineer I don't know; yet I function perfectly well afterward, showing none of the three effects of helplessness. What has limited the effects of helplessness?

The crucial factor is the slippage between the experience of uncontrollability and forming the expectation that events are uncontrollable. Under what conditions will the expectation that events are uncontrollable *not* be formed, even though an experience with actual uncontrollability has occurred? I suspect that there are at least three factors limiting an expectation of uncontrollability: immunization by a contrary expectancy, immunization by discriminative control, and relative strength of the outcomes.

A past history of experience with controllability over a given outcome will lead to an expectation that the outcome is controllable. If a subject is finally faced with a situation in which the outcome is actually uncontrollable, he will have difficulty becoming convinced that it is now uncontrollable. This is at the heart of the concept of immunization. Prior expectations are, of course, a two-edged sword. A past history of uncontrollability will make it difficult to believe that an outcome is controllable, even when it actually is; indeed, this is the finding of our basic helplessness experiment: the dog continues to expect that shock is uncontrollable even in the face of controllable shock.

Immunization by discriminative control is a second limitation on the generality of helplessness. If a person has learned in one place, his office for example, that he has control, and becomes helpless in a second place, a train for example, he will discriminate between the different controllability of the two contexts. Just as the dog who has had control over shock in the shuttle box continues to escape in the shuttle box, even after intervening helplessness in the hammock, railroad helplessness should not affect my office performance. C. S. Dweck and

N. D. Reppucci (1973) reported discriminative control over helplessness in school children: when a teacher who had presented the pupils with unsolvable problems presented solvable ones, the children failed to solve them, even though they readily solved the identical problems if they were presented by other teachers. Steven Maier, however, in an unpublished study, found lack of discriminative control over helplessness in dogs. During a tone, shock was escapable by panel pressing in the hammock, while during a light it was inescapable. To Maier's dismay, dogs were helpless in the shuttle box during both light and tone.

It need not be tones or lights that exert discriminative control over helplessness. Being told—particularly by someone "who should know"—that a given event is uncontrollable will create an expectation that the event is uncontrollable, even without experience of the contingency. Conversely, just being told that an event is controllable will also short-circuit experiencing the contingency. Recall that merely telling a person he has a panic button that will turn off loud noise, even if he doesn't use it, is enough to prevent many of the effects of helplessness.

The final factor that may limit the transfer of helplessness from one situation to another is the relative significance of the two situations: helplessness may generalize readily from more traumatic or important events to less traumatic or important ones, but not vice-versa. My intuition is that, if I learned that the elevator in my office building was uncontrollable, I would not thereupon become helpless in intellectual disputes; but if I suddenly found myself helpless in intellectual matters, I might give up button pressing to get the elevator to come more readily. Bob Rosellini and I found that, when given very mild inescapable shock and tested on escape from that same mild shock, rats became mildly helpless: they escaped shock rather more poorly than rats who had not been shocked previously. If strong shock was used in both training and testing, however, the helpless animals were much poorer at escaping than unshocked rats. At the moment I know of no laboratory evidence that being helpless in a trivial situation fails to produce helplessness in a more important situation, while being helpless in an important situation produces helplessness in trivial situations.

ALTERNATIVE THEORIES

The theory of helplessness fits well with the data presented in Chapter Three; indeed, historically speaking, the theory predicted much of it. In addition, it has suggested successful means of prevention and cure of helplessness. Over the last decade, a number of alternate approaches have been suggested.[17] None of these accounts, incidentally, explains the wide range of effects we have reviewed; rather they focus specifically on explaining how inescapable shock can interfere with later escape.

Competing motor responses

Traditional learning theory has not only been conservative about how simple the contingencies for learning must be, but also about what could be learned. For example, learning theorists have been comfortable saying a pigeon had learned a response, like pecking a key for food, but uncomfortable saying a pigeon had learned *that* key pecking led to food. Such a cognition has usually been excluded from the realm of what animals (and even people!) could learn. The reason for the conservatism has to do with observability and simplicity: response learning is observable, but cognitions can only be inferred. Furthermore, response learning was thought to be simple and basic, while cognitions were seen as complex and derivative. While the controversy has lost much of its heat in the last two decades, it is worth considering response-learning alternatives to our cognitive theory of helplessness.

Why do the dogs fail to escape in the shuttle box? Not

because they have learned that responding does not matter, but because they have learned, in the hammock, some motor response that they perform in the shuttle box and that competes with barrier jumping. There are three ways a competing response might be learned.

One way, based on the idea of superstitious reinforcement, claims that some specific motor response happens to occur at the moment that shock terminates in the hammock. This magic moment reinforces the particular response, and increases the probability that it will happen when shock terminates on the next trial; in this manner, the response will acquire great strength. If this response is incompatible with barrier jumping and if shock elicits it in the shuttle box, then the dog will not jump the barrier.

This view is weak empirically: we observed the dogs and rats closely, yet saw no evidence of superstitious responding. Furthermore, the argument is logically unsound: if some response is superstitiously reinforced by shock termination, and so is more likely to recur, it will be more likely happen when shock goes on, as well as when shock goes off. This response will be punished by shock onset and continuation, as well as reinforced by shock termination, and it will therefore *decrease* in probability. Moreover, even if acquired in pretraining, why should the specific response persist in spite of hundreds of seconds of shock during testing? It seems that such a response should disappear.

A second hypothesis claims that active responses are occasionally punished by shock onset. Such superstitious punishment decreases the probability of active responding in the hammock, and this transfers to the shuttle box. This hypothesis entails the same logical difficulty as does superstitious reinforcement. Active responding may be occasionally punished by shock onset, but it will also be reinforced by shock termination. Furthermore, as active responding is eliminated by punishment, passive responding will increase in frequency. At this point, punishment will begin to eliminate passive responding, thereby increasing the probability of active responding, and so on. Moreover, even if passive responding were acquired through superstitious punishment in the harness, why would it persist in spite of hundreds of seconds of shock in the shuttle box? The reader by now should begin to appreciate how many degrees of freedom superstitious-motor-response explanations have, and therefore how they can "explain" virtually any result—after the fact.

A third version of the competing-motor-response interpretation is that the animal, by means of some specific motor response, reduces the severity of electric shocks received in the harness. This explicitly reinforced motor response might interfere with barrier jumping. Because inescapable shocks in the harness are delivered through attached electrodes held on by electrode paste, it is unlikely that the dog could change the intensity by any particular motor response. It is conceivable, however, that some unknown pattern of movement may reduce pain. Overmier and Seligman (1967) eliminated this possibility: their dogs were completely paralyzed by curare during inescapable shocks in the harness, and so could not move any of their muscles. These dogs subsequently failed to escape shock in the shuttle box, just like unparalyzed dogs who received inescapable shocks. In contrast, dogs merely paralyzed, but given no shock, later escaped normally. If a dog under curare can reduce shock, he is not doing it with his muscles.

Regardless of how the response is alleged to come about, we are convinced that helplessness is not any form of competing motor response. S. F. Maier's (1970) passive-escape experiment most emphatically rules it out. In response to the possible criticism that what is learned during uncontrollable trauma is not the cognitive set of helplessness that we have proposed, but some motor response like freezing,[18] which antagonizes barrier jumping, Maier reinforced the most antagonistic responses he could find. As the reader will recall, one group (passive-escape) of dogs had panels arranged 1/4 inch from the sides and tops of their heads. Only by not moving their heads, by remaining passive and still, could these dogs terminate shock. Another group (yoked) received the same shocks in the hammock, but independently of responding. A third group received no shock. A response-learning hypothesis predicts that, when the dogs were later tested in the shuttle box, the passive-escape group would be the most helpless, since they had been trained *explicitly* not to move in the face of trauma. The helplessness hypothesis makes the opposite prediction: these dogs could control shock, albeit by being passive; some response, even a competing one, was effective in producing relief, and they should not learn that responding doesn't matter. The passive-escape group should learn to escape by jumping, and this is exactly what happened. Similarly, in the rat: it seems unlikely that the rat learns a competing response after inescapable shock; for in the experiments on the rat discussed in Chapter Three the rat responded well on schedules which called for one bar press or one shuttle, but became helpless when two or more responses were called for.[19] Competing responses would interfere with the first response at least as much as the second and third.

While response-learning explanations of behavior have been convenient devices, they just will not do the job of explaining helplessness—helplessness is not a peripheral alteration of the response repertoire, but a change central to the whole organism.

Adaptation, emotional exhaustion,
and sensitization

Several motivational hypotheses have been offered to explain failure to escape following uncontrollable shock. Theories of adaptation and emotional exhaustion both claim that animals who have received uncontrollable shock become adapted to trauma and no longer *care* enough to respond. They are so exhausted or adapted that their motivational level is insufficient. This seems implausible for several reasons:

(1) The animals do not look adapted: during the initial shocks of escape-avoidance testing, they are frantic; they become passive on later trials, but even then they vocalize when shocked.

(2) Adaptation to repeated, intense electric shock has never been directly demonstrated in the literature on pain.

(3) Even if adaptation occurs, it is unlikely to persist through the time periods that intervene between helplessness training and escape-avoidance testing.

(4) We have disconfirmed the adaptation hypothesis experimentally. Bruce Overmier and I gave very intense shocks in the shuttle box, but this did not reduce the interfering effects of prior inescapable shocks; the dogs were more upset, but they did not try to escape. If a dog fails to respond, or responds slowly, in the shuttle box only because shock is not motivating enough, then increasing the intensity of shock should produce responding.

(5) A series of escapable shocks received in the hammock does not interfere with barrier jumping, although the same shocks, if inescapable, produce helplessness. Both escapable and inescapable shocks should lead to the same degree of adaptation or exhaustion, yet their effects are strikingly different.

(6) Dogs that first escaped shocks in the shuttle box, and then received inescapable shocks in the hammock, continued to respond efficiently when returned to the shuttle box. There is no reason why prior escape training should reduce adaptation or exhaustion resulting from the series of inescapable shocks.

(7) Failure to escape in the shuttle box was eliminated when we dragged the dog back and forth over the barrier. There is no reason why forcibly exposing the dog to the escape and avoidance contingencies should make the dog less adapted or exhausted.

A complementary motivational hypothesis invokes sensitization. According to this view, dogs fail to escape because prior shock has so upset them that they are too frantic to organize an adaptive response. This is compatible with our premise of the enhanced emotionality produced by inescapable shock; however, it does not explain the basic data. If prior inescapable shocks make the dog overmotivated, then reducing the shock intensity in the shuttle box should induce the dog to respond. We found that the interference effect was *not* eliminated when the shock intensity used in the shuttle box was very low. Furthermore, arguments (5), (6), and (7) above invalidate the sensitization hypothesis as well as the adaptation hypothesis.

The existence of a time course of helplessness, at least in dogs and goldfish, makes an emotional-exhaustion theory especially palatable. Why does one session of inescapable shock lose its ability to produce helplessness after about 48 hours? Why, in the catastrophe syndrome, does the emotional bottom drop out and then recover in about 48 hours?

The simplest answer is that some substance is first exhausted and then renewed. As we shall see later in this chapter, it has been claimed that *norepinephrine* (NE) may be depleted by uncontrollable trauma, and take about 48 hours to be restored.[20] On the other hand, a learning explanation is also possible. Remember that multiple experiences with uncontrollability abolish the time course. Does repeated exposure to uncontrollability prevent the depleted substance from ever being restored? Possibly; but consider that before an animal or a man experiences uncontrollable trauma, he has usually had a wealth of previous experience controlling events of importance to him. If something is learned first, like an association between A and B, and then something contrary is learned, like A with C, the memory of the second experience weakens with time. So if I test you immediately after the second experience by asking you what letter follows A, you will say C; but if I ask a few days later what follows A, you will probably say B. This is called *proactive inhibition* (PI) and is often used to explain forgetting.[21] Because proactive inhibition (and therefore forgetting) in both humans and animals increases with time, the dissipation of helplessness might result from such forgetting. Twenty-four hours after inescapable shock, the earlier memories of control are not strong enough to counteract the new expectation that responding does not control shock; forty-eight hours later, they are. Perseveration of helplessness occurs because the extra experience with inescapable shock makes the helplessness too strong to be counteracted by the earlier experience of control. Future experimentation will reveal whether the time course is a physiological phenomenon or a forgetting phenomenon. My best guess is that, as for helplessness itself and for depression, phenomena at both the psychological and physiological levels of analysis usually act in concert.

PHYSIOLOGICAL APPROACHES TO HELPLESSNESS

I have opted for a behavioral-cognitive explanation of the motivational, cognitive, and emotional disturbances that accompany uncontrollability; but this is not meant to exclude a physiological explanation. Rather, it simply reflects the fact that we know a great deal more—at this moment—about the cognitive and behavioral basis of helplessness than we do about its physiological underpinnings. But helplessness must have some neural and biochemical basis, and two investigators have proposed intriguing physiological theories.

J. M. Weiss and his associates have uncovered some preliminary facts about the physiological consequences of uncontrollable shock: aside from the ulcers and weight loss produced in the yoked rats, the contents of the brain show deficits as well.[22] Norepinephrine (NE), one chemical by which a neuron fires another neuron in the central nervous system, is the basic *adrenergic* transmitter substance. (*Cholinergic* substances are other basic transmitters that will concern us.) Weiss has found that when a rat can control shock, the level of NE in the brain goes up compared to the rats who are not shocked; but when a rat gets uncontrollable shock, NE goes down. On this basis, Weiss has suggested that NE depletion may be the explanation of helplessness.

He believes that the deficits produced by inescapable shock are not caused by learning or cognition, but *directly* caused by NE depletion. Inescapability causes weight loss, loss of appetite, ulcers, and NE depletion. These deficits in turn cause failure to escape and a generally lowered level of activity. NE depletion is both necessary and sufficient to produce helpless behavior; invoking a cognition of helplessness is, according to Weiss, unnecessary.

In an experiment supporting this, Weiss plunged rats into very cold water for six minutes. Among many other things, this depleted NE; when tested a half hour later in shuttle box escape, the rats were helpless. A six-minute swim in warm water does not deplete NE and does not produce helplessness. A more specific NE depletor, α-methyl-para-tyrosine (AMPT) also produces failure to escape in rats.[23]

In his most impressive experiment, Weiss tried to play off a cognitive view against a physiological explanation. It turned out that, for unknown reasons, while a course of 15 consecutive daily sessions of very intense inescapable shock at first depleted NE, by the end of the course, NE depletion did not occur. A cognitive view of helplessness predicts that rats should seem very helpless after so much inescapable shock; an NE-depletion view, which holds cognition to be irrelevant, predicts no helplessness. These rats escape and avoid like unshocked controls. This is important evidence, but before criticizing the NE hypothesis and discussing its implications, I want to present another exciting new finding on the physiological substratum of helplessness.

Let me first say a few words about some nerve tracts in the higher mammalian brain. There is a large tract of neurons called the median forebrain bundle (MFB), the stimulation of which is thought to be the physiological basis for pleasure and positive reward.[24] The MFB is adrenergic, incidentally, and norepinephrine is the primary transmitter substance in it. A neighboring cholinergic structure, called the septum, when stimulated shuts down or inhibits the MFB. E. Thomas noticed that when he stimulated the septum directly with electricity, his cats became passive and lethargic.[25] Rewards did not seem as rewarding as usual, and punishment less disturbing. This led Thomas to propose that septal excitation, which inhibits the MFB, was the cause of helplessness.

To test this, Thomas produced learned helplessness in cats by inescapable electric shock. Each cat had a cannula, which is a small hypodermic needle, implanted in its septum. Thomas injected atropine into the septa of cats that had received inescapable shock. (Atropine, a cholinergic blocking agent, shuts off the activity of the septum.) These cats were not helpless in the shuttle box, but cats without atropine who had experienced inescapable shock were helpless. Thomas then gave all of these cats more inescapable shock in the hammock and returned them to the shuttle box. The cats who had been helpless now got atropine; this cured their helplessness. The cats who previously had atropine, and had escaped normally in the shuttle box, now got no atropine; they became helpless. This confirmed Thomas's view that helplessness is explained by the cholinergic action of the septum, since blocking it with atropine broke up helplessness.

These data on NE depletion and cholinergic activity will undoubtedly help us to find the physiological basis of helplessness, and also, perhaps, of human depression. But what exactly do they portend for the cognitive theory of helplessness that I have proposed? There are two ways of determining this: by asking (1) what facts NE depletion explains that the cognitive theory can't, and (2) what facts the cognitive theory explains that NE depletion can't.

The cognitive theory is not greatly troubled by most of the data concerning NE depletion. In fact, the data may lead us to the neural and biochemical basis of the cognition of helplessness. For example, NE depletion in rats follows a time course somewhat like that of helplessness in dogs that have received only one session of inescapable shock. This could either be because NE depletion is caused by the presence and waning of a belief in helplessness, or because NE depletion is a correlate of the cognition; it need not imply that the cognition does not exist or even that NE depletion causes the cognition. Similarly, atropine might work by producing a cognition of not being helpless, the cognitive change then causing the behavioral change. As I shall mention in Chapter Five, atropine seems to reverse depressive cognitions in man.

How about the cold-water swim producing interference with escape? The cognitive theory does not hold that the cognition of uncontrollability is the *only* way of producing the inability to escape shock. Cutting off an animal's legs will interfere with escape, but that does not mean that inescapable shock interferes with escape by means of "legotomy." When we put rats, for a few minutes, in water as cold as Weiss used, they were numb and half dead when taken out. Sportsmen who canoe in Maine know that, if you capsize in cold water, you have only a very few minutes to make it to shore before you die of exposure; it may well have been that Weiss's rats failed to escape 30 minutes after the cold swim because they were near death, not because of NE depletion.

The 15-day course of inescapability is more troubling. With the other NE data, the cognitive view makes no prediction in advance about what particular chemical changes are associated with the cognition; it is merely not inconsistent with the findings. But in the case of the rats who received 15 days of inescapable shock, the cognitive theory makes a prediction opposite to the NE-depletion theory. Recently Steven Maier and his co-workers, and Robert Rosellini and I, have tried to reproduce Weiss's findings. We gave rats either 10 or 15 consecutive days of inescapable shock; contrary to Weiss's findings, our rats failed completely to escape shock after this pretreatment. It seems that Weiss's 15-day finding awaits further empirical exploration.

There is a great deal of data, on the other hand, that the NE-depletion theory cannot handle, but the cognitive theory can. Here is a reminder of some: It is most unlikely that humans or hungry rats who receive unsolvable discrimination problems thereby become NE depleted; yet they fail to solve subsequent problems. It is most unlikely that rats who receive noncontingent food become NE depleted, yet they have trouble later learning to press a bar for food. In rats after one session of inescapable shock or in dogs after several sessions, helplessness is permanent; yet NE depletion is transient. Similarly, rats who receive inescapable shock at weaning fail to escape shock as adults; yet NE depletion should have disappeared long before adulthood. Rats who have received inescapable shock are not less active than control rats in an open field, either 24 hours or one week later; yet they fail to escape shock. NE depletion predicts that they should be less active, and fail to escape 24 hours later, but not fail to escape one week later. Rats or dogs who have been immunized by early experience escaping shock do not become helpless after inescapable shock; yet why should learning mastery prevent NE depletion? If NE depletion undermines performance only by reducing activity, why should rats fail to learn FR1 escape only when the contingency is obscured by delay of shock termination? Finally, showing a rat or a dog how to turn off shock, by dragging him through the response, breaks up helplessness, although merely random dragging does not; yet there is no reason to believe that this suddenly restores NE. In fact, showing a rat NE-depleted by AMPT how to escape breaks up helplessness.[26]

So the cognitive view can handle the NE-depletion data—indeed, the discovery of NE depletion may help explain the cognition of uncontrollability. NE depletion alone, however, cannot account for many of the facts that the cognitive theory predicts, since NE depletion seems to be neither necessary nor sufficient to produce learned helplessness.

If further research bears out the importance of septal activity or NE depletion in helplessness, what will we say the *cause* of helplessness is? Does the physiology cause the cognition, or does the cognition cause the physiological change? This is a very thorny problem.

Many laymen believe in a pyramid of the sciences—physics explains chemistry, which explains biology, and so on up to economics or politics. A parallel of this in psychology is the belief that physiology causes behavioral and cognitive states, but that cognition and behavior don't cause physiological changes. But the arrow of causation goes both ways. On the one hand, the physiological changes caused by lack of blood sugar may cause feelings of fatigue and faintness. On the other hand, if I tell you that your house is on fire, this information, processed cognitively, causes adrenalin flow, sweating, and dryness of the mouth. Similarly, change in the prime interest rate, an economic phenomenon, causes heart-rate change, a physiological phenomenon, in Wall Street investors.

The relation of physiology to cognition in helplessness also shows both causal directions. As Thomas showed, direct blockade of the septum alleviates helplessness; since no behavioral or cognitive manipulation has occurred, in this case physiology causes behavioral and perhaps cognitive changes. On the other hand, when dragging a dog back and forth across the shuttle box shows him that responding works, this cognitive information breaks up the behaviors of helplessness and almost surely causes physiological changes. Moreover, keep in mind the basic triadic design: here the difference between escapability and inescapability is not physical; it is information that can only be processed cognitively. It is this cognitive change that begins the chain of physiological, emotional, and behavioral events that together make up helplessness.

Both cognition and physiology influence helplessness. The two levels of change usually act in concert, but there are indications that either one *alone* can produce helplessness. Future research will tell us whether NE depletion or septal activity is sufficient to produce helplessness even in animals or people who believe that events are controllable. If it is, does it act by changing their cognitions or does it produce helpless behavior directly? Conversely, is merely learning uncontrollability sufficient to produce helplessness in animals that have NE artificially elevated or have the septum artificially blocked? If these subjects escape, do they now believe that shock is controllable? Or do they still believe that shock is uncontrollable, but escape well anyway? In our discussion of depression in the next chapter, we will raise this question again: Is depression basically a physiological, an emotional, or a cognitive disorder? The answer will be parallel: influences at all three levels seem to cause changes in each other, and all finally pour into the common channel of depression.

I have presented a theory of helplessness which claims that organisms, when exposed to uncontrollable events, learn that responding is futile. Such learning undermines the incentive to respond, and so it produces profound interference with the motivation of instrumental behavior. It also proactively interferes with learning that responding works when events become controllable, and so produces cognitive distortions. The fear of an organism faced with trauma is reduced if it learns that responding controls trauma; fear persists if the organism remains uncertain about whether trauma is controllable; if the organism learns that trauma is uncontrollable, fear gives way to depression. We shall now turn to an examination of depression, the most common form of human psychopathology.

CHAPTER FIVE

DEPRESSION

Recently, a 42-year-old business executive, temporarily unemployed, came to see me for some vocational advice. Actually, it was his wife who first contacted me; having read a popular article of mine on helplessness, she asked me to talk with her husband, Mel, because he looked helpless to her. For the last twenty years, Mel had been a rising executive; up until a year ago, he had been in charge of production for a multimillion-dollar company involved in the space program. When the government decreased its financial support of space research, he lost his job, and was forced to take a new executive position in another city, in a company he described as "backbiting." After six miserable and lonely months he quit. For a month he sat listlessly around the house, and made no effort to find work; the slightest annoyance drove him into a rage; he was unsocial and withdrawn. Finally his wife prevailed on Mel to take some vocational guidance tests that might help him find a satisfying job.

When the results of the tests came back, they revealed that he had a low tolerance for frustration, that he was unsociable, that he was incapable of taking on responsibility, and that routine, prescribed work best fit his personality. The vocational guidance company recommended that he become a worker on an assembly line.

This advice came as a shock to Mel and his wife, since he had twenty years of high executive achievement behind him, was usually outgoing and persuasive, and was much brighter than most sewing-machine operators. But the tests actually reflected his present state of mind: he believed himself incompetent, he saw his career as a failure, he found every small obstacle an insurmountable barrier, he was not interested in other people, and he could barely force himself to get dressed, much less to make important career decisions. But this profile did not give a true picture of Mel's character; rather it reflected a process, probably temporary, that had been going on since he lost his job—the disorder of depression.

Depression is the common cold of psychopathology and has touched the lives of us all, yet it is probably the most dimly understood and most inadequately investigated of all the major forms of psychopathology. In this chapter, I shall present a learned-helplessness model of depression that may shed some light on the causes, treatment, and prevention of this disorder.

What is depression? Mel, as well as two of the people described in the introductory chapter, are typical examples of depression: Recall the middle-aged woman, formerly active and vivacious, who now lies in bed all day and cries; her troubles began when her sons went away to college and her husband was promoted. And there was Nancy, the "golden girl" who, after many high-school successes, entered the University, and is now feeling empty and worthless; she is, in fact, a failure.

We can sympathize with these three people, because every

one of us, at one time or another, has felt the mood of depression: we feel blue, small exertions tire us out, we lose our sense of humor and our desire to do much of anything—even the things that usually excite us the most. For most people, these moods are usually infrequent and lift in a short time; for many others, however, this mood is recurrent, pervasive, and can be of lethal intensity. When depression is this severe, what most people pass off as just a mood has become a syndrome, or the symptom of a disorder. As depression progresses from mild to severe, the dejected mood intensifies, and with it, erosion of motivation and loss of interest in the world. The depressed person often becomes aware of strong feelings of self dislike; he feels worthless and guilty about his shortcomings. He believes that nothing he can do will alleviate his condition, and the future looks black. Crying spells may set in, the person loses weight, finds himself unable to go to sleep, or unable to get back to sleep when he wakes up very early in the morning. Food no longer tastes good, sex is not arousing, and people, even his wife and children, become wholly uninteresting. He may begin to think about killing himself. As his intention becomes more serious, the suicidal musings may change to desire; he will evolve a plan and begin to carry it out. There are few psychological disorders as completely debilitating, and none that produce such misery, as severe depression.

The prevalence of depression in American today is staggering. Excluding the mild depressions we all occasionally suffer, the National Institute of Mental Health estimates that "four to eight million Americans may be in need of professional care for the depressive illness." Unlike most other forms of psychopathology, depression can be lethal. "One out of every 200 persons affected by a depressive illness will die a suicidal death." This estimate is probably on the low side. In addition to the unmeasurable cost in individual misery, the economic cost is large: treatment and loss of time at work alone cost between 1.3 and 4.0 billion dollars a year.[1]

TYPES OF DEPRESSION

Confusion is rampant in the literature on depression, and it is often caused by a proliferation of categories. In discussing problems of classification, J. Mendels (1968) listed some of the subtypes of depression that have been described:

> A short list would include psychotic, neurotic, reactive, psychotic reactive, involutional, agitated, endogenous, psychogenic, symptomatic, presenile, senile, acute, chronic, and, of course, manic-depressive psychosis and melancholia (minor and major); as well as depression in sexual perversion, alcoholic depression, and depressive symptoms resulting from organic disorder.

I will suggest that, at the core, there is something unitary that all these depressions share.

The most useful and best-confirmed typology of depression is the *endogenous-reactive dichotomy*.[2] The *reactive depressions* are by far the most common, and the kind familiar to us all. Roughly 75 percent of all depressions are reactions to some external event, such as the death of a child. Reactive depressions do not cycle regularly in time, are not usually responsive to physical therapies like drugs and electroconvulsive shock (ECS), are not genetically predisposed, and are usually somewhat milder in their symptoms than endogenous depression.

Endogenous depressions, are a response to some unknown internal or endogenous process. These depressions are not triggered by any external event; they just sweep over the sufferer. They usually cycle regularly in time, and can be either *bipolar* or *unipolar*. Bipolar depression is called *manic-depression*—the individual repeatedly cycles through despair, a neutral mood, a hyperactive and superficially euphoric state of mania, and back through neutrality to despair. Early in this century, all depressions were mistakenly called manic-depressive illnesses, but it is now known that depression usually occurs without mania, and that mania can occur without depression. Unipolar endogenous depression consists of a regular alternation of despair and neutrality, without the occurrence of mania. Endogenous depressions often respond to drug treatments and ECS, and may be hormonal. They may also be genetically predisposed,[3] and are often more severe in their symptoms than reactive depressions.

While reactive depressions are at the primary focus of the learned-helplessness model of depression, I will suggest that endogenous depressions have much in common psychologically with reactive depressions.

THE LEARNED-HELPLESSNESS
MODEL OF DEPRESSION

It has happened more than once that investigators have discovered striking maladaptive behaviors in their laboratories and suggested that the behaviors represented some form of naturally occurring psychopathology. Pavlov (1928) found that conditioned reflexes of dogs disintegrated when discrimination problems became very difficult. H. Liddell (1953) found that sheep gave up making conditioned flexion responses after very many trials of signals paired with shock. Both Pavlov and Liddell claimed they had demonstrated experimental neuroses. J. H. Masserman (1943) found that hungry cats stopped eating in compartments where they had been shocked; he claimed that he had brought phobias into the laboratory. The experimental analyses of such phenomena were reasonably thorough, but the claim that they analyzed real psychopathology was usually unconvincing. Worse, they usually employed "plausibility" arguments that are very hard to confirm.[4] How, for example, would one ever *test* whether Pavlov's dogs had anxiety neuroses, rather than compulsions or psychoses? I believe that psychopathology in man, like physical pathology, can be captured and analyzed in the laboratory. To do this, however, a superficial validity argument of the form "this looks like a phobia" is insufficient. Therefore, I want to suggest some necessary ground rules for testing whether some laboratory phenomenon, either animal or human, is a model of a natural form of psychopathology in man.

Ground rules

There are four relevant lines of evidence for asserting that two phenomena are similar: (1) behavioral and physiological symptoms, (2) etiology or cause, (3) cure, and (4) prevention. If two phenomena are similar on one or two of these criteria, we can then test the model by looking for similarities predicted on the other criteria. Suppose that learned helplessness has symptoms and etiology similar to reactive depression, and further, that we can cure learned helplessness in dogs by forcing them to respond in a way that produces relief. This makes a prediction about the cure of depression in man: the central issue in successful therapy should be the patient's recognition that his responding is effective. If this is tested and confirmed, the model is strengthened; if disconfirmed, the model is weakened. In this case, the laboratory phenomena suggest what to look for in real-life psychopathology, but it is also possible to strengthen the model empirically from the other direction: for example, if the drug imipramine helps reactive depression, it should also relieve learned helplessness in animals.

A suitable model not only improves testability, but helps to sharpen the definition of the clinical phenomenon, since the laboratory phenomenon is well defined, while the definition of the clinical phenomenon is almost always fuzzy. For example, consider whether learned helplessness and depression have similar symptoms. Because it is a laboratory phenomenon, helplessness has necessary behaviors that define its presence or absence. On the other hand, there is no one symptom that all depressives have, since depression is a convenient diagnostic label that embraces a family of symptoms, no one of which is necessary.[5] Depressives often feel sad, but sadness need not be present to diagnose depression; if a patient doesn't feel sad, but is verbally and motorically retarded, cries a lot, has lost twenty pounds in the last month, and the onset of symptoms can be traced to his wife's death, then depression is the appropriate diagnosis. Motor retardation also is not necessary, for a depressive can be quite agitated.

A laboratory model does not have the open-endedness of the clinical phenomenon; it clips the clinical concept off at the edges by imposing necessary features on it. So if our model of depression is valid, some phenomena formerly called depressions will probably be excluded. The label "depression" applies to passive individuals who believe they cannot do anything to relieve their suffering, who become depressed when they lose an important source of nurture—the perfect case for learned helplessness to model; but it also applies to agitated patients who make many active responses, and who become depressed with no obvious external cause. Learned helplessness need not characterize the whole spectrum of depressions, but only those primarily in which the individual is slow to initiate responses, believes himself to be powerless and hopeless, and sees his future as bleak—which began as a reaction to having lost his control over gratification and relief from suffering.

The definition and categorization of illness is customarily refined by the verification of a theory about the illness. The presence of little poxes on the body was once the defining feature of smallpox. When a germ theory of smallpox was proposed and confirmed, the presence of the germ became part of the definition. As a result, some cases previously called smallpox were excluded, and others, previously ignored, were included. Ultimately, if the learned-helplessness model of depression proves adequate, the very concept of depression may be reshaped: if learned helplessness significantly illuminates some depressions, others, such as manic-depression, may eventually be seen as a different disorder, and still other problems, such as the disaster syndrome, that are not usually thought of as depression, may be called depression.

Symptoms of depression and
learned helplessness

In the previous chapters, six symptoms of learned helplessness
have emerged; each of them has parallels in depression:

(1) Lowered initiation of voluntary responses—animals
and men who have experienced uncontrollability show reduced
initiation of voluntary responses.

(2) Negative cognitive set—helpless animals and men
have difficulty learning that responses produce outcomes.

(3) Time course—helplessness dissipates in time when
induced by a single session of uncontrollable shock; after
multiple sessions, helplessness persists.

(4) Lowered aggression—helpless animals and men initiate fewer aggressive and competitive responses, and their
dominance status may diminish.

(5) Loss of appetite—helpless animals eat less, lose
weight, and are sexually and socially deficient.

(6) Physiological changes—helpless rats show norepinephrine depletion and helpless cats may be cholinergically
over-active.

Lowered initiation of voluntary responses.   Depressed men and
women don't do much; the word *depression* itself probably has its
etymological roots in the reduced activity of the patient. I
recently suggested to a depressed woman patient, who had let
her appearance go to seed, that she go out and buy herself a
new dress. Her response was typical: "Oh, Doctor, that's just
too hard for me."

Systematic studies of the symptoms of depression characterize this behavioral manifestation in a number of ways:

*Isolated and withdrawn, prefers to remain by himself, stays in bed much
of the time.*

*Gait and general behavior slow and retarded. Volume of voice decreased,
sits alone very quietly.*

Feels unable to act, feels unable to make decisions.

Gives the appearance of an "empty" person who has "given up."[6]

Paralysis of the will is a striking feature of severe depression:

In severe cases, there often is complete paralysis of the will. The patient has no desire to do anything, even those things which are essential to life. Consequently, he may be relatively immobile unless prodded or pushed into activity by others. It is sometimes necessary to pull the patient out of bed, wash, dress and feed him. In extreme cases, even communication may be blocked by the patient's inertia.[7]

Lowered response initiation is documented by experimental studies of *psychomotor retardation* in depression, as well as by clinical impressions. When depressives are tested in a variety of psychomotor tasks, such as reaction time, they prove to be slower than normals[8] — chronic schizophrenics are the only other patients who are as slow as depressives. Furthermore, depressed people engage in fewer of the activities that they used to find pleasant.[9]

Lowered response initiation may also be the cause of a variety of other so-called intellectual deficits in depressed patients. For example, the tested IQ's of hospitalized depressives drop during the disorder, and their ability to memorize definitions of new words deteriorates.[10] It must be remembered that when a patient takes an IQ test or memorizes definitions, this is not a pure test of intellectual abilities irrespective of how motivated the patient is. If the person does not believe that he will do well, or if he feels helpless, he will not try as hard: he will not make voluntary cognitive responses, such as memory-scanning or multiplication, as quickly or as well as someone whose motivation is not impaired. So a belief in helplessness may produce apparent intellectual deficits in depressives indirectly, through a motivational impairment.

Incidentally, the same reasoning applies to the racial IQ controversy. Jensen (1969, 1973) has reviewed rather strong data showing that American blacks score 15 points lower than whites on IQ tests, even on so-called culture-fair tests. If this is true, I know of no evidence that rules out a motivational impairment, rather than "intellectual" inferiority, as the explanation. I would not be surprised to find that blacks in America historically have believed themselves to be considerably more helpless than whites; I shall discuss this more fully in Chapter Seven.

Lowered response initiation in depression is also manifested in social deficits. P. Ekman and W. V. Friesen (1974) have done a fascinating series of filmed studies of the hand motions that depressives make in the course of chatting with an interviewer. Two categories of hand motion accompany conversation: *Illustrators* are sweeping gestures that accompany words to emphasize and illustrate what is being said. These are voluntary and conscious, for if you interrupt and ask the speaker what he just did, he can tell you accurately. *Adaptors* are small, tic-like motions, such as nose picking or hair pulling. These are involuntary and are not conscious; if interrupted, the speaker usually cannot report them. When a depressive arrives at the hospital, he makes many adaptors, but few illustrators. As he gets better, he makes more illustrators and fewer adaptors, indicating a recovery of voluntary response initiation.

Other social responses are also diminished in depressives. When someone says "Good morning" to a depressed person, he will be slow to answer.[11] Moreover, it will take him longer to reply with a social amenity, such as "And how are *you?*" The reader can verify this in any phone conversation with a friend he knows to be depressed.

In summary, the lowered voluntary response initiation that defines learned helplessness is pervasive in depression. It produces passivity, psychomotor retardation, intellectual slowness, and social unresponsiveness; in extreme depression, it can produce stupor.

Negative cognitive set. Suppose that I was able to convince my depressed patient that it wouldn't be too hard for her to go out and buy a dress. Her next line of defense would be: "But I'd probably take the wrong bus, and even if I found the right store, I'd pick out the wrong size, style, and color. Anyway,

I'd look just as bad in new clothes as in old clothes, because I'm basically unattractive." Depressed people believe themselves to be even more ineffective than they actually are: small obstacles to success are seen as impassible barriers, difficulty in dealing with a problem is seen as complete failure, and even outright success is often misconstrued as failure. A. T. Beck[12] views this *negative cognitive set* as the universal hallmark of depression.

The discrepancy is striking between the depressive's objective performance, which as we have seen isn't all that good to begin with, and his subjective appraisal. A. S. Friedman (1964) found that depressed patients performed more poorly than normals in reaction to a light signal, and they took longer to recognize common objects; but even more striking was their subjective estimate of how poorly they thought they would do:

> *When the examiner would bring the patient into the testing room, the patient would immediately protest that he or she could not possibly take the tests, was unable to do anything, or felt too bad or too tired, was incapable, hopeless, etc. . . . While performing adequately the patient would occasionally and less frequently reiterate the original protest, saying "I can't do it," "I don't know how," etc.*

This has also been our experience in testing depressed patients in the laboratory. If you ask a depressive after an intellectual speed test how slow he was, he will tell you that he was even slower than he had actually been.

This struck me most forcefully when my colleagues and I were trying out the *graded-task assignment*, a new therapy for depression. The instructions to the patient routinely begin: "I have some tasks here I should like you to perform." One day, after chatting amiably with a depressed middle-aged woman, I brought her to the testing room and began the instructions. When I said the word *task*, she burst into tears and was unable to continue. A mere task is seen by a depressive as a labor of Hercules.

William Miller and I have tested this aspect of the learned-helpless model on depressed students and patients.[13] If learned helplessness is a model of depression then helplessness produced by inescapable noise or unsolvable problems should result in the same symptoms seen in naturally occurring depression. Recall that in Chapter Three I mentioned that the experience of inescapable noise produced a negative cognitive set: subjects thereafter showed small changes in their expectancies of success or failure in a skill task (p. 37). They treated their successes and failures in a task of skill just as if it had been a task of chance in which their responses didn't matter. In contrast, subjects who received escapable noise or no noise showed large expectancy changes when they failed or succeeded in skill, but small changes when they performed chance tasks. None of these subjects was depressed. We then wondered if depression itself, without pretreatment with noise, would produce the same negative set as that produced by helplessness in nondepressed subjects.

According to our model, depression is not generalized pessimism, but pessimism specific to the effects of one's own skilled actions. We therefore placed groups of depressed and nondepressed subjects in tests of skill and of chance; in both tests the subjects were to experience the same pattern of success and failure. We found that depressed and nondepressed students did not differ in their initial expectancies of success. After each success and each failure, we asked the subjects how well they thought they would do on the next trial, as we had earlier with the subjects who had experienced noise. Depressed and nondepressed people differed greatly, once the two groups had experienced success and failure. The nondepressed people, believing that their responses mattered in the skill task, showed much greater expectancy changes than they did in the chance task. The depressed group, however, did not change their expectancies any more in skill than they did in chance. Further, the more depressed an individual was, the less his expectancies changed in skill tasks: he apparently believed that his responses mattered no more in skill than they did in chance. When depressive subjects were matched for anxiety with non-depressed subjects, only the depressives showed the negative cognitive set, indicating that this deficit is not produced by anxiety, but is specific to depression.[14] These results show experimentally that both depression as found in the real world and helplessness induced by uncontrollable events result in a negative cognitive set, the belief that success and failure are independent of one's efforts.

Miller and Seligman (1974b), by looking at anagram solution, provided more evidence for the symmetry of depression and learned helplessness. In Chapter Three, I mentioned that prior inescapable noise impairs the ability to solve anagrams (p. 38). Uncontrollability increased the time to solve an anagram, the number of failures to solve, and the number of trials to catch on to a pattern in the anagrams. These subjects were not depressed, however. Does naturally occurring depression produce the same negative cognitive set, as measured by impairment of anagram solution, as laboratory-induced helplessness? To test this, we gave three groups of students escapable noise, inescapable noise, or no noise. Half of each group was depressed, as measured by the Beck Depression Inventory (BDI), a mood scale; the other half was not depressed. As predicted, depressed subjects who had heard no noise, like nondepressed subjects who had experienced inescapable noise, did very badly on anagrams: they failed to solve more anagrams, took longer on the ones they did solve, and had more trouble catching on to the pattern. In addition, the more depressed a person was, the worse he did on anagrams. Again we see that depression produces the same deficits as laboratory-induced helplessness.[15]

One other group showed important results: the depressed group that had experienced escapable noise. This experience appeared to reverse their negative cognitive set, as measured by anagram solutions: this depressed group did much better than the depressed group who had heard no noise at all; in fact, they did just as well as *non*depressed subjects who had heard no noise at all. In summary, depressed people have a negative cognitive set, or difficulty believing that their responding works. We have been able to demonstrate this experimentally by looking at perception of reinforcement, anagram solution, and noise escape by depressives: the deficits shown by depressives in these tasks parallel exactly the deficits produced in nondepressed persons by uncontrollable events. These results offer strong support for the learned-helplessness model of depression.

Time course. Sometimes, when a man's wife dies he is depressed for only a few hours; at other times for weeks, months, or even years. (Sometimes, of course, he is euphoric.) But time usually heals. When catastrophe strikes, time courses of depression are found that parallel laboratory helplessness in the dog. When a team of researchers flew into Worcester, Massachusetts following a tornado, they found that people had functioned well during the catastrophe.[16] But 24 to 48 hours later there was emotional collapse—the residents meandered about listlessly or just sat in the rain. Within several days, however, the symptoms lifted. Time plays a role in almost all depressions.[17] In endogenous depressions, mood often cycles with regularity. In reactive depressions, mood is self-limiting, and it is therapeutically important for depressed patients to know that their despair will lift if they wait long enough.

There has been much talk lately about the civil rights of people who want to kill themselves. Most of our states have laws against suicide, and steps, such as suicide-prevention centers, are almost universally taken to prevent it. Civil libertarians have argued that if a person decides to take his own life, no agent should interfere with that decision.[18] He has a right to dispose of himself, just as he has a right to dispose of his property as he desires. I believe that this view is misguided. Suicide usually has its roots in depression, and depression dissipates in time. When a person is depressed, his view of the future is bleak; he sees himself as helpless and hopeless. But in many cases, if he waited a few weeks, this cognitive set would be changed, and by reason of time alone; the future would seem less hopeless, even though the actual circumstances remained the same. In other words, the force of the depressive's wish to kill himself would weaken, even though his reasons might remain the same. One of the most tragic aspects of suicide is that often, if the person could be rendered inactive for a week or two, he would no longer wish to kill himself.

Lack of aggression.   Depressed people are virtually drained of overt hostility toward others. So striking is this symptom that Freud and his followers made it the basis of the psychoanalytic theory of depression.[19] Freud believed that when a love object is lost, the depressive becomes angry; he turns this freed anger inward on himself, since the person who "abandoned" him is no longer available to bear the brunt of the depressive's hostility. This introjected hostility causes depression, self hate, suicidal wishes, and, of course, the characterizing symptom, lack of outward hostility.

Unfortunately, there has been no systematic evidence to support this view; indeed, the theory is so remote from observables that it is almost impossible to test directly. Even so, some dream evidence has been gathered. The psychoanalytic theory holds that the bound-up hostility of the depressive should have free rein in dreams; whereas in fact, the dreams of depressives, like their waking life, are drained of hostility.[20] Even in dreams, they see themselves as passive victims and losers.

Theory aside, the psychoanalytic observation that depressives seemed drained of aggression corresponds to the lack of aggression seen in learned helplessness. I see the symptom not as the psychoanalyst does, as causing depression, but as resulting from the belief in helplessness that causes the depression: aggression is just one more voluntary response system that is undermined by the belief in helplessness.

We have found depressed people to be less competitive in the laboratory. In Chapter Three, I mentioned that Kurlander, Miller, and I found that college students who first had been given unsolvable discrimination problems were somewhat less competitive and made more withdrawal responses in the prisoner's dilemma game than nonhelpless subjects, who had been given solvable problems or no problems (p. 35). These subjects were not depressed. We replicated the experiment using depressed subjects, and found that depressed subjects who had received no problems were much less competitive in the game and more withdrawn than nondepressed subjects who had received no problems. Again, both naturally occurring depression and helplessness induced by uncontrollability reduce competitiveness and increase passivity.

In studies of depression in primates, young monkeys have been separated from their mothers or placed in a dark pit; social and aggressive deficits ensued, as well as response-initiation deficits. These deficits parallel the deficits produced by uncontrollability and found in human depression. In Chapter Seven, I shall discuss the infant-separation studies, but I should mention the pit study here.

S. Suomi and H. Harlow put 45-day-old rhesus monkeys into a 2-foot-deep, 6-inch-wide vertical chamber, where they remained undisturbed for 45 days; since the pit was opaque, the monkeys received a minimum of stimulation.[21] At the end of this period their social responses were extensively tested. These monkeys displayed much greater social deficits than controls raised alone in cages or monkeys raised without mothers; they were profoundly depressed when tested in unrestricted environments: they made very little social contact with other monkeys, and showed virtually no play behavior; rather they would lie huddled in a corner clasping themselves. The emotional growth of the pitted monkeys seemed permanently stunted, for they subsequently developed almost no social interaction with their peers.

It is possible that the depressive behaviors induced by pitting occur because, like uncontrollable shock or unsolvable problems, pitting produces helplessness. While in the pit a monkey is helpless, according to the definition of uncontrollability. He has very little control over anything at all: food and water arrive independently of his behavior; there are no objects or fellow monkeys in the pit for him to control; he cannot even look out when he wants to. Almost all the good things in the life of a young monkey are absent, and therefore uncontrollable; even when they do occur it is without respect to his behavior.

Loss of libido and appetite. To a depressed person, food has lost it savor. Severe depressives eat less and lose weight. Sexual interest wanes, and impotence can accompany severe depression. People the depressive once found exciting and amusing become uninteresting; life loses its zest. These symptoms correspond to the appetitive, sexual, and social deficits seen in helpless animals.

Norepinephrine depletion and cholinergic activity. The most prominent hypothesis of a physiological origin of depression is called the *catecholamine hypothesis*.[22] It claims that norepinephrine is depleted at appropriate sites in the central nervous system of depressives. The evidence for it is indirect: Two kinds of antidepressant drugs, *monoamine oxidase* (MAO) *inhibitors* and *tricyclics*, have the common property of keeping NE available in the brain.[23] A drug, *reserpine*, first used to lower the blood pressure of heart patients, occasionally causes depression and also depletes NE, among many other effects. AMPT, a rather specific NE depletor, produces social withdrawal and other depressive-like behavior in monkeys, and produces in rats failure to escape shock.[24] These findings may correspond to the NE deficits seen in helpless rats by Weiss and his associates (1970, 1974).

One recent finding supports the possibility of cholinergic activity in depression. When normal people are injected with *physostigmine*, a drug that activates the cholinergic system, depression ensues within minutes.[25] Feelings of helplessness, suicidal wishes, and self-hate sweep over the subject. (Marijuana, incidentally, magnifies these effects.) When these people are then injected with atropine, a cholinergic blocker, the symptoms rapidly disappear and the subjects return to normal. This may parallel the finding that injecting atropine into the septum cured learned helplessness in cats.

Even though the symptoms of learned helplessness and depression have a great deal in common, there are two symptoms found with uncontrollable shock that may or may not correspond to depression. First, stomach ulcers occur more frequently and severely in rats receiving uncontrollable shock than in those receiving controllable shock;[26] I know of no study examining the relationship of depression to stomach ulcers. Second, uncontrollable shock produces more anxiety than controllable shock, measured subjectively, behaviorally, and physiologically; there is no clear answer to the question of whether depressed people are more anxious than people who aren't depressed. Both depression and anxiety can be observed at the same time in some individuals, but only a small positive correlation exists among inpatients. W. Miller and co-workers (1974) found very few depressed college students who were not also anxious, although it was easy to find anxious students who were not depressed. I have stated earlier my belief that anxiety and depression are related in the following way: when a man or animal is confronted with a threat or a loss, he responds initially with fear; if he learns that the threat is wholly controllable, fear disappears, having served its function; if he remains uncertain about controllability, fear remains; if he learns or is convinced that the threat is utterly uncontrollable, depression replaces fear.

There are also a number of features of depression that have been as yet insufficiently investigated in learned helplessness. Preeminent among these are the depressive symptoms that cannot be investigated in animals: dejected mood, feelings of self-blame and self-dislike, loss of mirth, suicidal thoughts, and crying. Now that learned helplessness has been reliably produced in man, it can be determined whether any or all of these states occur in helplessness. If such studies are undertaken, the investigators must take great care to undo any effects that the laboratory manipulation produces.

These, then, are the gaps that are yet to be filled in. I know of no evidence, however, that directly disconfirms the symptomatic similarity of learned helplessness and depression. Indeed, when depressives are asked about what they feel, the most prominent feelings they report are helplessness and hopelessness.[27]

Etiology of depression and learned helplessness

Learned helplessness is caused by learning that responding is independent of reinforcement; so the model suggests that the cause of depression is the belief that action is futile. What kind of events set off reactive depressions? Failure at work and school, death of a loved one, rejection or separation from friends and loved ones, physical disease, financial difficulty, being faced with insoluble problems, and growing old.[28] There are many others, but this list captures the flavor.

I believe that what links these experiences and lies at the heart of depression is unitary: the depressed patient believes or has learned that he cannot control those elements of his life that relieve suffering, bring gratification, or provide nurture— in short, he believes that he is helpless. Consider a few of the precipitating events: What is the meaning of job failure or incompetence at school? Often it means that all of a person's efforts have been in vain, that his responses have failed to achieve his desires. When an individual is rejected by someone he loves, he can no longer control this significant source of gratification and support. When a parent or lover dies, the bereaved is powerless to elicit love from the dead person. Physical disease and growing old are helpless conditions par excellence; the person finds his own responses ineffective and is thrown upon the care of others.

Endogenous depressions, while not set off by an explicit helplessness-inducing event, also may involve the belief in helplessness. I suspect that a continuum of susceptibility to this belief may underlie the endogenous-reactive continuum. At the extreme endogenous end, the slightest obstacle will trigger in the depressive a vicious circle of beliefs in how ineffective he is. At the extreme reactive end, a sequence of disastrous events in which a person is actually helpless is necessary to force the belief that responding is useless. Consider, for example, premenstrual susceptibility to feelings of helplessness. Right before her period, a woman may find that just breaking a dish sets off a full-blown depression, along with feelings of helplessness. Breaking a dish wouldn't disturb her at other times of the month; it would take several successive major traumas for depression to set in.

Is depression a cognitive or an emotional disorder? Neither and both. Clearly, cognitions of helplessness lower mood, and a lowered mood, which may be brought about physiologically, increases susceptibility to cognitions of helplessness; indeed, this is the most insidious vicious circle in depression. In the end, I believe that the cognition-emotion distinction in depression will be untenable. Cognition and emotion need not be separable entities in nature simply because our language separates them. When depression is observed close up, the exquisite interdependence of feelings and thought is undeniable: one does not *feel* depressed without depressing thoughts, nor does one have depressing thoughts without feeling depressed. I suggest that it is a failure of language, not a failure of understanding, that has fostered the confusion about whether depression is a cognitive or an emotional disorder.

I am not alone in believing that cognitions of helplessness are the core cause of depression. The psychodynamic theorist E. Bibring (1953) sees matters this way:

> What has been described as the basic mechanism of depression, the ego's shocking awareness of its helplessness in regard to its aspirations, is assumed to represent the core of normal, neurotic, and probably, also psychotic depression.

F. T. Melges and J. Bowlby (1969) see a similar cause of depression:

> Our thesis is that while a depressed patient's goals remain relatively unchanged his estimate of the likelihood of achieving them and his confidence in the efficacy of his own skilled actions are both diminished . . . the depressed person believes that his plans of action are no longer effective in reaching his continuing and long range goals. . . . From this state of mind is derived, we believe, much depressive symptomology, including indecisiveness, inability to act, making increased demands on others and feelings of worthlessness and of guilt about not discharging duties.[29]

P. Lichtenberg (1957) sees hopelessness as the defining characteristic of depression:

> Depression is defined as a manifestation of felt hopelessness regarding the attainment of goals when responsibility for the hopelessness is attributed to one's personal defects. In this context hope is conceived to be a function of the perceived probability of success with respect to goal attainment.

Behaviorally inclined theorists believe that depression is caused by a loss of reinforcers or the extinction of responding.[30] There is no contradiction between the learned-helplessness and extinction views of depression; helplessness, however, is more general. This distinction may need some elucidation. *Extinction* refers to the contingency in which reinforcement is withdrawn altogether, so that the subject's response (as well as lack of response) no longer produces reinforcement. Loss of reinforcers, as in the case of the death of a loved one, can be viewed as extinction. In conventional extinction procedures the probability of the reinforcer is zero, whether or not the subject responds. This is a special case of independence between responding and reinforcement (the origin of the $45°$ line in the response contingency space, Figure 2-3). Reinforcement, however, may also occur with a probability greater than zero, and still be independent of responding. This is the typical helplessness paradigm; such contingencies cause already established responding to decrease in probability.[31] The helplessness model, which refers to independence between responding and reinforcement, subsumes the extinction view and, in addition, suggests that even conditions under which reinforcers occur, but independently of responding, will cause depression.

Can depression actually be caused by contingencies other than extinction, contingencies in which reinforcements still occur, but are not under the individual's control? Is a net loss of reinforcers necessary for depression, or can depression occur when there is only loss of control? Would a Casanova who slept with seven new girls every week become depressed if he discovered that his success was due not to his amatory prowess, but to his wealth or his fairy godmother? This is a theoretically interesting case, but we can only speculate about what would happen. Our theory of helplessness suggests that it is not the loss of reinforcers, but the loss of control over reinforcers, that causes depression; success depression and related phenomena provide some indication that this is so.

A speculation about success and depression

> Now the longed-for signal has appeared. When happiness comes it brings less joy than one expected.
>
> C. P. Cavafy

My emotional reaction to large metaphysical and political propositions depends on how I'm feeling about myself. Take, for example, "Man must create his own meaning; no larger purpose is foreordained," which I happen to believe. When I'm feeling badly about myself because I've given a bad lecture or I've found out that someone dislikes me, this metaphysical statement makes me feel sad. "Life is absurd," I say to myself. "There is no greater meaning to my acts." On the other hand, when I'm feeling good about myself because I've given a good lecture or someone has bestowed love on me, I feel euphoric about the proposition. "Man must carve out his own destiny," I think. "No one can dictate the terms of my life to me." In general, I believe that how we feel about large statements that do not have immediate impact on our lives reflects how we feel about ourselves at that time.

In the last few years, many of my students have come to tell me that they felt depressed. Often they attributed their depression to their belief that life had no intrinsic meaning, that the Vietnam war would never end, that the poor and the black are oppressed, or that our leaders are corrupt. These are legitimate concerns and to devote so much thought and energy to them is certainly justifiable. But was the feeling, the actual depression, caused directly by these issues? Clearly, for a poor person, a black, or a student about to be drafted, these propositions could directly cause depression. But most of those I saw were neither poor, nor black, nor about to be drafted; these propositions were remote from their daily lives. Yet they said they were depressed about them—not just concerned or angry, but depressed. To me, this meant that they were feeling bad about something much closer to home, bad about themselves, their capacities, and their daily lives. Such existential depressions are rampant today, I daresay much more than when I was a student ten years ago.

At first it seems paradoxical. More of the good things of life are available now than ever before: more sex, more records, more intellectual stimulation, more books, more buying power. On the other hand, there have always been wars, oppression, corruption, and absurdity; the human condition has been pretty stable along these lines. Why should this particularly fortunate generation find itself especially depressed?

I think the answer may lie in the lack of contingency between the actions of these students and the good things, as well as the negative events, that came their way. These reinforcers came about less through the efforts of the young individuals who benefited from them, than because our society is affluent. They have experienced a minimum of hard work followed by reward. From where does one get a sense of power, worth, and self-esteem? Not from what he owns, but from long experience watching his own actions change the world.

I am claiming, then, that not only trauma occurring independently of response, but noncontingent *positive* events, can produce helplessness and depression. After all, what is the evolutionary significance of mood? Presumably, sentient organisms could just as well be constructed without mood—complex computers are. What selective pressure produced feeling and affect? It may be that the hedonic system evolved to goad and fuel instrumental action. I suggest that joy accompanies and motivates effective responding; and that in the absence of effective responding, an aversive state arises, which organisms seek to avoid. It is called depression. It is highly significant that when rats and pigeons are given a choice between getting free food and getting the same food for making responses, they choose to work.[32] Infants smile at a mobile whose movements are contingent on their responses, but not at a noncontingent mobile.[33] Do hunters hunt from a lust to kill or mountain climbers scale peaks for glory? I think not. These activities, because they entail effective instrumental responding, produce joy.

Dysphoria produced by the cessation of effective responding may explain "success depression." Not infrequently, when a person finally achieves a goal toward which he has been striving for years, depression ensues. Officials elected to public office after arduous campaigns, presidents of the American Psychological Association, successful novelists, and even men who land on the moon can become severely depressed soon after achieving the pinnacle. For a theory of depression by loss of reinforcers, these depressions are paradoxical, since successful individuals continue to receive most of their old reinforcers, plus more new reinforcers than ever before.

This phenomenon is not a paradox for the theory of helplessness. Depressed, successful people tell you that they are now rewarded not for what they're doing, but for who they are or what they *have* done. Having achieved the goal that they strove for, their rewards now come independently of any ongoing instrumental activity. There are more depressed and suicidal beautiful women than it seems there should be; few people get more rewards: attention, cars, love. What they disgustedly say when reminded how fortunate they are is: "I got these things for what I look like, not for what I really am."

In summary, I suggest that what produces self-esteem and a sense of competence, and protects against depression, is not only the absolute quality of experience, but the perception that one's own actions controlled the experience. To the degree that uncontrollable events occur, either traumatic or positive, depression will be predisposed and ego strength undermined. To the degree that controllable events occur, a sense of mastery and resistance to depression will result.

Cure of depression and learned helplessness

Forced exposure to the fact that responding produces reinforcement is the most effective way of breaking up learned helplessness. Helplessness also dissipates in time. Furthermore, two physiological therapies seem to have an effect: electroconvulsive shock (ECS) broke up helplessness in three out of six dogs,[34] and atropine cannulated to the septum broke it up in cats.

There is no scientifically established panacea for depression. Left alone, depression often dissipates in a few weeks or months; but there are therapies that are reported to alleviate depression and that are consistent with the theory of learned helplessness. According to this view, the central goal in successful therapy should be to have the patient come to believe that his responses produce the gratification he desires—that he is, in short, an effective human being. Bibring (1953) saw the matter similarly:

> The same conditions which bring about depression (helplessness) in reverse serve frequently the restitution from depression. Generally one can say that depression subsides either (a) when the narcissistically important goals and objects appear to be again within reach (which is frequently followed by a temporary elation), or (b) when they become sufficiently modified or reduced to become realizable, or (c) when they are altogether relinquished, or (d) when the ego recovers from the narcissistic shock by regaining its self-esteem with the help of various recovery mechanisms (with or without any change of objective or goal).[35]

A. T. Beck's (1970, 1971) cognitive therapy is aimed at similar goals.[36] In his view, successful manipulations change the negative cognitive set to a more positive one: he argues that the primary task of the therapist is to change the negative expectation of the depressed patient to a more optimistic one, in which the patient comes to believe that his responses will produce the outcomes he wants.

Melges and Bowlby (1969) also see the reversal of helplessness as the central theme in the treatment of depression:

> If the argument that hopelessness in one or another of its forms is a central dynamic in certain kinds of psychopathology turns out to be valid, treatment measures would need to be evaluated in terms of the degree to which they help the patients to change their attitude toward the future. . . . A principal aim of insight-oriented therapy is to help a patient recognize some of the archaic and unreachable goals towards which he may still be striving, and some also of the impracticable plans to which he may still be wedded, aims that are especially clear when a patient is suffering from a pathological form of mourning. By psychoanalytic techniques, it is be-

lieved, a patient can sometimes be freed from the conditions that led him to become hopeless, and given opportunity both to set himself more reachable goals and to adopt more effective plans. Behavioral techniques also are being explored to see how successful they can be in setting up more positive attitudes in the future.[37]

Other therapies are claimed to be successful in alleviating depression and providing the patient with control over important outcomes. The "Tuscaloosa Plan" of a Veterans Administration hospital in Alabama puts severely depressed patients in an "anti-depression room."[38] In this room the patient is subjected to an attitude of "kind firmness": He is told to sand a block of wood, and then reprimanded when he sands against the grain. He then sands with the grain, only to be reprimanded for that. Alternatively, he is told to begin counting about a million little seashells scattered about the room. This systematic harassment continues until the depressed patient finally tells the guard "Get off my back!" or says something like "I've counted my last seashell." He is then promptly let out of the room with apologies. The patient has been forced to emit one of the most powerful responses people have for controlling others—anger, and when this response is dragged out of his depleted repertoire, he is powerfully reinforced. This breaks up depression—lastingly.

In assertive-training therapy, the patient actively rehearses making assertive social responses, while the therapist plays the role of the boss who is being told off or the henpecking wife who repents her ways and begs forgiveness. Here, too, the patient makes responses that have powerful outcomes.[39] It probably benefits mildly depressed people to return faulty merchandise to department stores, or to ring the bell at the meat counter to get exactly the cut they want.

Gradual exposure to the response-reinforcement contingencies of work reinforces active behaviors, and may be effective against depression. In a graded-task treatment of depression, E. P. Burgess (1968) first had her patients emit some minimal bit of behavior, like making a telephone call. She emphasizes that it is crucial that the patient succeed, rather than just start and give up. The task requirements were then increased, and the patient was reinforced for successfully completing the tasks by the attention and interest of the therapist.

Burgess and others have pointed to the role of *secondary gain* in depression: depressives are often alleged to *use* their symptoms instrumentally to gain sympathy, affection, and attention. By lying in bed all day and crying, rather than going to work, a depressed man may cause his philandering wife to pay more attention to him, and may even win her back. Secondary gain is annoying, and one is tempted during therapy to remove the rewards that maintain it. But caution is in order here: secondary gain may explain the persistence or maintenance of some depressive behaviors, but it does not explain how they began. The theory of helplessness suggests that failure to initiate active responding originates in the patient's perception that he cannot control outcomes. So a depressed patient's passivity can have two sources: (1) patients can be passive for instrumental reasons, since staying depressed brings them sympathy, love, and attention; and (2) patients can be passive because they believe that no response at all will be effective in controlling their environment. Comparing the first to the second, one might conclude that secondary gain, while a practical hindrance to therapy, is a hopeful sign in depression: it means that there is at least *some* response (even a passive one) that the patient believes he can effectively perform. Remember that dogs whose passivity was reinforced by shock termination were not nearly as debilitated as dogs for whom all responding was independent of shock termination (p. 26). Similarly, patients who use their depression as a way of controlling others may have a better prognosis than those who have given up.

My colleagues and I have used a graded-task treatment like Burgess's on 24 hospitalized depressives.[40] These patients were given verbal tasks of gradually increasing difficulty in a one-hour session, and were praised upon successful completion of each task. First they were asked to read a paragraph aloud. Then they were asked to read a new paragraph aloud and with expression. They were asked to read yet another with expression and interpret it in their own words; then reading aloud with expression, plus interpretation and arguing for the author's point of view. At the top of the hierarchy, the patients were asked to choose one of three topics and give an extemporaneous speech. All patients reached and successfully completed the speech. (Anyone who has worked with hospitalized depressives knows they do not ordinarily make extemporaneous speeches.) Nineteen of the 24 showed substantial, immediate elevation in mood as measured by a self-rating mood scale. Although we did not observe how long the improvement lasted, what one smiling patient said was illuminating: "You know, I used to be a debater in high school and I had forgotten how good I was."[41]

There are other parallels to learned helplessness in therapy for depression. Electroconvulsive shock seems to be effective in about 60 percent of depressions, although these are mostly endogenous depressions. Atropine may possibly be an antidepressant.

Individuals often adopt their own strategies for dealing with their own minor depressions. Asking for help and getting it or helping someone else (even caring for a pet) are two strategies that entail gaining control and may alleviate minor depressions. My own strategy is to force myself to work: sit down and write a paper, read a difficult text or an article from a technical journal, or do a math problem. What better way is there for an intellectual to see that his efforts can still be effective and bring gratification than to plunge into writing, heavy reading, or problem solving? To be sure, persistence is essential: if I begin to solve the math problem, but give up halfway through, the depression gets worse.

Many therapies, from psychoanalysis to T-groups, claim to be able to cure depression. But we do not yet have sufficient evidence from well-controlled studies to evaluate the effectiveness of any form of psychotherapy for depression. The evidence I have presented is selected: only those treatments that seem compatible with helplessness were discussed. It is possible that when other therapies work it is because they, too, restore the patient's sense of efficacy. What is needed now is experimental evidence isolating the effective variable in the psychological treatment of depression. It is also essential that untreated control groups be run, since depression dissipates in time, of its own accord.

Prevention of depression and learned helplessness

Learned helplessness can be prevented if the subject first masters outcomes before being exposed to their uncontrollability. Can depression be prevented? Almost everyone loses control over some of the outcomes that are significant to him: parents die, loved ones reject him, failure occurs. Everyone becomes at least mildly and transiently depressed in the wake of such events, but why are some people hospitalized by depression for long periods, and others so resilient? I will discuss this in more detail in Chapter Seven, on child development; at this point, I can only speculate, but the data on immunization against helplessness will guide my speculations.

The life histories of those individuals who are particularly resistant to depression, or resilient from depression, may have been filled with mastery; these people may have had extensive experience controlling and manipulating the sources of reinforcement in their lives, and may therefore see the future optimistically. Those people who are particularly susceptible to depression may have had lives relatively devoid of mastery; their lives may have been full of situations in which they were helpless to influence their sources of suffering and relief.

The relationship of adult depression to childhood loss of parents is relevant: it seems likely that children who lose their parents experience helplessness and are more susceptible to later depression. The findings on this topic are mixed, but they tend to establish parental death as a factor predisposing to depression. Overall it seems statistically somewhat more likely that children who suffer early parental loss will become depressed more often and even attempt suicide more.[42]

A caveat is in order here, however, While it seems reasonable that extended experience with controllable outcomes will make a person more resilient from depression, how about the person who has met only with success? Is a person whose responses have always succeeded especially susceptible to depression when confronted with situations beyond his control? We all know of people who were stunningly successful in high school, but who collapsed on encountering their first failure in college. Everyone eventually confronts failure and anxiety; too much success with controlling reinforcers, just like too little, might not allow the development and use of responses for coping with failure.

Successful therapy should be preventative. Therapy must not focus just on undoing past problems; it should also arm the patient against future depressions. Would therapy for depression be more successful if it strove explicitly to provide the patient with a wide repertoire of coping responses that he could use at times when he found his usual responses ineffective?

SUMMARY

I have reviewed the findings from two converging literatures, those of depression and learned helplessness. As summarized in Table 5-1, the major symptoms of learned helplessness all have parallels in the symptoms of depression. This suggests that reactive depression, as well as learned helplessness, has its roots in the belief that valued outcomes are uncontrollable. The central goal of therapy for depression, therefore, is the patient's regaining his belief that he can control events important to him. Selected therapeutic findings lend some support to this proposition. Finally, I have speculated that early experience with uncontrollable events may predispose a person to depression, while early experience with mastery may immunize him.

TABLE 5-1
Summary of Features Common to Learned Helplessness and Depression

	Learned Helplessness	Depression
SYMPTOMS	Passivity	Passivity
	Difficulty learning that responses produce relief	Negative cognitive set
	Dissipates in time	Time course
	Lack of aggression	Introjected hostility
	Weight loss, appetite loss, social and sexual deficits	Weight loss, appetite loss, social and sexual deficits
	Norepinephrine depletion and cholinergic activity	Norepinephrine depletion and cholinergic activity
	Ulcers and stress	Ulcers (?) and stress
		Feelings of helplessness
CAUSE	Learning that responding and reinforcement are independent	Belief that responding is useless
CURE	Directive therapy: forced exposure to responses that produce reinforcement	Recovery of belief that responding produces reinforcement
	Electroconvulsive shock	Electroconvulsive shock
	Time	Time
	Anticholinergics; norepinephrine stimulants (?)	Norepinephrine stimulants; anticholinergics (?)
PREVENTION	Immunization by mastery over reinforcement	(?)

CHAPTER SIX

ANXIETY AND UNPREDICTABILITY

In the early hours of a February morning in 1971, a powerful earthquake struck Los Angeles. Marshall's experience was typical for an eight-year-old in the San Fernando Valley, the epicenter of the quake: He awakened at 5:45 to find himself in what sounded like a railroad tunnel, with a train bearing down on him. Dazed and frightened he looked up out of his bed; the ceiling was moving! As it swayed back and forth bits of plaster dropped down on him. The floor undulated; he screamed and from the next room heard the frightened screams of his mother and father. Although it was only about thirty seconds, it seemed like an eternity of terror while the very ground shook beneath him.

Three years later, Marshall still showed psychological aftereffects of that morning. He was timid and jumpy; slight, unexpected sounds terrified him. He had trouble getting to sleep, and once he had, his sleep was very light and restless; he occasionally woke up screaming.

Earthquakes, like many traumatic events, have strong elements of uncontrollability. There is nothing that a person can do to prevent an earthquake, although there are safety precautions that he can take and responses he can make once it strikes. A much more salient feature of earthquakes is their utter unpredictability: they come out of nowhere; the first shock is completely unheralded. Marshall's symptoms fit a pattern of anxiety related not to uncontrollability, but to the related concept of *unpredictability*.

DEFINITION OF UNPREDICTABILITY

We can define predictability and unpredictability in a way wholly parallel to our definition of controllability and uncontrollability. For example, consider some astronauts who have landed on Mars and are trying to predict when sandstorms will occur. The occurrence of the sandstorms is, of course, uncontrollable; the best the astronauts can do is try to predict them and then batten down the hatches. After being there for three days, each cloudy with dust, they note that a sandstorm has occurred on each day. At this point, they have observed the probability of a sandstorm on a cloudy day [p(Sandstorm/ Clouds)] to be 1.0, and they hypothesize that clouds predict sandstorms perfectly. But then come two cloudy days without a sandstorm; now the probability of a sandstorm on a cloudy day is 0.6. Clouds still tell them they had better watch out, but are no longer a perfect predictor of sandstorms.

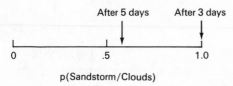

Figure 6-1
Probability of a sandstorm on a cloudy day

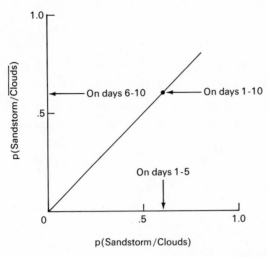

Figure 6-2
Probability of a sandstorm on a cloudy day and on a clear day

On days 6 through 10 no dust clouds occur; on three of these five days there are sandstorms, but on two there are no sandstorms. During these five days, the probability of a sandstorm given no clouds [p(Sandstorm/$\overline{\text{Clouds}}$)] is 0.6.

Do clouds bear any predictive relationship to sandstorms? The answer is no. The probability of a sandstorm, whether or not clouds occur, is 0.6; dust clouds don't give any information at all about sandstorms.

We can now define predictability and unpredictability generally. Recall that when I defined controllability I referred to instrumental learning, or the relationship of a voluntary response to an outcome (p. 17). Predictability is related to classical or Pavlovian conditioning contingencies, which relate an outcome, or an unconditioned stimulus (US), to a signal, or conditioned stimulus (CS). For the moment, I will assume that the US is uncontrollable and concentrate on its predictability by the CS. Suppose we are presenting tones and brief electric

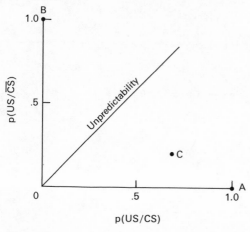

Figure 6-3
The Pavlovian conditioning space

shocks to a rat who cannot do anything about either. We can arrange the relationship between tones and shocks in a number of ways. For example, we can present a shock every time we present a tone, but never present a shock without a tone—this is represented by point A in Figure 6-3. Here the tone is a perfect predictor of shock, while absence of tone is a perfect predictor of no shock.

Alternatively, we can present shocks whenever the tone is not on, but never present shocks if the tone is on. Here (point B) absence of tone is a perfect predictor of shock, while tone perfectly predicts no shock. Predictability need not be all or none, however. Suppose we present shocks seven out of ten times we sound the tone, and also present shocks two out of ten times we withhold the tone (point C). At point C, when the tone goes on the rat does have some information—shock is more likely to occur than if tone is absent.

Finally, shocks can be presented unpredictably with respect to tones. At any point along the 45° line, the probability of a shock is the same whether or not a tone occurs. In general, therefore, a US is unpredictable by a CS if the probability of the US in the presence of the CS is equal to the probability of the US in the absence of the CS:

$$p(US/CS) = p(US/\overline{CS})$$

When this is true of *all* CS's, the US is *unpredictable*.

Conversely a CS *predicts* a US when the probability of the US in the presence of the CS is *not* equal to the probability of the US in the absence of the CS:

$$p(US/CS) \neq p(US/\overline{CS})$$

These definitions parallel our definition of controllability in that US is substituted for outcome (O), and CS is substituted for response (R), throughout. This raises the question of what kinds of events can be CS's or signals for outcomes in our conditioning space. The answer is any event that the organism can perceive. The CS need not be an explicit external event like a tone. It can be an internal event like heartburn. It can be a temporal pattern: if shocks are presented every fifth minute with no external signal, the passage of four minutes and 59 seconds from the last shock is a CS that predicts shock. The CS can also be the feedback from making a response, or the feedback from *not* making the response. Suppose, for example, a rat is shocked if and only if he presses a bar; when he presses the bar he can predict shock by using his perception of the fact that he has pressed the bar (the feedback from responding) as the CS. He can also predict that he will not be shocked when he perceives that he has not pressed the bar. So when an animal can control an event by a response he can also use the feedback from the response to predict the event. The reverse is not always true, however: if he can predict an event, he may not be able to control it.

ANXIETY AND THE SAFETY-
SIGNAL HYPOTHESIS

Anxiety, like *depression*, is a term from ordinary English, and as such does not have necessary and sufficient defining conditions.[1] However, a helpful distinction between anxiety and fear is made in the psychoanalytic literature: fear is a noxious emotional state that has an object, such as fear of rabid dogs; anxiety is a less specific state, more chronic, and not bound to an object. I have observed in the laboratory two emotional states that roughly correspond to this distinction, and may in fact provide a well-defined model of it. I shall call *fear* the acute state that occurs when a signal predicts a threatening event, such as an electric shock. I shall call *anxiety* the chronic fear that occurs when a threatening event is in the offing but is unpredictable. Having defined unpredictability so that we can recognize such situations, we can examine the disruptive emotional consequences of unpredictability. The data on unpredictability is diverse and is most easily organized around what is called the *safety-signal hypothesis*.[2]

The safety-signal hypothesis

How does the unpredictability of an earthquake produce the anxiety, jumpiness, and insomnia that Marshall suffers? Consider a world in which earthquakes are reliably predicted by a ten-minute tone. In such a world, the absence of the tone reliably predicts safety, or the absence of earthquake. As long as the tone isn't on, you can relax and go about your business; when the tone *is* on, you're probably terrified, but at least you have usable safety signals. When traumatic events are predictable, the absence of the traumatic event is also predictable— by the absence of the predictor of the trauma. When traumatic events are unpredictable, however, safety is also unpredictable: no event reliably tells you that the trauma will not occur and that you can relax.[3]

The contrast between earthquakes and the bombing of London in the Second World War highlights this point. After a time, the British air-raid warning system worked quite well: each raid was predicted by sirens some minutes in duration. When no sirens were on, Londoners carried on admirably, without undue tension and in good cheer. On the other hand, there is no stimulus that predicts earthquakes, and therefore no stimulus whose absence predicts no earthquakes; Marshall has no safety signal, no event during which he can be sure an earthquake won't occur. The anxiety he shows—the jumpiness, the midnight wakening, and the inability to get to sleep—points to the lack of a safe haven in his life, a time at which he can relax, knowing that no earthquake will occur.

This is the heart of the safety-signal hypothesis: in the wake of traumatic events, people and animals will be afraid all the time, except in the presence of a stimulus that reliably predicts safety. In the absence of a safety signal, organisms remain in anxiety or chronic fear. On this view, people and animals are safety-signal seekers: they search out predictors of unavoidable danger because such knowledge also gives them knowledge of safety.

Many people instruct their doctors that they wish to be told when they are soon to die. I believe that two motivations underlie this request: In the first place, when a person is told he will die, he can tie up the loose ends of his life—sell the business, settle old feuds, go to Paris and dissipate his savings. More important than this, and often overlooked, are the safety signals that this arrangement provides. Suppose you are worried about your heart, and your doctor has examined you. If you have not made the "death knowledge" agreement, you will probably be anxious regardless of what he tells you; your life will be spent in anxiety about death. If you have made the agreement, you can relax as long as your doctor does not tell you that you are going to die; you are in the presence of a safety signal. What you buy with such an agreement—if you trust your doctor—is a lifetime of safety signals and less anxiety when you are not, in fact, going to die. What you give up is the likelihood of a blissful and unsuspecting death.

UNPREDICTABILITY AND MONITORING FEAR

Fear and anxiety are hypothetical constructs used widely in psychological theory today. Like hunger, they can never be observed directly, but are inferred from observation of behavior, physiology, and subjective report. Number of hours of food deprivation, amount of shock a rat will tolerate to get to food, how hard a person will work to get food, and an open-ended list of other variables define the state of hunger. Similarly, *galvanic skin response* (GSR) change, crouching and trembling, ulcers, heart rate changes, and many other dependent variables are taken to measure the states of fear and anxiety. Perhaps the most widely used index is the *conditioned emotional response* (CER), first used by W. K. Estes and B. F. Skinner in 1941 in their classic paper "Some quantitative properties of anxiety." In their technique, a rat is first taught to press a bar at a high and constant rate for food. Some stimulus such as a tone is then paired with electric shock during the bar-pressing session. Bar pressing is independent of shock presentation: the shock is uncontrollable. The rat learns to become afraid of the tone by Pavlovian conditioning and shows this by crouching in a corner and failing to press the bar for food. The decrease in bar-pressing rate is called the conditioned emotional response to the tone and is probably the most reliable and widely used index of fear.

This technique allows fairly direct testing of the safety-signal hypothesis, and a substantial number of studies have been carried out with CER produced by predictable and unpredictable shock.[4] Since these studies are uniform in their results, I shall detail only one of them here [Seligman (1968)].

Two groups of hungry rats first learned to press a bar for food at a high rate. One group, "predictable," then received fifteen daily fifty-minute sessions during which three one-minute signals (CS's) ended in electric shocks. The "unpredictable" group received the same signals and shocks, but they were interspersed so that the probability of shock was the same whether or not the signal was on. Food continued to be available by means of bar pressing.

The results were striking. At first the predictable group stopped bar pressing, both in the presence and absence of the signal. As they learned to discriminate between the fact that they were shocked during the signal, but not shocked in its absence, they suppressed their response only during the signal and pressed the bar for food in the absence of the CS: they showed fear during the CS, but no fear in its absence. The unpredictable group had no safety signal during which shock would not occur. They stopped bar pressing completely, both during the signal and during its absence, and never pressed again for the remainder of the 15 sessions. Huddled in a corner throughout each session, they showed chronic fear or anxiety. Unlike the predictable group, the unpredictable group developed massive stomach ulcers.

Davis and McIntire (1969), in a parallel experiment, found some recovery of bar pressing in their unpredictable-shock group after many sessions. Seligman and Meyer (1970) speculated that this recovery might have been caused by the fact that exactly three shocks occurred in each session. The rats might have been able to count to three and learn that, after the third, no further shock would occur; therefore recovery would occur only after the third shock, since the rats were using the third shock itself as a safety signal. If true, this would not disconfirm but actually confirm and extend the safety-signal hypothesis. To test this, Seligman and Meyer (1970) gave two groups daily sessions of unpredictable shock for seventy consecutive days. One group received exactly three shocks a day while the other group received from one to five unpredictable shocks, with an average of three a day. During the last thirty sessions the first group showed some recovery: they did 61.6 percent of all their bar pressing during the last 25 percent of the session remaining after the third shock. The second group did not recover: they did 25 percent of their meager bar pressing during the 25 percent of the session remaining after the third shock. Rats, apparently, can count to three and use the occurrence of the third shock as their safety signal.

The galvanic skin response, an index of fear related to sweating, has been measured during predictable and unpredictable trauma.[5] Price and Geer (1972) presented undergraduate men with a series of gory pictures of dead bodies. For the predictable group, an eight-second tone heralded each photograph, so that during the absence of the tone, no dead bodies would appear and the subjects could relax. For the unpredictable group, no tones occurred: both dead bodies and safety were unpredictable. The predictable group showed high GSR during the tone, but not between tones. As expected, the unpredictable group sweated throughout. Thus measurement of CER and GSR suggest that fear is chronic during unpredictable traumatic events because no signal for safety exists.

STOMACH ULCERS

Jim and George are brothers. Jim is the family success story: he has risen from a lower-class Polish background to become vice president of a good-sized bank. He is a very busy man: his day begins at 7 A.M.; by 8 o'clock he has already made several telephone calls—juggling an account, closing a deal, and arranging loans for several customers. At any moment he can be on two telephones, simultaneously supervising a couple of assistants and dictating a letter. He slaves away at this sort of thing—and says he enjoys it—until 6 o'clock in the evening.

After a rushed supper, he can typically be found running the treasurer's office of his country club or arranging a meeting of his church group.

George is the black sheep of the family; he has not held a job in three months. He has been fired from a string of menial jobs, none of which lasted longer than a year, but he doesn't understand why he keeps getting fired, and attributes it to bad luck. His wife has left him. He spends his days looking for work and his nights struggling with loneliness.

One of these brothers has ulcers. A decade ago, most psychologists would have predicted that Jim, the overworked executive, was the one. They would have based this prediction on a famous study by J. V. Brady, the "executive monkey" study, which I mentioned in Chapter Three.[6] To refresh your memory: Brady exposed eight monkeys to electric shock, allowing them to avoid shock by pressing a bar. The first four monkeys to learn avoidance became the executives; the slowest four were assigned to the yoked group. The executives' bar pressing avoided shock, both for themselves and for their four yoked partners, who were helpless, receiving uncontrollable and unpredictable shock. Like real-life executives, the avoiders made all the relevant decisions: their bar presses predicted and controlled whether shock would occur. As is widely known, all four of the executives developed severe ulcers, while the helpless partners did not. A decade of homilies followed on how leading an executive's life was bad for health. These homilies were a disservice both to psychologists and to the general public, for Brady's results were probably an artifact of his experimental design.

Notice that these results are strikingly different from the scores of experimental studies reviewed in this book: here the animals that exert control over their environment are worse off than helpless animals. You will recall that Brady's monkeys were not randomly assigned to be executives or yoked subjects; rather the first four to start banging away at the bar when shocked became the executives, while the others were assigned to the helpless condition. Animals who are more susceptible to ulcers may learn an avoidance response faster because they are more emotional or because the shock hurts them more.[7] Thus Brady's results may have been produced not by the difference in controllability, but by assigning the more emotional monkeys to the executive slots.

J. M. Weiss, who first made this criticism of the executive-monkey study, has performed the most extensive sets of studies on ulceration, predictability, and control.[8] In his 1968 study, he assigned rats randomly to executive, helpless, or no-shock conditions and found that the helpless animals got the most ulcers, contrary to the executive-monkey study. This is consistent with the view that helplessness usually produces more stress than control does. Weiss's later series of studies indicate, further, that the ulceration differences apparently caused by controllability may actually reflect differences in predictability: when a monkey presses a bar and avoids shock, the feedback from bar pressing predicts safety; the yoked monkey cannot control shock, but he also has no prediction of safety. Weiss's results highlight the role of predictability rather subtly, so that is worth discussing his data at some length.

When no control is allowed, stomach ulceration occurs with unpredictable rather than predictable shock.[9] Weiss (1970), for example, restrained triads of rats and exposed them to signalled or unsignalled shock, or no shock. Shock was uncontrollable for all groups. Rats receiving unpredictable shock formed many more ulcers than rats receiving predictable shock or no shock. To a lesser degree, increased body temperature and higher plasma-corticosteroid level were also associated with unpredictable shock.

In a follow-up study, Weiss (1971a) varied both predictability and controllability of shock. Triads of rats were exposed to escapable or inescapable shock, or no shock; a

TABLE 6-1
Median Number of Ulcers and Wheel Turns [adapted from Weiss (1971a)]

	Ulcers	Wheel Turns
Escape groups		
Signalled shock	2.0	3,717
Unsignalled shock	3.5	13,992
Yoked groups		
Signalled shock	3.5	1,404
Unsignalled shock	6.0	4,357
No shock		
Signal	1.0	60
No signal	1.0	51

wheel was present in the small chamber for all groups, but served as the instrumental response for only the escape-avoidance group. Shocks were either signalled, progressively signalled, or unsignalled; for simplicity's sake, I shall not consider the progressively signalled groups. Table 6-1 summarizes the median data for each of the six remaining groups.

There were four basic findings: (1) *predictability difference* — both the yoked and the escape rats had more ulcers with unsignalled than with signalled shock; (2) *controllability difference* — both the signalled and the unsignalled rats had more ulcers in the yoked than in the escape condition; (3) *wheelturning frequency* — both the yoked and the escape rats made more wheel turns with unsignalled than with signalled shock; both the signalled and the unsignalled rats made more wheel turns in the escape than in the yoked condition (recall that wheel turning turned off shock only for the escape rats); (4) *correlation of wheel turning with ulcers* — the unsignalled rats had more ulcers and did more wheel turning. Weiss claimed, further, that in *every* group the more responses an individual rat made, the more ulcers it had.

Weiss proposed that two factors accounted for these results: less *relevant feedback* causes more ulcers, and more *coping responses* cause more ulcers. I believe that these two factors boil down to the safety-signal hypothesis. Consider first the concept of relevant feedback, which is supposed to account for why helpless rats ulcerate more than escape rats. Weiss defines relevant feedback as a stimulus that follows the response and is *not* associated with the stressor; in other words, the stimuli that Weiss refers to are associated with the *absence* of the stressor—they are safety signals. When a rat learns to escape shock, it thereby learns a safety signal, a signal for the absence of shock, and it ulcerates less because it spends less time in fear than a helpless rat who has no safety signal.

The second factor—the more coping responses, the more ulcers—is proposed to account for more ulcers with unpredictability and for the correlation of ulcers with number of wheel turns. There are two very different ways this factor may be construed: causally or correlationally. Causally (the construction that Weiss opts for) it would mean that making more responses actually *produces* more ulcers. This implies, for example, that if you could force yourself to sit back and accept shock with resignation, you wouldn't ulcerate. The other sense is shallower and more descriptive, but also more tenable: that some third factor causes both frantic responding, as manifested by wheel turning, and ulceration. There is a prime candidate for such a third factor, which Weiss himself proposed to criticize the executive-monkey study: animals that are more emotional, more afraid, or more pained by the shock will be more reactive, and so turn the wheel more; they ulcerate more not because they turn the wheel more, but because they are more afraid.

Recall that rats receiving unpredictable (unsignalled) shock ulcerated more and responded more than rats receiving predictable shock under the same conditions of controllability. Weiss would have us believe that they ulcerated *because* they responded more. In contrast, the safety-signal hypothesis explains both why they ulcerated more and why they responded more. If turning the wheel in a very confined chamber reflects fear and emotional arousal,[10] then rats in the unsignalled group will turn the wheel more; since they have no safety signal, they will engage in wheel turning at all times. Signalled rats will turn the wheel only during their danger signal, since they can relax during the safety signal. Thus the greater fear, due to the absence of a safety signal with unpredictable shock, will produce both more wheel turning and more ulceration. As for the correlation between individual wheel turning and ulceration, it is reasonable to believe that more emotional subjects will turn the wheel more and develop more ulcers because they are more emotional. In other words, it will do you no good to refrain from coping attempts if you don't want to have ulcers.

In summary, Weiss's theory reduces to the safety-signal hypothesis: relevant feedback is synonymous with the more exact notion of safety signal, and the high rate of responding reflects the lack of safety signals. So it appears that the fact that more ulcers occur when shock is uncontrollable reflects the fact that shock is also unpredictable, and unpredictable shock produces more ulcers than predictable shock.

PREFERENCE FOR PREDICTABILITY

It is not known whether the state, which I have called anxiety, that results from unpredictable shock is different from or merely a chronic version of the state of fear that occurs during predictable shock. Be it anxiety or fear, according to the safety-signal hypothesis more of it occurs with unpredictable than predictable trauma. This is because during unpredictable shock, anxiety occurs all the time; on the other hand, during predictable shock fear occurs only during the signal for shock while relaxation occurs the rest of the time. Therefore, we expect that predictable noxious events will be preferred to unpredictable ones.

Such a preference has been observed in the laboratory many times in both men and rats.[11] I will detail one study here, since it is perhaps the most elegant one performed. Badia and Culbertson (1972) gave seven rats a choice between signalled and unsignalled shock. Shock itself was uncontrollable, but the rat could control whether or not he received it in the presence of a warning signal. While a white light was on, shocks occurred at random intervals, and no warning stimulus predicted exactly when a shock would occur—there was no safety signal. Pressing a bar turned the white light off; during this period shocks occurred, but they were heralded by a brief tone. So the absence of the white light—whenever the tone was also off—was a safety signal, and the absence of light with the tone on was a danger signal. To put it another way, anxiety occurred during the white light, but only acute fear occurred in its absence. All rats pressed the bar, showing a marked preference for the period in which the white light was off, even though the same number of shocks occurred as during the white light.[12] Figure 6-4 summarizes the design.

In addition to a literature on signalled vs. unsignalled shock, there exists a literature on preference by both animals and men for immediately delivered shock over delayed shock. A preference for immediate shock can be expected since the onset of shock is more predictable with immediate than with delayed shock. Studies on humans all find a preference for immediate over delayed shock.[13] The animal literature, however, is inconsistent. R. K. Knapp and co-workers (1959) found that rats preferred to get shocked right away rather than wait. But Renner and Houlihan (1969) found the preference only when the rats were allowed to escape the chamber after being shocked.

In general, men and animals prefer predictable to unpredictable aversive events. I believe that this reflects the fact that no safety is available with unpredictable shock, while

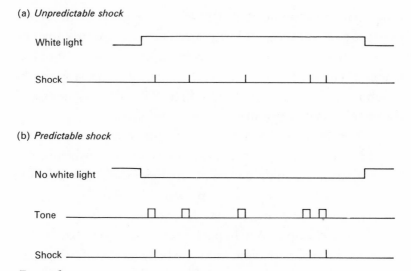

(a) *Unpredictable shock*

White light

Shock

(b) *Predictable shock*

No white light

Tone

Shock

Figure 6-4
In condition a, *white light is dangerous throughout; in condition* b, *absence of white light is safe throughout, except when tone is on.*

safety can be predicted by the absence of the signal for predictable shock. So acute fear is preferred to the anxiety or chronic fear that unpredictability produces.

THE RELATIONSHIP OF PREDICTABILITY TO CONTROLLABILITY[14]

A sixty-five-year-old man reports bursts of anxiety. He is afraid he is going to die of a heart attack—his heart is in good shape, but his constant anxiety is certainly bad for his circulatory system. A typical anxiety attack looks like this: He is momentarily concerned and stops to think about his heart. After introspecting deeply for a moment, he detects what he thinks might be a slight irregularity in heartbeat. He says to himself, "This might be the first sign of a heart attack." He begins to sweat. His blood pressure increases and he concentrates more on what's going on in his chest; the increased blood pressure and heart rate convince him that he really might have another heart attack. His panic mounts, his blood pressure goes up, and his heart pounds faster. Now he knows he must stop thinking about it because just thinking about it makes it worse. He is clammy with sweat. He can't stop thinking about an imminent heart attack; he is in full panic now, and the vicious cycle continues.

After he consults a psychiatrist, a tranquilizer is prescribed. He is told that the medicine is a very powerful drug and will stop his anxiety even at the height of an attack. He carries the drug in his chest pocket wherever he goes; no anxiety attack reappears. He has never taken the drug.

In the example, our hypochondriac believes that he has potential control over his anxiety; he believes that if he were to take the pill, his anxiety would subside. What is the operative variable here, *controllability* of anxiety or the *predictability* that anxiety will be suppressed if he takes the pill?

These two variables are very hard to separate; for when control is present, prediction is as well. In discussing Weiss's ulceration results, I contended that the effects of control over shock amounted to the effects of the predictability of shock. However, I suspect that, in general, control does add something to the effect of predictability. Incidentally, I believe that control might reduce to predictability only in its effects on fear and anxiety—the effects of uncontrollability on response initiation, on sudden death, and on depression do *not* reduce to the effects of unpredictability.

Even in its effects on anxiety there may well be more to controllability than just predictability. Perhaps the key lies in the study of self-administered aversive stimulation and of perceived potential control. Consider two subjects, one who administers shock to himself, and the other who receives the same sequence of shocks, without having any control over them, but so that he can predict when they will occur. If the shocks are equally predictable and unmodifiable by the subject who administers them to himself, the only difference is controllability. Alternatively, consider two groups each of whom receive totally unpredictable shock; but one group, like our hypochondriac, is told that they have a panic button and can exit from the experiment. If only the subjects who do not leave the experiment are considered, they have equal unpredictability, but they differ in controllability. Only a few such studies have been run using such self-administration and perceived potential control.

Self-administration

L. A. Pervin (1963) gave college students all permutations of controllable, uncontrollable, predictable, and unpredictable shock. In this study, controllability meant self-administration, for subjects could not actually modify the shock. Each subject was run in each condition for three one-hour sessions; when asked which conditions they would choose to go through again, the subjects significantly preferred predictability to unpredictability and preferred control to no control. Subjects who had control tended to report less anxiety, though not to a significant degree.[15]

E. Stotland and A. Blumenthal (1964) used sweating of the hands as a measure of anxiety concerning an upcoming examination. Subjects were all told that they would be taking tests measuring important abilities. Half of the subjects were told that they could administer the tests to themselves by taking the parts in any order they pleased, whereas the others were told that they would have no choice about the order. The subjects did not actually take the tests, but galvanic skin response was measured immediately following the instruction. In the choice condition, sweating did not increase, while it increased in the no-choice condition.

Self-administration has played a significant role in an animal brain-stimulation study. Positive brain stimulation consists of a very small current delivered to the brain through an implanted electrode, and it is considered positive or pleasurable when an animal will work to get it. S. S. Steiner and coworkers (1969) gave rats positive brain stimulation for bar pressing. The experimenters then presented the stimulation in exactly the same temporal pattern that the rats had just given themselves; the rats now found the stimulation aversive and learned to escape from it, even though they had found it positive when they administered it to themselves. It is unclear, however, whether it was the act of self-administration that was critical or the lowered predictability of the stimulus when it was not self-administered.

These studies are inadequate to definitively separate predictability and controllability, because subjects who control a stimulus may also have more finely tuned predictability; making an uncontrollable stimulus equally predictable to a controllable one may be practically impossible. Perhaps the advantage that controllability yields in self-administration is that it gives such fine tuning of predictability. For example, when you drive a car, every small turn of the wheel has a predictable result. A passenger, even one watching every small movement of the driver, just does not have the exact predictability that the driver has. I tend to get motion sick in small, ocean-going boats, but I have found a technique that prevents illness: if I steer, turn the wheel, and control the boat as it breaks over the four-foot swells, I don't become nauseated.

What is needed are yoked designs comparing perfectly predictable onsets and offsets of stimulation: one subject himself makes the response that turns the stimulus on and off; the other subject is yoked, although he can predict the occurrence of the stimulus. In such a design, self-administration contributes no predictability, only controllability. To my knowledge only the following study approximately fulfills these criteria.

J. H. Geer and E. Maisel (1972) presented color photographs of victims of violent death to students in each of three conditions: (1) An escape group, whose subjects could terminate the photographs by pressing a button; the onset of each photograph was signalled by a 10-second tone. (2) A predictability group, whose subjects were informed that they would be shown each photograph for a certain number of seconds, but had no control over termination. The onset of each photograph for this group was also signalled by a 10-second tone. (3) A no-control, no-predictability group, whose subjects were randomly presented with tones and photographs, without any instrumental control. Both groups 2 and 3 were yoked to the escape group for mean duration of the photographs.

Escape subjects gave significantly lower GSR to the photographs than subjects in the other groups. Moreover, the predictability group subjects gave higher GSR's to the onset of tone than the escape subjects did. These results suggest that controllability contributes some relief of anxiety over that contributed by predictability. A methodological improvement that should be incorporated into future studies of this sort is to provide predictability subjects more exact predictability by some means of externally timing the duration of aversive stimulation (for example, a clock). This would insure that predictability subjects have as finely tuned prediction of offset of stimulation as escape subjects do.

Perceived control

The second line of evidence suggesting that control adds some anxiety relief over and above predictability comes from perceived, but not actual, control.[16] There are two ways a subject can perceive control without obtaining concomitant predictability: he never exercises control and merely believes it to be potential, as in the case of the heart patient; or he actually responds and continues to believe he has control, although he really does not.

D. C. Glass and J. E. Singer (1972) played two groups of college students a melange of loud sounds; the noise was unpredictable for both groups. One group was told it had potential control: "You can terminate the noise by pressing the button; that is, pressing the button will end the noise for the remainder of today's session. Of course, whether or not you press is up to you. Some people who come here do press the button, others do not; we'd prefer that you do not." None of the subjects actually pressed the button, so noise was equally predictable for both groups. Glass and Singer found that noise perceived as controllable caused no disruption of later performance; whereas the group without perceived control did show disrupted performance. Comparing groups from several of these studies, Glass and Singer concluded that "perceived control appears to reduce the aftereffects of unpredictable noise to a point where they resemble performance following predictable noise or no noise at all."[17]

J. H. Geer and co-workers performed a study in which subjects believed falsely that they were controlling shock.[18] They pressed a switch as soon as they felt a 6-second shock, which was preceded by a 10-second ready signal. In the second half of the experiment, half the subjects were told that they could reduce the length of the shocks if they reacted fast enough, while the others were simply told that their shocks would be shorter. All subjects actually received shocks of 3-second duration. The results indicated that subjects who believed they had control showed fewer spontaneous GSR's and lower GSR to shock onset than subjects who did not believe that they had control. Even though shock was exactly equally predictable for the two groups, the group which believed it had control seemed less anxious.[19] Ultimately the problem of disentangling the effects of controllability from predictability may be next to logically impossible; for even in the face of the perceived control data, it can still be argued that the anxiety reduction actually stemmed from a belief in the more exact predictability of shock that potential control must provide.

So, if we take the controllability results at face value, controlling an aversive event reduces anxiety; when people administer outcomes to themselves, they are less upset than yoked subjects. But it is possible that self-administration does this by means of providing very finely tuned predictability. The advantage of finely tuned predictability is probably eliminated in studies of perceived control. Here, when subjects believe they are controlling events, even when they are not, anxiety is lessened. The reduction of anxiety by perceived control provides us insight into the working of a very successful psychotherapy for anxiety.

SYSTEMATIC DESENSITIZATION AND CONTROLLABILITY

Since predictability and controllability play such a strong anxiety-reducing role, I suggest that these dimensions are an active ingredient in systematic desensitization, perhaps the most effective form of psychotherapy used to treat anxiety.[20] In this therapy, a patient complaining of an anxiety neurosis, for example a cat phobia, is first taught deep muscle relaxation; while relaxing, he then imagines scenes of successively more fearful events. For example, he imagines hearing the word *cat* in *catsup* while he relaxes; and so on up a hierarchy of fear until he can, with equanimity, imagine petting a cat. This technique seems to produce rapid remission of specific phobias in 80 to 90 percent of cases.

J. Wolpe, the founder of systematic desensitization, believes that the mere contiguity of relaxation with the feared object *counterconditions* the fear of the object. The feared object is eventually neutralized by pairing with a response—relaxation—that is incompatible with fear. Yet counterconditioning has been severely criticized as an inadequate explanation of the therapeutic effectiveness of desensitization.[21] A major criticism has been that cognitive factors also play a role. While I believe that counterconditioning may play a fear-reducing role in systematic desensitization, I also believe that the cognitive factor of controllability plays a role.

Relaxation seems to work best in systematic desensitization when it is a voluntary and active process, when the patient strongly believes that he can control his anxiety. However, systematic desensitization also works, at least partially, when relaxation is passively induced, and when actual mastery is not emphasized; obviously control is not the whole story.

One source of data concerning the importance of voluntary control over anxiety comes from drug-induced relaxation. Because it is sometimes difficult to get patients to relax adequately during systematic desensitization, several investigators have tried to induce relaxation by intravenous injections of a chemical muscle relaxant (methohexitone). It was noted, however, that this method resulted in a decline in therapeutic effectiveness. According to J. L. Reed (1966), some patients found the period of drug-induced relaxation very unpleasant. Their main complaint was an intense feeling of loss of control. In these cases the drug was withdrawn and replaced by relaxation induced by strictly muscular techniques; the patients found this acceptable and relaxed well.

Similarly J. P. Brady (1967) claims that successful use of drug-induced relaxation hinges on several procedural details:

> I no longer rely on methohexitone alone to produce the desired state of deep muscular relaxation and emotional calm. Rather I begin the first session with instructions and training in muscle relaxation. This may be regarded as a brief course (4-5 min.) in progressive relaxation. As the patient continues to relax he is advised that the drug he is about to receive will facilitate further relaxation and calm, but that he must "work along with it." As soon as the injection is started, further suggestions of relaxation are given such as might be used to induce hypnosis.

Relaxation by itself does not inhibit anxiety as much as relaxation that an individual produces himself.

The effects of self-produced controllability have led some behavior therapists to emphasize to their patients that desensitization is an active mastery procedure, not a passive outcome of the effects of counterconditioning. P. J. Lang

(1969) stresses the subject's control over the procedure of desensitization:

> The subject's control of the imagined fear stimulus—its length, frequency, and sequence of presentation is another important cognitive element in the desensitization procedure. When this control element was eliminated in Davison's experiment (1968) positive reduction in fear was not obtained. It may be that the aversiveness of phobic stimuli lies in the helplessness of the subject, the fact that he has no organized response except flight and avoidance.

Not only actual control, but perceived control, may also play some fear-reducing role in systematic desensitization. Phobics often panic at the mere thought of the phobic object or an anxiety-provoking situation. This helplessness-induced panic precludes their using any available coping responses. The perception of potential control, which arises once the subject has learned that he can relax in the presence of the phobic object, prevents this panic. Consider a client who has come to a behavior therapist for treatment of a phobia: After initial discussion the therapist decides to use systematic desensitization and explains to the client that he intends to use a proven technique that will enable him to master his fear and anxiety. A hierarchy is constructed and the client begins to work his way up; at every stage of the hierarchy the client's expectancy of gain is confirmed, that is, he is no longer afraid or anxious. As time goes on the client no longer panics at the sight of the phobic stimulus, but expects to be able to control fear. For the first time in his life the phobic has at his disposal the ability to short-circuit anticipatory panic and time to marshal his coping resources. He confirms this belief by successfully applying his newly learned mastery to realistic situations. So believing that one can control fear may reduce panic and allow more effective coping.

The treatment of premature ejaculation provides an interesting parallel with the last example. Premature ejaculators are not only unable to control sexual arousal, but they often have anticipatory fears when sexual involvement is inevitable. This anticipatory panic nullifies attempts to control ejaculation and may result in *secondary impotence*.[22] By the use of a penile squeeze technique and graduated exposure to real-life sexual situations, premature ejaculators learn that they can control their sexual arousal and, as a result, short-circuit their anticipatory panic. This further increases their ability to control ejaculation. Here again the belief in control reduces anxiety concerning sexual adequacy and allows more adequate coping.

CONCLUSION

A US is unpredictable when its probability is the same whether or not any CS occurs. When aversive events are unpredictable, no safety signal exists and anxiety ensues. Monitoring of anxiety during predictable and unpredictable shock confirms the safety-signal hypothesis: when animals and men receive unpredictable shock they show continual conditioned emotional responses and strong galvanic skin responses. Stomach ulceration is produced by unpredictability as well as uncontrollability of shock; the ulcer-inducing effects of helplessness may well result from the lack of response-produced safety signals. Animals and men choose predictable over unpredictable shock, as expected from the safety-signal hypothesis. While controllable events are predictable by the feedback from the response that controls them, controllability may have anxiety-reducing consequences in addition to this predictability—perceived potential control and nonveridical control of aversive events also relieve anxiety. Finally, I suggest that the perception of control and predictability may play a major therapeutic role in systematic desensitization.

In the last two chapters, I have examined the sources of two emotional states—depression and anxiety. Some people are more prone to depression and anxiety than others. For some fortunate people, the perception of helplessness and the state of depression will occur only after repeated, excruciating hardship. For others the smallest mishap will trigger a depression; for them depression is more than a state, it is a personality trait. What makes a human being so ready to perceive helplessness and to find himself depressed? The experiences of infancy, childhood, and adolescence are the most likely places to look for the foundations of helplessness. In the next chapter, I will examine the development of helplessness as a personality trait.

CHAPTER SEVEN

EMOTIONAL DEVELOPMENT AND EDUCATION

Ten years ago as a beginning graduate student, I decided to investigate emotional and motivational development. I found that, while the development of cognition, language, motor skills, morals, and intelligence had all been investigated and were represented by scientifically grounded theories, motivational development had only speculations and case histories. "This is a subject that we just don't know much about," said one of my professors. "Come back in ten years."

The ten years are up, but the state of our knowledge has not changed. The study of cognitive development, in its many forms, is flourishing, but almost no one seems willing to tackle motivational development. This chapter presents my speculations about motivational and emotional development. What I have to say is schematic, with much less experimental basis than I would like, but it is a beginning.

American psychologists, probably for reasons stemming from democracy and egalitarian ideals, have usually been interested in phenomena that are changeable and moldable. The behaviorism of J. B. Watson epitomized this noble endeavour:

> Give me a dozen healthy infants, well-formed, and my own specified world to bring them up in and I'll guarantee to take any one at random and train him to become any type of specialist I might select—doctor, lawyer, artist, merchant-chief and, yes, even beggar-man and thief.[1]

Let's stand back for a moment and make a guess about the future of our enthusiasm for plastic processes. From many sides, plasticity and environmentalism are under attack—deep, sustained, scholarly attack, and environmentalism of Watson's sort is in retreat in the scientific community. Piagetian psychology, for example, views the cognitive development of the child as not heavily determined by experience. On the contrary, the child's cognitive abilities are seen to grow and interact with the world much as a mussel accretes layer after layer of shell. A great mass of evidence supports this view. Children do not learn language in the way a rat learns to press a bar by reward and punishment. Or so the influential work of Chomsky, Brown, and Lenneberg tells us. Under all but the most impoverished conditions, children will come to speak and understand their native tongue. This is assured by elaborate neural preprogramming for language in *Homo sapiens*; the weight of evidence here also is not easy to challenge. Intelligence, as measured by IQ, cannot be raised very much by manipulating the environment, as Jensen, Herrnstein, Eysenck, and others have found. The bulk of the variance in IQ scores is produced not by environmental shaping, but by the IQ of the biological parent. Degree of economic deprivation, we are told, does not predict very well at all how smart a child will be; but his genes do.

My own work on learning, other than on helplessness, is no exception to the trend away from plasticity. I recently co-edited a book whose main theme was that evolutionary constraints place severe limits on what an organism can learn.[2] Different genetic preparedness, I argued, makes it easy for a given species to learn about some kinds of contingencies, and virtually impossible for it to learn about others. For example, pigeons easily learn to peck keys for food, but have great difficulty learning to peck a key to avoid shock.

As a diligent reader of the American psychological literature, I have almost been convinced. The cognitive development of a child is not nearly as plastic as I had hoped. This realization is not a cause for rejoicing. A few years ago, I attended a lecture by a famous old German psychologist. For four decades, right through the Nazi era, he had gathered data on different types of personality. He defined and described his typology at great length. At the end of the lecture I asked him, "How do different men get to be that way?" His answer was brief and remarkable; ten years ago I would have considered it frivolous at best, but in light of recent developments, it now has a deeper ring.

"That, young man, depends on character," he replied blandly.

I, for one, am not ready to abandon the search for plasticity. The democratic, egalitarian ideals that motivated American (and Soviet) environmentalism run too deep and mean too much to give them up lightly. If cognition cannot be molded at will in a child, psychologists must find what can.

I believe that motivation and emotion are more plastic than cognition, more shaped by the environment. I am no longer convinced that special, intensive training will raise a child's IQ by twenty points, or allow him to talk three months early, or induce him to write piano sonatas at age five, as Mozart did. On the other hand, I *am* convinced that certain arrangements of environmental contingencies will produce a child who believes he is helpless—that he cannot succeed—and that other contingencies will produce a child who believes that his responses matter—that he can control his little world. If a child believes he is helpless he will perform stupidly, regardless of his IQ. If a child believes he is helpless he will not write piano sonatas, regardless of his inherent musical genius. On the other hand, if a child believes that he has control and mastery, he may outperform more talented peers who lack such a belief. And most important, how readily a person believes in his own helplessness or mastery is shaped by his experience with controllable and uncontrollable events.

THE DANCE OF DEVELOPMENT

Human infants begin life more helpless than infants of any other species. In the course of the next decade or two, some acquire a sense of mastery over their surroundings; others acquire a profound sense of helplessness. Induction from past experience determines how strong this sense of helplessness or mastery is. Consider a third grader who has been beaten in every schoolyard fight he has had. The very first time he fought, he may not have sensed defeat until he was completely subjected. After nine defeats in a row, however, he probably feels beaten early, and at only the first hint of defeat. How ready he is to believe himself defeated is shaped by how regularly he has won or lost. So it is with more general beliefs, like helplessness and mastery. If a child has been helpless repeatedly, and has experienced little mastery, he will believe himself to be helpless in a new situation, with only minimal clues. A different child with the opposite experience, using the same clues, might believe himself to be in control. How early, how many, and how intense the experiences of helplessness and mastery are will determine the strength of this motivational trait.

When a baby is deposited, naked and screaming, into the waiting hands of his mother's obstetrician, he can exert almost no control over outcomes. Most of the responses of a neonate seem to be reflexive; he exhibits a very limited range of voluntary responses—actions that can be instrumentally shaped. For example, a newborn's sucking can be shaped.[3] The sucking response has two components: expression, or squeezing the nipple between the tongue and palate; and suction, or creating a vacuum to pull milk out of the nipple. A. J. Sameroff (1968) reinforced either expression or suction with milk. When expression was followed by milk, suction disappeared. In addition, neonates changed the force of their nipple squeezing to match changes in the minimum pressure at which milk was given. But this was a weak form of learning, showing no signs of being remembered from one feeding to the next. Neonates also may be able to exert some control over reinforcement with head turning, since when they get sugar water for turning their heads, the rate of head turning goes up.[4]

As the infant matures, more and more voluntary responses come to control outcomes. He cries, and his mother comes; consequently, his crying increases in frequency when next his mother is absent. He laboriously finds a comfortable position while lying in his crib; when next set down, he assumes that position more efficiently. His eyes get better and better at following objects—at least slowly moving objects.

At this point, it is worth reminding the reader of the distinction between actual control and the perception of control. The infant's voluntary actions, by definition, show control over certain outcomes. This does not necessarily imply that the infant, at the early stages, perceives that he has such control, and I do not assert that the neonate has such a perception.[5] Somewhere along the developmental course, however, such perceptions begin to develop—just when is an open question. Only future research on the transfer of helplessness and mastery across situations will pin down the beginnings of these perceptions. Objective control, however, is a necessary condition for the development of the perception of control.

The infant begins a dance with his environment that will last through childhood. I believe it is the outcome of this dance that determines his sense of helplessness or mastery. When he makes some response, it can either produce a change in the environment or be independent of what changes occur. At some primitive level, the infant calculates the correlation between response and outcome. If the correlation is zero, helplessness develops. If the correlation is highly positive or highly negative, this means the response is working, and the infant learns either to perform that response more or to refrain from performing it, depending on whether the correlated outcome is good or bad. But over and above this, he learns that responding works, that in general there is *synchrony* between responses and outcomes. When there is *asynchrony* and he is helpless, he stops performing the response, and further, he learns that in general responding doesn't matter. Such learning has the same consequences that helplessness has in adults: lack of response initiation, negative cognitive set, and anxiety and depression. But this may be more disastrous for the infant since it is foundational: it is at the base of his pyramid of emotional and motivational structures.

As I write this paragraph, my three-month-old son is nursing at his mother's breast. The dance of development is conspicuous: He sucks, the world responds with warm milk. He pats the breast, his mother tenderly squeezes him back. He takes a break and coos, his mother coos back. He gives a happy chirp; his mother attempts to chirp back. Each step he takes is synchronized with a response from the world.

J. S. Watson's experiments with two-to-three-month-old babies capture the essence of this dance.[6] Watson's view, like mine, is that the infant engages at every opportunity in a contingency analysis of the relationship between his responses and their outcomes. For about eight weeks the infant is contingency-deprived, because he makes so few voluntary responses and his memory span is so short that he has trouble remembering about the last pairing of a response with an outcome. But at the age of about eight weeks, a new capacity emerges. Watson and his colleagues gave three groups of infants of this age special contingency training for ten minutes a day, with striking results. They had designed a very sensitive air pillow that closed a switch every time the infant pressed it with his head. In the contingent group, a mobile made of colored balls hanging over the crib spun for one second following each press. The noncontingent group also saw a spinning mobile, but it was not under their control. A third group saw a stabile.

The contingent infants, unlike the others, appreciably increased their activity over the course of the experiment, showing that they had learned about the contingency. Only the mothers of the contingent infants reported (unanimously) that their babies vigorously smiled and cooed starting on the third or fourth day of the experiment.

Watson applied his procedure to a severely retarded eight-month-old girl who had developed behaviorally only to the age of one and a half months. She had been termed a developmental failure and had never displayed any instrumental activity or any appreciable smiling and cooing. Within eleven days of exposure to the contingent mobile, her activity increased tenfold, and she smiled and cooed vigorously when the mobile was around.

The contingency-analysis game exemplifies the earliest stages of the dance of development. Controlling the environment is powerfully pleasurable to a developing infant. Lack of control does not produce pleasure and may even be aversive, even if the environment is "interesting" and contains spinning mobiles. Why does the sound of a rattle please an infant? Not because of the physical properties of the sound, its novelty, or its familiarity, but because the infant himself makes it rattle. The basic evolutionary significance of pleasure may be that it accompanies effective instrumental responses and thereby encourages those activities that lead to the perception of control. Boredom, on the other hand, may drive the child away from stimulation that he cannot control, into games in which he can learn that he is an effective human being.

Reafference

What happens when an infant is deprived of synchrony between responding and outcome?

The earliest and perhaps most fundamental synchrony that can be interrupted is *reafference*. Reafference refers to the contingent relationship between action and visual feedback. When you take a step toward a wall, your motor action is synchronized precisely with the sight of a wall looming larger. Any normal infant can be seen to learn that the act of moving his hand in a certain way results in the sight of his hand moving.

Reafference is so fundamental that it is hard to imagine how, without it, an infant would even perceive a difference between himself and the rest of the world. What does distinguish the self from the world, after all? Those things that are part of *me* yield very high correlations when I voluntarily move them: I decide my hand is part of me, not part of others, because certain motor commands are almost invariably followed by the sight and feeling of the hand stretching out. Indeed, a contingency analysis that discovers synchrony between a given motor command and a given feedback seems the most likely way that we learn which motor command produces a particular response. To his grief each infant learns that mother is not part of self, but part of the world: the synchrony between motor commands and the sight of mother moving around is much less than a perfect correlation—although it is not zero except in the most impoverished environment. I suggest that those "objects" become self that exhibit near-perfect correlation between motor command and visual and kinesthetic feedback; while those "objects" that do not, become the world. Then, of course, begins the lifelong struggle to raise the correlation of the world's changes with motor commands— the struggle for control.

R. Held, A. Hein, and their colleagues at M.I.T. have conducted an impressive series of studies on depriving infant organisms of reafference.[7] Eight pairs of kittens were raised in darkness until they were eight to twelve weeks of age. Each pair was then literally yoked together in a carousel; one kitten was active and the other was carried passively in a gondola. The active kitten could walk around more or less freely; when it made a motor movement, synchronous visual feedback occurred. The passive kitten in the gondola received the same visual stimulation as the active kitten. All changes in the visual world of the passive kitten were independent of its actions; whether it moved its paw (or anything else) did not alter the probability that its visual world would change. There was no synchrony between its motor output and visual outcomes. The kittens spent three hours a day in the apparatus; at other times they were kept in the dark with their mother and littermates.

After thirty hours in the carousel, each pair was tested. The active kittens blinked at approaching objects, put out their paws to ward off collisions when they were carried downward to a surface, and avoided steep places. The passive kittens showed none of these behaviors, although after being allowed to run freely in light for a few days, they finally began to develop them.

In this case the damage caused by asynchrony of motor output and visual feedback was reversible. The reversibility may have been due to the relatively mild asynchrony. Even the passive kitten was provided with many synchronies; for even though it was raised in the dark, motor commands and tactual or auditory feedback were present: When the cat moved one leg and touched the other leg, he could feel the legs touching.

When he sucked at his mother's teats, milk flowed. When he put out his claws, the clawed object shrieked. More radical asynchrony could be expected to produce more pervasive and perhaps irreversible damage.

L. B. Murphy (1972) paints a bleak picture of radical asynchrony between a baby's actions and his mother's reaction in extremely impoverished American homes:

> *It is precisely this active exchange of play signals . . . which the extremely deprived baby with a destitute, exhausted mother does not have any more than do babies in some foundling homes. The discouraged, apathetic mother just sits, passively holding the baby, without face-to-face communication, much less active, playful mutual responses to the baby. The deprived baby does not have the experience which . . . leads him to the realistic expectation that reaching out, exploring the outside, trying out new impacts upon it would bring pleasant results.*

Helplessness may be a major result of maternal deprivation and institutional child rearing, and it is to these depressing circumstances we now turn.

MATERNAL DEPRIVATION

Human infants seem to suffer severe psychological damage when they are raised in certain institutional environments. One factor is common to all of them—the lack of control over outcomes. The observations of R. Spitz (1946) are typical and chilling:

> *In the second half of the first year, a few of these infants developed a weepy behavior that was in marked contrast to their previously happy and outgoing behavior. After a time this weepiness gave way to withdrawal. The children in question would lie in their cots with averted faces, refusing to take part in the life of their surroundings. When we approached them we were ignored. . . . If we were insistent enough, weeping would ensue and, in some cases, screaming. . . . During this period some of these children lost weight . . . the nursing personnel reported that some suffered from insomnia. . . . All showed a greater susceptibility to intercurrent colds or eczema. . . .*

*This behavior syndrome lasted three months. Then the weepiness
subsided, and stronger provocation became necessary to provoke it. A sort
of frozen rigidity of expression appeared instead. These children would
lie or sit with wide-open, expressionless eyes, frozen immobile face, and a
faraway expression as if in a daze, apparently not perceiving what went
on in their environment. This behavior was in some cases accompanied by
autoerotic activities. . . . Contact with children who arrived at this stage
became increasingly difficult and finally impossible. At best, screaming
was elicited.*[8]

This phenomenon has been variously called anaclitic
depression, hospitalism, and morasmus. It can arise from two
different circumstances. One is removal of a mother who has
formed a good relationship with her child of 6 to 18 months.
It is interesting that, if the relationship is weak or negative, the
condition tends not to develop. Alternatively it occurs when
children are raised in foundling homes, lying on their backs day
in and day out, with only white sheets to look at and with only
minimal, mechanical, human contact. If the mother soon returns, the condition usually remits, sometimes dramatically.
Without intervention, however, the prognosis is grim. Thirty-
four of the ninety-one foundling-home infants observed by
Spitz died in the first three years; stuporous depression and
idiocy resulted in other cases.

An infant deprived of stimulation is an infant thereby
deprived of *control* over stimulation. There can be no dance of
development when there is no partner. How can a bottle that
comes exactly every four hours regardless of what the child is
doing produce a sense of synchrony between action and outcome? Recall the experiments of Suomi and Harlow (1972), in
which infant monkeys were placed in a pit with no stimulation,
and remained there for forty-five days (p. 90). Like anaclitically
depressed children, these monkeys displayed profoundly depressed behavior even when taken out of the pit. They did not
play; they huddled in a corner and shrieked when approached
by peers. I suggest that it is not deprivation of stimulation in

itself, but deprivation of synchrony, that produces these effects.

An infant who loses his mother is an infant deprived not only of love, but of control over the most important outcomes in his life. The dance of development is impoverished indeed, if the mother is not available to be the primary partner. With no mother, there is often no one to hug back when you hug. Your coos and smiles are unreturned. Cries and shrieks fall on the deaf ears of a nursery staff too busy to respond and provide you with control. Food, diaper changing, and cuddling are not usually provided in response to your demands, but in response to the demands of a clock.

Most of our systematic knowledge of the effects of maternal deprivation comes from studies of monkeys. H. F. Harlow (1962) describes the behavior of motherless rhesus monkeys.[9]

> We observed the monkeys which we had separated from their mothers at birth and raised under various mothered and nonmothered conditions. The first 47 baby monkeys were raised during the first year of life in wire cages so arranged that the infants could see and hear and call to other infants but not contact them. Now they are five to seven years old and sexually mature. As month after month and year after year have passed, these monkeys have appeared to be less and less normal. We have seen them sitting in their cages strangely mute, staring fixedly into space, relatively indifferent to people and other monkeys. Some clutch their heads in both hands and rock back and forth—the autistic behavior pattern that we have seen in babies raised on wire surrogates. Others, when approached or even left alone, go into violent frenzies of rage, grasping and tearing at their legs with such fury that they sometimes require medical care.

The behavior of monkeys reared with no mother is similar to the behavior of monkeys reared with a "mother" made out of wire.[10] These monkeys do not explore and manipulate their world. Both in the presence and absence of their "mothers," what little contact they initiate with objects is frantic and erratic. They do not aggress when at play with other monkeys. G. P. Sackett (1970) has found similar deficits in monkeys reared in isolation from mother and peers. They no longer initiate or solicit physical contact, their aggression wanes, and their motor activity drops drastically. Like helpless dogs, these isolates also show deficits in their responsiveness to electric shock: when shocked for drinking from an electrified tube, they take a much higher level of shock before quitting than nonisolated controls.

What is missing here? The traditional answer is "mother's love." I think this answer is shallow. In any deprivation or enrichment study, it is easy to overlook the deprivation and enrichment of control. When an experimenter adds toy blocks and mazes to the laboratory environment of a rat, he not only adds more things, but he adds more *control* over things. The environment is enriched not because the block is there, but because the animal interacts with it: he sniffs it, overturns it, chews it. I doubt very much that adding objects, without allowing concomitant control, would yield any effects of enrichment. The opposite is also true. When a person is exposed to the chronic lack of something, he also lacks control over that thing. It is pertinent that deficits similar to those produced by maternal deprivation occur when young monkeys are merely given uncontrollable shock.[11] I suggest that maternal deprivation results in a particularly crucial lack of control. Mother is the primary partner in the dance of development, the fountain of synchronies with the infant's responses, and the main object of his contingency analyses. His sense of mastery or of helplessness develops from the information provided by mother's responses to his actions. If mother is absent, a profound sense of helplessness should arise—particularly if no surrogate, or an unresponsive one, is provided. Presumably even a mechanical mother, but one that danced with the infant and provided synchronies, would help stave off helplessness.

Mother also provides frustration and conflict for the infant—but *resolvable* frustration and conflict. B. L. White

(1971) emphasizes the role mother plays in providing difficulties that become resolved when the child acts:

> They design a physical world, mainly in the home, that is beautifully suited to nurturing the burgeoning curiosity of the one-to-three-year-old. . . . These effective mothers do not always drop what they are doing to attend to his request, but rather if the time is obviously inconvenient, they say so, thereby probably giving the child a realistic small taste of things to come. . . . Though they do volunteer comments opportunistically, they mostly act in response to overtures by the child.

As the dance of development goes on, it becomes more elaborate and challenging. No longer does each response of the child bring an outcome from mother. Problems occur, frustration ensues. When the child, by his own actions, copes with anxiety and frustration, his sense of effectiveness increases. If either the frustrations remain unresolved or the parents resolve them for the child, helplessness tends to build.

Not only helplessness with respect to mother, but helplessness with respect to the brutality of peers, can produce disastrous consequences. J. B. Sidowski (1971) isolated rhesus monkeys both from peers and their mothers until they were six months old. At six months these monkeys began to spend one hour a day taped to a restraining device, in the presence of other young monkeys who were unrestrained. The immobilized monkeys were subjected to uncontrollable abuse by their peers: the unrestrained monkeys gouged their eyes, pried their mouths open, pulled their hair and skin. The responses of the monkeys made helpless in this way were striking:

> After two or three months of stressful vocalizing and active struggle against the bonds, the restrained S's emotional reactivity slowly declined and appeared to give way to hopeless acceptance. Grimaces and screeches were present but ignored and no advantage was taken of numerous opportunities to bite the oppressor which thrust fingers or sex organs against or into its mouth.

These effects persisted when the monkeys were no longer restrained. When they were introduced to other monkeys, they were terror-stricken. One screeched, jumped, and convulsed so violently that the otherwise hardened experimenters considered terminating the session. The other formerly restrained monkey, when first touched by another animal, tilted and fell like a solid concrete block. He stirred only after the other monkey moved to another part of the cage. The growth of these monkeys was permanently stunted, for they subsequently developed almost no social interaction with their peers.

Several other recent animal experiments enlarge our knowledge of the effects of early helplessness on later development. J. M. Joffe and co-workers (1973) reared two groups of rats in a contingent and a noncontingent environment. In the contingent environment, pressing one lever produced food pellets, pressing another produced water, and pressing a third turned the house lights on or off. The noncontingent group received the same food, water, and lighting changes, but independently of their behavior. At about sixty days of age, each animal was tested in an open field, a standard test of anxiety. The contingency-reared animals explored more and defecated less, indicating lower anxiety. Being reared with mastery may produce less anxiety than being reared helpless.

R. D. Hannum, R. A. Rosellini, and I (1974) recently extended these findings to response initiation. Three groups of rats, shortly after they were weaned, received escapable, inescapable, or no shock. As adults they were tested on a new escape task. Rats who had received inescapable shock at weaning were helpless; they failed to escape shock. Rats who had received escapable shock or no shock escaped well. Furthermore, if a weanling rat had extensive experience with escapable shock, he would not become helpless when given inescapable shock as an adult. Early experience with control can immunize against adult helplessness.

Recently Peter Rapaport and I wondered if, by any chance, a helpless mother could communicate anything about her helplessness to her offspring.[12] It had been demonstrated that if a rat mother was given fear conditioning with signalled shock, and the signal was presented repeatedly during pregnancy, the offspring were more fearful.[13] Our question, however, was about the more subtle effects of control over shock presented only before pregnancy. We therefore gave three groups of female rats one session of inescapable, escapable, or no shock sixteen days before pregnancy. No further experimental manipulations were carried out. The cycle of ovulation was lengthened for the rats who received inescapable shock, indicating the expected greater stress of inescapability. All the rats became pregnant, gave birth to pups, and reared them until the pups were weaned at twenty-one days of age. Two of the five mothers who received inescapable shock died during pregnancy, a distressing but not surprising fact, as we shall see in Chapter Eight. When the pups grew to adulthood all of them were tested in an open field. The pups of mothers who had received inescapable shock did not explore the open field, while the pups whose mothers had received escapable shock or no shock explored the open field vigorously. When tested later on bar-press escape from shock, the "inescapable" offspring also tended to do worse, particularly the males.

Mothers who receive inescapable trauma, even before pregnancy, somehow can transmit their fear to the next generation. We don't know how they do this, but there are two possible sets of mechanisms: (1) *Uterine factors.* Inescapable shock may produce illness or some subtle and unknown, but lasting, abnormality in the sexual hormones that later bathe the fetus. The lengthening of the estrous cycle suggests this; the more the mother's cycle had been lengthened, the more her offspring froze when they were tested. (2) *Rearing factors.* Mothers who receive inescapable shock may become incompetent or hyperanxious, rearing their offspring badly. This study is as yet unreplicated, so generalization from it is premature and somewhat hazardous.

In another demonstration of the disruptive effects of uncontrollability on developing organisms, P. L. Bainbridge (1973) gave two groups of rats experience with discrimination problems at about fifty days of age. For one group the problem was unsolvable—food reward was independent of responses and stimuli. The second group's discrimination problem was solvable—a response to the appropriate stimulus always produced food. A third group received no problems. Later in life, the helpless animals were inferior at solving new discrimination problems and finding their way through mazes.

These types of developmental studies with animals are in their infancy. Although there is abundant literature on the effects of shock, handling, food deprivation, and maternal deprivation in animals, investigators have largely overlooked the dimension of controllability. If the line of argument I have followed is correct, deprivation of control over these events is a crucial manipulation. Those few studies that have varied controllability directly have done so for only a limited set of outcomes. If we are to discover the effects of chronic helplessness on motivational development, we must compare totally uncontrollable with controllable environments.[14]

My view of motivational development in infancy has now emerged. A child's or an adult's attitude toward his own helplessness or mastery has its roots in infant development. When an infant has a rich supply of powerful synchronies between his actions and outcomes, a sense of mastery develops. Responsive mothering is fundamental to the learning of mastery. On the other hand, if the child experiences independence between voluntary responding and outcome, helplessness will take root. Absence of mother, stimulus deprivation, and non-responsive mothering all contribute to the learning of uncontrollability. Helplessness in an infant organism has the same consequences as in adults: lack of response initiation, difficulty in seeing that responding works, anxiety, and depression. Since helplessness in an infant, however, is the foundational motivational attitude around which later motivational learning must crystallize, its debilitating consequences will be more catastrophic.

Is there any practical child-rearing suggestion that emerges from this? I think so. When my daughter, Amy, was eight months old, my wife and I and a group of my students went out to a tavern for pizza and beer. Amy sat in a highchair and gurgled while the adults discussed helplessness. At one point in the conversation, Amy, apparently bored, banged both her hands on the metal surface of the highchair. Since we had been talking about the importance of control in child development, I illustrated the point by banging both my hands on the table in front of me in response to Amy. A bright smile lit up Amy's face and she banged again. So we all banged in response. Amy banged back, laughing heartily. We all banged back. This continued for half an hour; the sight of eight adults and one child banging on the table at each other must have astonished the waitress and customers.

If what is commonly called *ego strength* proceeds from a child's sense of mastery over his environment, parents should go out of their way to play "synchrony games" of this sort with their young children. Rather than do things your child likes when the whim strikes you, wait for him to make some voluntary response, and then act. When the child repeats and intensifies his actions, repeat and intensify yours. If this chapter is wrong, and early childhood synchronies are unimportant, little is lost—a few hours of special play with a delighted child. If I am right, however, parents who go out of their way to "dance" with their children will thereby augment the sense of mastery that the children will develop.

PREDICTABILITY AND CONTROLLABILITY IN CHILDHOOD AND ADOLESCENCE

When my wife and I began to leave our daughter with baby-sitters during her first year, we noticed that Amy went from being placid to being increasingly fretful. We had adopted this strategy: when the babysitter arrived for the first time, I introduced the babysitter to Amy; then when they were engrossed in playing, my wife and I sneaked off. Our fading away, we hoped, would avoid the traumatic separation, with Amy wailing and protesting, that we knew would otherwise occur. It certainly seemed like the path of least resistance, and it is a course many parents take.

After we did this several times, we noticed Amy's increased anxiety. Kerry then objected to our strategy: "The safety-signal theory has definite predictions about sneaking off."

"How so?" I asked.

"When we leave Amy with no clear warning signal, that's just like unpredictable shock," she said. "Amy is beginning to spend a lot of time in anxiety about separation, since she has learned that there is no predictor of leaving and therefore no predictor of our staying around. If, on the other hand, we go through an elaborate and explicit departure ritual, then Amy will learn that if the ritual hasn't occurred she doesn't have to worry."

This made a great deal of sense to me, so the next time, we told Amy at length that we were going out for a few hours, took her and the babysitter out to the car, waved bye-bye, exchanged hugs and kisses, and let them watch the car drive away. Amy understood enough of what we were doing to scream and protest, but we did go, and have followed this ritual ever since. Soon thereafter, Amy went back to being placid. Incidentally, Amy at age five is a calm child, who does not seem at all worried about her parents leaving her. The reader may ask where our experimental control is. Actually, since we now have another child of appropriate age, we could provide a "sneak off" control. But since the procedure appeared to work so well, I don't think we will.

Young children are bound to encounter all sorts of traumatic experiences—going to the dentist, parents' departure, hypodermic injections. To the extent that these occur unannounced, I should expect anxiety to develop because the child has no way of knowing when he is safe. To the degree that the event is predicted and exactly so ("This is really going to hurt."), the child will learn that he is safe when Mommy says "This isn't going to hurt," or says nothing. I will return to this subject when I discuss self-esteem.

The classroom

Controllability and helplessness play a major role in the child's encounters with our educational system. School is a trying experience for almost every child, and along with reading, writing, and arithmetic, I believe that the schoolchild is learning just how helpless or how effective he is. J. Kozol, in one of the most moving books about education in the 1960's, *Death at an Early Age*, has described helplessness in the classroom:

> *The boy was designated a "special student," categorized in this way because of his measured I.Q. and hence, by the expectation of most teachers, not teachable within a normal crowded room. On the other hand, owing to the overcrowding of the school and lack of special teachers, there was no room for him in our one special class. Again, because of the school system's unwillingness to bus Negro children into other neighborhoods, he could not attend class in any other school which might have room. The consequence of all this, as it came down through the channels of the system, was that he was to remain a full year mostly unseen and virtually forgotten, with nothing to do except to vegetate, cause trouble, daydream or just silently decay. He was unwell. His sickness was obvious, and it was impossible to miss it. He laughed to near crying over unimaginable details. If you didn't look closely it seemed often that he was laughing over nothing at all. Sometimes he smiled wonderfully with a look of sheer ecstasy. Usually it was over something tiny: a little dot on his finger or an imaginary bug upon the floor. The boy had a large olive head and very glassy rolling eyes. One day I brought him a book about a little French boy who was followed to school by a red balloon. He sat and swung his head back and forth over it and smiled. More often he was likely to sulk, or whimper or cry. He cried in reading because he could not learn to read. He cried in writing because he could not be taught to write. He cried because he couldn't pronounce words of many syllables. He didn't know his tables. He didn't*

know how to subtract. He didn't know how to divide. He was in this Fourth Grade class, as I kept on thinking, by an administrative error so huge that it seemed at times as if it must have been an administrative joke. The joke of HIM was so obvious it was hard not to find it funny. The children in the class found it funny. They laughed at him all day. Sometimes he laughed with them since it's quite possible, when we have few choices, to look upon even our own misery as some kind of desperate joke. Or else he started to shout. His teacher once turned to me and said very honestly and openly: "It's just impossible to teach him." And the truth, of course, in this case, is that the teacher didn't teach him; nor had he really been taught since the day he came into this school.[15]

By taking this boy under his wing in special sessions, Kozol was able to teach him.

What is often passed off as retardation or an IQ deficit may be the result of learned helplessness. The child has learned that when English words go up on the blackboard, nothing he does will be right. As he falls farther behind, the helplessness deepens. Intelligence, no matter how high, cannot manifest itself if the child believes that his own actions will have no effect.

Two helplessness experiments with young school children have captured the problem in the laboratory. The first experiment verified that the *learning set* of helplessness can be produced in school children. Learning set is widely used in comparative psychology to measure the acquisition of learning strategies.[16] In a typical experiment, a monkey or a young child is placed in a two-choice discrimination apparatus. On one side is a junk object such as a spoon; on the other side, another junk object such as a handkerchief. The child then picks one—the spoon, for example. If this is correct, he is given an M&M. If wrong, he gets nothing. By trial and error the child learns, over the course of ten or twenty trials, to always pick the spoon. The second problem set is then given: a can is rewarded, a glass is not. Eventually, the child learns to always pick the can. After many such problem sets, the child will learn something more general than "Cans and spoons are correct." He will learn a cognitive strategy: if the object picked on the first trial is correct, stay with it; if wrong, shift immediately, and stay with the other object.[17] Once the child has learned the strategy, he will be 100-percent correct after the first trial on every new problem, and will no longer have to use trial and error learning.

R. A. O'Brien (1967) added a helplessness contingency to the usual learning-set design. One group of kindergarteners received a solvable series of junk-object problems. Another, helpless, group had a long series of problem sets in which reward was presented independently of responding—no cognitive strategy was appropriate, other than "Responses don't matter." A third group received no problems. Finally, all groups were set to a series of solvable learning-set problems. The helpless group was by far the slowest to learn, the no-experience group next, and the "solvable" group fastest.

This indicates that the acquisition of higher-order cognitive strategies of the kind necessary to academic success can be severely retarded by learning that responses do not produce solution. When a child fails in school, he may be forming the higher-order cognition that his responses are ineffective in general.

Fortunately it is common to see a child who is a failure at school but not in other aspects of his life. Children discriminate helplessness: in the classroom, with a certain teacher or with a certain subject, the child may feel helpless. Many of my otherwise excellent college students are paralyzed when faced with a mathematical equation. Outside the classroom, with other teachers, or with subjects other than mathematics, the student may feel competent.

C. S. Dweck and N. D. Reppucci (1973) have demonstrated such discriminative helplessness in the classroom. Forty fifth-graders received solvable and unsolvable visual problems from two different teachers. At first, one teacher gave only solvable problems, the other only unsolvable ones. Finally, the children were given solvable problems by the "unsolvable" teacher. They failed to solve these problems—even if they were identical to the problems they had just solved with the "solvable" teacher. A child can discriminate and come to believe that he is helpless under one set of circumstances, but not under others. Faced with a solvable problem under the wrong set of circumstances, he will greatly underperform.

This discriminated helplessness may be related to certain (although certainly not all) failures to learn how to read. P. Rozin and his students took over a class of inner-city children with severe reading problems.[18] When he tried to teach them to read English they showed him consistent failure, just as they showed their regular English teachers. One day Dr. Rozin brought in a set of Chinese characters, and told the children that each one stood for a spoken English word. Within hours, these children were reading entire paragraphs in "Chinese." Obviously the capacity for reading was present but something was damming it up. Rozin suggested that the association of a whole word with each character was cognitively more accessible to these children than the ordinary association of a sound with each letter or letter-group. If this was the whole story, however, why did they have such trouble associating whole written English words with spoken words? I suspect that discriminated helplessness may have been at work. The children had learned through repeated failure that they could not read English. The written English word, like the mathematical equation for my verbal students, controlled helplessness discriminatively. When written "Chinese" replaced the written English word, the children did not know they were having a reading lesson. Their natural abilities then took over, unhampered by learned helplessness.

C. S. Dweck (1973) was able to alleviate learned helplessness displayed by ten-to-thirteen-year-olds with respect to arithmetic. She selected 12 classroom failures as the most helpless of 750 students in two New Haven public schools. These children were notorious for the ease with which they gave up and stared into space when they failed on arithmetic problems. She divided them into two treatment groups, a "success only" (SO) group and an "attribution retraining" (AR) group, and gave them 25 days of special training. The SO group always received arithmetic problems they could successfully complete—failure was avoided or glossed over by the choice of problem. The AR group received the same easy problems, but twice a day they received problems that were beyond their abilities. When they failed, they were told: "Time's up. You didn't finish in time. You needed to solve three and you only solved two. That means you should have tried harder." In other words, they were trained to attribute failure to their own lack of effort. After retraining, both groups were tested on their response to failing at new arithmetic problems. The SO group continued to go to pieces after failure. The AR subjects, in marked contrast, showed no impairment following failure, and even improvement, as well as reduced test anxiety.

This is an important experiment. It indicates that helplessness caused by failure in the classroom can be reversed, even in apparently intractable cases. The crucial manipulation was training the schoolchildren to cope with failure by attributing it to their own lack of effort. Such an attribution replaces the belief of a helpless child that he fails because there is nothing he can do. On the other hand, exposure to repeated success in which failure is avoided or glossed over leaves the child helpless, or makes him more so. To reverse classroom helplessness, it is necessary to experience some failure and to develop a way to cope with it.

The lack of experience coping with failure produces helplessness not only in grade school, but at advanced levels of education. If a young adult has no experience of coping with anxiety and frustration, if he never fails and then overcomes, he will not be able to cope with failure, boredom, or frustration when it becomes crucial. Too much success, too coddled an existence, makes a child helpless when he is finally confronted with his first failure. Recall the "golden girl" who fell apart in college when she found that rewards did not fall into her lap as readily as they had in high school.

Every year a few straight-A, advanced undergraduates elect to do a project in my laboratory. Every year I warn each of them that laboratory work is not as glamorous as they might believe: it means coming in seven days a week for months on end; looking at endless, boring printouts of data; having equipment break down in the middle of a session. Every year, half of them give up in the middle of their experiment. They do not lack intelligence, imagination, or wit. What they lack, and lack deeply, is a sense of *project*. What they have is a "Sesame Street" view of education, carried inappropriately to the college level: "If it's not titillating, exciting, colorful, I won't do it." The sense of project that is necessary for scientific discovery, as well as for any creative act, consists of an ability to tolerate failure, frustration, and, most of all, boredom. If the discovery had been easy, colorful, and titillating, someone else, probably, would have made it already. The only real, visceral gratification comes at the end of the experiment, if at all.

I believe that many of my "failures," through too much success, have developed insufficient coping mechanisms. Their parents and their teachers, out of a misguided sense of kindness, made things much too easy for them. If a reading list was too long and the student protested, the teacher shortened it— rather than have the students put in extra hours of work. If the teenager was picked up for vandalism, the parents bailed him out—rather than have the child find out that his actions have serious consequences. Unless a young person confronts anxiety, boredom, pain, and trouble, and masters them by his actions, he will develop an impoverished sense of his own competence. Even at the hedonic level, creating shortcuts around difficulties for children is not kind—depression follows from helplessness. At the level of ego strength and character, making the road too easy is a disaster.

I am not a crotchety old educator, but I enter here a plea for standards. At a time when students are protesting the existence of grades, long reading lists, and competition, I suggest that it is only when an individual matches his ability to a harsh standard, and overcomes, that ego strength emerges. If these standards disappear, the students will lose what they themselves want most—a sense of their own worth. S. Coopersmith (1967), in an extensive statistical study of self-esteem and its antecedents, concluded that children with high self-esteem came from backgrounds with clear and explicit standards, while children with low self-esteem did not have such standards to measure themselves against.[19]

A sense of worth, mastery, or self-esteem cannot be bestowed. It can only be earned. If it is given away, it ceases to be worth having, and it ceases to contribute to individual dignity. If we remove the obstacles, difficulties, anxiety, and competition from the lives of our young people, we may no longer see generations of young people who have a sense of dignity, power, and worth.

Poverty

My final speculations in this chapter are reserved for the relationship between helplessness and poverty. It would be glib to equate poverty with helplessness. Having an annual income of $6,000 a year, instead of $12,000, does not automatically produce helplessness. The lives of poor people are replete with instances of courage, of belief in the effectiveness of action, and of personal dignity. But a low income restricts choices and frequently exposes a poor person to independence between outcome and effort. Extreme, grinding poverty does produce helplessness, and it is a rare individual who can maintain a sense of mastery in the face of it. A child reared in such poverty will be exposed to a vast amount of uncontrollability. When he cries to have his diaper changed, his mother may not be there—or if there, too exhausted or harried to react. When he is hungry and asks for food, he may be ignored or even struck. In school, he often will find himself far behind, bewildered, and even abused.

E. C. Banfield (1958) poignantly describes the uncontrollable lot of South Italian peasants:

> What for others are misfortunes are for him calamities. When their hog strangled on its tether, a laborer and his wife were desolate. The woman tore her hair and beat her head against a wall while the husband sat mute and stricken in a corner. The loss of the hog meant they would have no meat that winter, no grease to spread on bread, nothing to sell for cash to pay taxes, and no possibility of acquiring a pig the next spring. Such blows may fall at any time. Fields may be washed away in a flood. Hail may beat down the wheat. Illness may strike. To be a peasant is to stand helpless before these possibilities.

These conditions of objective helplessness have their cognitive consequences, which in turn diminish voluntary response initiation:

> The idea that one's welfare depends crucially upon conditions beyond one's control—upon luck or the caprice of a saint . . . this idea must certainly be a check on initiative. Its influence on economic life is obvious: one who lives in so capricious a world is not likely to save and invest in the expectation of ultimate gain. In politics, too, it must have an effect. Where everything depends upon luck or Divine intervention, there is no point in community action. The community, like the individual, may hope or pray, but it is not likely to take its destiny into its own hands.[20]

K. A. Clark (1964) describes similar helplessness, powerlessness, and poverty in Harlem:

> In short, the Harlem ghetto is the institutionalization of powerlessness. Harlem is made up of the socially engendered ferment, resentment, stagnation, and potentially explosive reactions to powerlessness and continued abuses. The powerless individual and community reflect this fact by increasing dependency and by difficulty in mobilizing even the latent power

to counter the most flagrant abuses. Immobility, stagnation, apathy, in-difference, and defeatism are among the more obvious consequences of personal and community impotence. Random hostility, aggression, self-hatred, suspiciousness, seething turmoil, and chronic personal and social tensions also reflect self-destructive and non-adaptive reactions to a per-vasive sense and fact of powerlessness.

It is banal to point out that poverty is bad for children and other living things. Easily overlooked, however, is the way that many aspects of poverty converge in their effects by pro-ducing helplessness. Psychological explanations are often over-looked when economic or political explanations are apparent. Economic and political factors, however, can only have their effects via psychological mediators. Economic historians are wont to point out that, in the 1930's, the unavailability of capital caused suicide. Such an explanation is necessarily in-complete: capital or its lack cannot cause suicide directly; there must be a psychological state, such as depression, which in turn causes suicide. Similarly, poverty in itself is not a com-plete explanation of anomie. How does poverty work psycho-logically to produce stagnation, hostility, and rootlessness? I suggest that among its effects, poverty brings about frequent and intense experiences of uncontrollability; uncontrollability produces helplessness, which causes the depression, passivity, and defeatism so often associated with poverty.

The welfare system, however well intentioned, adds to the uncontrollability engendered by poverty; it is an institu-tion that undermines the dignity of its recipients because their actions do not produce their source of livelihood. A young child left to walk the streets too soon sometimes develops great mastery by coping with and overcoming his conditions; but more often he finds himself in situations beyond his control.

Crowding, frequently associated with poverty, may be another mechanism that increases uncontrollability.[21] J. Rodin (1974) theorized that one consequence of crowding, and therefore of urban poverty, is learned helplessness. To test this she selected thirty-two black boys between the ages of six and nine from a New York City housing project. These children differed in the number of people with whom they shared identical three-room apartments—there were from three to ten people living in each unit. The children did not differ in IQ, neighborhood environment, or class or income level. They were placed on an operant reinforcement schedule, in which they received marbles that could later be exchanged for different brands of candy. In the crucial part of the study, the boys who collected enough marbles could select the candy they wanted themselves, or they could ask the experimenter to select the candy for them. Children who lived with only two other people always wanted to select the candy themselves. The more people the child lived with, the more he left it to the experimenter to select his candy. Rodin suggests that crowding produces a sense of helplessness that undermines the child's desire or ability to make active choices.

In order to further examine the relationship of crowding and helplessness, Rodin ran an experiment that parallels in design our experiment on the relationship of depression and helplessness (p. 86). Four groups of children were chosen from conditions similar to the first study; half of them lived with many people in the same apartment, the other half lived with few. Half of each of these groups was given an unsolvable problem, the other half, a solvable problem. Then all the children were tested on a new, solvable problem. Children who were both crowded and had been given the unsolvable problem did by far the worst on the new problem; uncrowded children with the unsolvable problem were next worse. It is interesting that, if the first problem had been solvable, both the crowded and uncrowded children did well. Solvability reversed the effects of crowding, at least temporarily. It appears that crowding of children as measured by Rodin acts in the same way as depression in adults: it reduces cognitive performance, but it can be reversed by the experience of mastery. It is probably significant that D. J. Goeckner and co-workers (1973) found that rats reared in crowded cages failed to escape and avoid shock.[22] These data, together with those of Rodin and Miller,[23] suggest that crowding can produce depression and helplessness.

The academic performance of poor black American children is substandard. It has frequently been argued that this is caused by genetically lower IQ.[24] My guess is that this is not the whole story, and that the deficits may be more environmental than some currently believe. Both IQ and school performance can be lowered by helplessness. As I mentioned in my discussion of lowered IQ in depression, successful cognitive performance requires that two elements be present: adequate cognitive capacity and motivation to perform. To the extent a child believes that he is helpless and that success is independent of his voluntary responses, he will be less likely to make those voluntary cognitive responses, like scanning his memory or doing mental addition, that result in high IQ scores and successful schoolwork. No study that I know of has ruled out such a belief in helplessness as a cause of the lower IQ scores and scholastic performance of poor black American children.

U. Bronfenbrenner (1970) has focused on a similar variable:

> Deutsch's observations indicate that the lack of persistence reflects not only an inability to concentrate but also a lack of motivation and an attitude of futility in the face of difficulty. Thus he reports (Deutsch, 1960, p. 9):
> "Time after time, the experimental child would drop a problem posed by the teacher as soon as he met any difficulty in attempting to solve it. In questioning after, the child would typically respond 'so what?' or 'who cares?' or 'what does it matter?' In the control group (white children of 'similar socio-economic level'), there was an obvious competitive spirit, with a verbalized anticipation of 'reward' for a correct response. In general, this anticipation was only infrequently present in the experimental group and was not consistently or meaningfully reinforced by the teachers."

Deutsch's observations are confirmed by a series of studies, cited by T. F. Pettigrew (1964), showing that "lower-class Negro children of school age typically 'give up the fight' and reveal unusually low need for achievement."

In a sobering and moving assessment of black education, T. Sowell (1972), a noted economist, advances just this argument. He traces his own academic history as a black child in the South and in New York. It was communicated to him almost daily that he was stupid and that little success could be expected of him. He was a rebellious, but rare, character who did not internalize this belief in helplessness. But he argues that many other blacks do, and that, because of this belief in helplessness, blacks do not persist equally with whites in the face of academic difficulty. Such a process could easily account for IQ discrepancies.

If a belief in helplessness is a central problem of race and poverty today, implications follow about undoing the cycle of poverty. G. Gurin and P. Gurin (1970) cite the common hope that we are now living in a period of increased opportunities for the poor and the black. The Gurins caution that poor blacks may be unable to benefit from increased economic opportunities because of their widespread belief that outcomes are not under their control. This parallels directly the paradigmatic learned-helplessness experiments: People, dogs, and rats first learn that relief is uncontrollable. Then, because the experimenter has changed the conditions, relief actually becomes attainable; but because of their expectancies of independence between relief and responding, the subjects have difficulty forming a new, hopeful expectancy. If this logic is correct, repeated experience with success, accompanied by real changes in opportunity, will be necessary to break the cycle of poverty. It is crucial that these successes be perceived by the poor as resulting from their own skill and competence, and not from the benevolence of others.

Historians have made us aware of "revolutions of rising expectations."[25] When the lower strata of society are ground underfoot, revolution tends not to occur; when people begin to expect, however, that their own actions might succeed, the time is ripe for it. A belief in uncontrollability should, of course, make the initiation of revolutionary acts impossible. When oppressed and impoverished people see all around them the possibility of power and affluence, their belief in uncontrollability shatters, and revolution becomes a possibility.

It is not difficult to understand both the appeal and self-esteem-enhancing nature of social action.[26] If poverty produces helplessness, then effective protest—changing one's conditions by one's own actions—should produce a sense of mastery. The resentment in the black community against liberals and social workers who try to alleviate black problems is understandable, for poverty is not only a financial problem, but, more significantly, a problem of individual mastery, dignity, and self-esteem.

CHAPTER EIGHT

DEATH

When, in early 1973, medical army officer Major F. Harold Kushner returned from five and a half years as a prisoner of war in South Vietnam, he told me a stark and chilling tale. His story represents one of the few cases on record in which a trained medical observer witnessed from start to finish what I can only call death from helplessness.

Major Kushner was shot down in a helicopter in North Vietnam in November 1967. He was captured, seriously wounded, by the Viet Cong. He spent the next three years in a hell called First Camp. Through the camp passed 27 Americans: 5 were released by the Viet Cong, 10 died in the camp, and 12 survived to be released from Hanoi in 1973. The camp's conditions beggar description. At any one time there were about eleven men who lived in a bamboo hut, sleeping on one crowded bamboo bed about sixteen feet across. The basic diet was three small cups of red, rotten, vermin-infested rice a day. Within the first year the average prisoner lost 40 to 50 percent of his body weight, and acquired running sores and atrophied muscles. There were two prominent killers: malnutrition and helplessness. When Kushner was first captured, he was asked to make antiwar statements. He said that he would rather die, and his captor responded with words Kushner remembered every day of his captivity: "Dying is easy; it's living that's hard." The will to live, and the catastrophic consequences of the loss of hope, are the theme of Kushner's story and of this chapter.

When Major Kushner arrived at First Camp in January 1968, Robert had already been captive for two years. He was a rugged and intelligent corporal from a crack marine unit, austere, stoic, and oblivious to pain and suffering. He was 24 years old and had been trained as a parachutist and a scuba diver. Like the rest of the men, he was down to a weight of ninety pounds and was forced to make long, shoeless treks daily with ninety pounds of manioc root on his back. He never griped. "Grit your teeth and tighten your belt," he used to repeat. Despite malnutrition and a terrible skin disease, he remained in very good physical and mental health. The cause of his relatively fine shape was clear to Kushner. Robert was convinced that he would soon be released. The Viet Cong had made it a practice to release, as examples, a few men who had co-operated with them and adopted the correct attitudes. Robert had done so, and the camp commander had indicated that he was next in line for release, to come in six months.

As expected, six months later, the event occurred that had preceded these token releases in the past. A very high-ranking Viet Cong cadre appeared to give the prisoners a political course; it was understood that the outstanding pupil would be released. Robert was chosen as leader of the thought-reform group. He made the statements required and was told to expect release within the month.

The month came and went, and he began to sense a change in the guards' attitude toward him. Finally it dawned on him that he had been deceived—that he had already served his captors' purpose, and he wasn't going to be released. He stopped working and showed signs of severe depression: he refused food and lay on his bed in a fetal position, sucking his thumb. His fellow prisoners tried to bring him around. They hugged him, babied him, and, when this didn't work, tried to bring him out of his stupor with their fists. He defecated and urinated in the bed. After a few weeks, it was apparent to Kushner that Robert was moribund: although otherwise his gross physical shape was still better than most of the others, he was dusky and cyanotic. In the early hours of a November morning he lay dying in Kushner's arms. For the first time in days his eyes focused and he spoke: "Doc, Post Office Box 161, Texarkana, Texas. Mom, Dad, I love you very much. Barbara, I forgive you." Within seconds, he was dead.

Robert's was typical of a number of such deaths that Major Kushner saw. What killed him? Kushner could not perform an autopsy, since the Viet Cong allowed him no surgical tools. To Kushner's eyes the immediate cause was "gross electrolyte imbalance." But given Robert's relatively good physical state, psychological precursors rather than physiological state seem a more specifiable cause of death. Hope of release sustained Robert. When he gave up hope, when he believed that all his efforts had failed and would continue to fail, he died.

Can a psychological state be lethal? I believe it can. When animals and men learn that their actions are futile and that there is no hope, they become more susceptible to death. Conversely, the belief in control over the environment can prolong life. The evidence for this that I shall now lay out comes from a wide range of sources, and has never been integrated before. Unlike the previous chapters, the review will not be theoretical, but descriptive; I hope only to make one proposition plausible: The psychological state of helplessness increases the risk of death. I do not know the physical reasons why this is so, but I shall mention some of the speculations about physical causes. Because of our ignorance we shall have to put physical cause aside and concentrate on the fact that these deaths have real and catastrophic psychological underpinnings.

Instances of death from helplessness are by no means rare, and they are often only slightly less dramatic than the ones Kushner saw. I shall first document the phenomenon in a variety of animals, then in humans, young and middle-aged, then among old people, and finally in young children. Along the way I shall speculate on how these tragedies could have been prevented, and how they can be prevented in the future.

DEATH FROM HELPLESSNESS IN ANIMALS

Observation of sudden death from helplessness has not been restricted to the death of humans; there is a small, but remarkable, experimental literature on animals.

The wild rat (*Rattus norwegicus*) is a fierce and suspicious creature. Wild rats react with astonishing vigor when one attempts to capture them, and they are constantly vigilant for avenues of escape. C. P. Richter observed sudden death in these creatures and attributed it to "hopelessness."[1] He had found that if a wild rat was placed in a large vat of warm water from which there was no escape, the rat would swim for about 60 hours before drowning in a state of exhaustion. Other rats were first held in the investigator's hand until they stopped struggling, and then they were put in the water. These rats swam around excitedly for a few minutes, then suddenly sank to the bottom and drowned without resurfacing. A few died even earlier—in the hand of the investigator. When restraint was combined with trimming of the whiskers, a primary sensory organ of the rat, all rats tested showed sudden death.

Richter reasoned that being held in the hand of a predator like man, having whiskers trimmed, and being put in a vat of water from which escape is impossible produces a sense of helplessness in the rat. This must have sounded like a radical speculation to his tough-minded readers, but he substantiated it: He first held rats in his hand until they stopped struggling, then let them go. Then he held them again and released them again. Finally, he held them and put them in the water. "In this way, the rats quickly learn that the situation is not hopeless; thereafter they again become aggressive, try to escape and show no signs of giving up." These immunized wild rats swam for 60 hours. Similarly, if Richter took a helpless rat out of the water before it drowned and put it in again several times, the rats would swim for 60 hours. In essence, sudden death could be prevented by showing the rat that escape was possible. These two procedures resemble our therapeutic and immunizing procedures for breaking up learned helplessness in rats and dogs (p. 56).

The physiological condition of the wild rats during sudden death was bizarre. In the most common forms of death in mammals, the heart speeds up (*tachycardia*) as death occurs. These are called *sympathetic deaths*, referring to the excited nature of the sympathetic nervous system: tachycardia and increased blood pressure quickly pump blood from the heart to the extremities—in short, emergency death. Richter's wild rats, in contrast, showed *parasympathetic death*, or death from relaxation: the heart rate slowed down (*bradycardia*) and the heart was found on autopsy to be engorged with blood. Richter pretreated some of his rats with atropine, which blocks the parasympathetic (and cholinergic) system. This prevented death in a significant minority of the rats. The net draws a bit tighter as we remember that Thomas and Balter used atropine to prevent learned helplessness in cats (p. 70), and that Janowsky and co-workers used atropine to reverse depression in normal humans (p. 92).[2] Richter concluded that he had found death from hopelessness, death caused by giving up the struggle.

Bennet Galef and I wondered whether inescapable shock in learned-helplessness experiments works upon the same mechanisms that Richter activated by restraining wild rats.[3] So we built a steel Skinner box, bought chain-mail gloves, and started a colony of wild rats. We used two groups of adult females. One received immunization with escapable shock followed by long-duration inescapable shock (of mild intensity). The second group was yoked: they received the same sequence of shocks, but *all* of them were inescapable. We had intended to put both groups in the vat of water, expecting that the escapable-shock group would swim for 60 hours and the yoked group might show sudden death. To our surprise, however, six of the twelve in the yoked group lay down, paws splayed beneath the grids, and died in the box during mild, long-duration shock. Their hearts were engorged with blood. None of the other group died.

Recently Robert Rosellini, Yitzchak Binik, Robert Hannum, and I tested laboratory rats in the sudden-drowning apparatus. We used white rats who at weaning had received escapable, inescapable, or no shock. Only those who had received inescapable shock at weaning were helpless at escaping shock as adults. We found that this group showed significantly more sudden death than the other two groups. These findings are tentative, since the helpless rats, because they failed to escape, had received more shock as adults than the others. Nevertheless, they suggest that inescapable shock and restraining a wild rat in the hand can produce similar effects. Again a relaxation, or giving-up death, rather than an emergency death, is implicated.[4]

There is another animal-restraint phenomenon that may be related to death from helplessness. When a predator, such as a chicken hawk, attacks a chicken and then lets the chicken go, the chicken may remain in a frozen posture for many minutes or even hours. This catatonic response has been called animal hypnosis, tonic immobility, death feint, playing possum, catalepsy, and mesmerism.[5] Examples of this from common folk knowledge include "putting a frog to sleep" by turning it on its back and stroking its stomach, and immobilizing alligators during alligator wrestling; people banding birds are warned that holding them may produce a state that looks like death. In the laboratory the effect is usually produced by seizing an animal and holding it on its side for about fifteen seconds. The animal struggles at first, then becomes rigid. A prolonged state of total unresponsiveness ensues, and immobilized animals may not even react to pinpricks. Eventually the animal comes out of it, usually abruptly, and runs away. This phenomenon is usually thought of as immobilization by fear, but it has features that tie it to helplessness and sudden death.

M. A. Hofer (1970) exposed a variety of rodents (chipmunks, kangaroo rats, and others) to an open space, a startling sound, the silhouette of a hawk, and a snake—all at once. Immobility was immediate and pronounced, and persisted for up to thirty minutes. So profound was it that no movement occurred even when the snake crawled under and around the bodies. Hofer's main variable of interest was cardiac rate. As in Richter's sudden-death study, the heart slowed greatly during immobility. During the bradycardia, frequent cardiac arrhythmias were observed. In spite of this, none of the rodents died during testing, although 26 percent of the rodents trapped had died of unknown cause during the first week in the laboratory. Several of the rodents showing arrhythmia died soon thereafter, but none died that hadn't shown arrhythmias. The crucial factors are here: an uncontrollable stressor, a reaction of passivity, and enhanced susceptibility to death.

J. Maser and G. Gallup have produced tonic immobility in domestic chicks by holding them on their sides, and reported that electric shock prolonged this immobility.[6] To test whether helplessness was involved in the phenomenon, they gave three groups escapable or inescapable shock, or no shock, before immobilization. The chickens receiving inescapable shock remained immobile about five times as long as the chickens receiving escapable shock. Gallup has also mentioned that some of his chickens never come out of immobility: they die during it.

H. J. Ginsberg (1974) immobilized chicks and later tested them for sudden death by drowning. One group of chicks were allowed to terminate their own immobility; they came out of it when the spirit moved them. Another group received uncontrollable termination of immobility; the experimenter prodded their breasts until they came out of it. A third group was not immobilized. Then all groups were tested in water. The helpless group died fastest, the naive group next, and the chicks who controlled immobility termination were slowest to drown.

I am reminded of birds caught in oil spills: When the tanker *Torrey Canyon* ran aground off England and disgorged its contents onto the beaches in the first of the major oil spills, many wild birds were covered with crude oil. Well-intentioned people who picked them up and began to wash them off were dismayed when many of the birds died in their hands. It was said that the detergent killed them. I cannot help speculating, however, that they died from helplessness produced by restraint, amplified by the helplessness produced by the inability of the birds to fly due to the oil. Handbooks urge gentle and very quick washing; perhaps if the birds were repeatedly released and recaptured, as were Richter's immunized rats, washing would be less lethal.[7]

Most of the species in which sudden death has been seen are wild.[8] Controllability may be a particularly significant dimension of life to a wild animal. When he is taken to a zoo and put in a cage, he is deprived not only of the plains, banyan trees, and ants, but of *control*. If the argument set forth here is well-founded, the astonishing rate of death in wild animals newly acquired by zoos makes sense.[9] I have heard that 50 percent of the tigers brought from India die en route to the zoo. Special procedures might cut such mortality, such as transportation in cages full of manipulanda enabling the captured animals to exercise instrumental control. Recently the *Washington Post* reported that Dr. Hal Markowitz of the Portland (Oregon) Zoo had instituted such procedures with his apes and monkeys.[10] Before this, the animals would look almost lifeless at feeding time as they sat near wilted food on the floor. Markowitz placed feeding under the animals' control: at a light signal they now rush to press lever one, race across the cage to press lever two, and then get a bite of food. Experts say they have never seen healthier zoo apes, and the animals have been free from the extensive illness that often plagues less active zoo animals.

Primates other than man also show death from helplessness. Dr. I. Charles Kaufman reported to me that two of the eleven rhesus infants he separated from their mothers died during the withdrawal phase of the loss reaction.[11]

The first death was in one of the first-born infants who was five months and seven days old. He died on the ninth day of separation. An autopsy revealed no pathology to account for the death. Nutritional state was excellent. The infant showed the usual sequence of agitation followed by depression, with a sharp fall in play. However, in the second week of separation there was a very marked withdrawal from all other animals and then sudden death. The other infant died on the sixth day of separation when he was five months old. He also showed the typical agitation followed by depression. Locomotion continually decreased after day 1. His posture crumbled on the second and third days of separation, more so than was seen in any other infant in his group. His play levels dropped to zero. He also was found dead in the morning. As with the other infant, autopsy revealed no explanation for his death, and his nutritional state was excellent.

Jane Goodall described the death of Flint, a young male chimpanzee, after his mother, Flo, died:

Flo lay down on a rock, toward the side of a stream and simply expired. She was quite old. Flint stayed near her corpse: he grabbed one of her arms and tried to pull her up by the hand. The night of her death he slept close to the body, and, by the following morning, he showed signs of extreme depression.

After that, no matter where he might wander off to, he kept returning to his mother's body. It was the maggots which, at last, drove him away; he'd try to shake the maggots off her and they would swarm on to him.

Finally, he stopped coming back. But he did remain in the area comprising about 50 square yards; and he wouldn't move any further away from the place where Flo had died. And in 10 days he had lost about a third of his body weight. He also developed a strange, glazed look.

At last Flint died too; he died very close to the spot where his mother had died. In fact, the day before he had returned to sit on the very rock where Flo had lain down (by then we had removed her body and buried her).

The results of the post mortem have been negative. They indicated that although he had a certain parasite load and one or two bugs, there was nothing sufficient in itself to cause death. And so the major cause of death had to be grief.[12]

Grief, perhaps, but again these ingredients are present: an uncontrollable situation—death of his mother; a passive, depressed reaction; no obvious disease (could bradycardia have been present?); and unexpected death.

DEATH FROM HELPLESSNESS IN HUMANS

A healthy, middle-aged man had spent most of his life in the shadow of his mother.[13] Fatherless, he described her as "a wonderful lady who made all the family decisions correctly and who never met a situation she could not control." At 31, financed by his mother, he bought a nightclub, and she helped him to run it. At 38 he married, and his wife, not surprisingly, began to resent his dependence on his mother. When he received a profitable offer to sell the nightclub, he told his mother he was considering it, and she became distraught. Finally, he decided to sell. His mother told him, "Do this, and something dire will happen to you."

Two days later he had his first asthma attack. He had no previous history of respiratory illness and had not even had a cold in ten years. The day after he closed the sale, his asthma attacks became much worse when his mother told him angrily that "something will strike you." He now became depressed and frequently protested that he was helpless. With psychiatric help, he began to see the connection between the asthma attacks and his mother's "curse"; he improved greatly. His psychiatrist saw him for a 30-minute session at 5:00 P.M. on August 23, 1960, and found him in excellent physical and mental shape. At 5:30 he called his mother to tell her that he planned to reinvest in a new business without her help. She reminded him of her curse and told him to prepare for "dire results." At 6:35 he was found gasping for breath, cyanotic, and in coma. He died at 6:55.

When a person believes that he is doomed, like the hexed woman described in Chapter One who died on her twenty-third birthday, death often ensues. Such deaths occur in many cultures. The great American physiologist W. B. Cannon was the first scientist to give respectability to such "hex death" or "voodoo death."[14] He reviewed many examples of psychogenic, sudden, and mysterious death:

A Brazilian Indian condemned and sentenced by a so-called medicine man, is helpless against his own emotional response to this pronouncement—and dies within hours. In Africa a young Negro unknowingly eats the inviolably banned wild hen. On discovery of his "crime" he trembles, is overcome by fear, and dies in 24 hours. In New Zealand a Maori woman eats fruit that she only later learns has come from a tabooed place. Her chief has been profaned. By noon of the next day she is dead. In Australia a witch doctor points a bone at a man. Believing that nothing can save him, the man rapidly sinks in spirits and prepares to die. He is saved only at the last moment when the witch doctor is forced to remove the charm.

The man who discovers that he is being boned by an enemy is, indeed, a pitiable sight. He stands aghast with his eyes staring at the treacherous pointer, and with his hands lifted to ward off the lethal medium, which he imagines is pouring into his body. His cheeks blanch, and his eyes become glassy, and the expression of his face becomes horribly distorted. He attempts to shriek but usually the sound chokes in his throat, and all that one might see is froth at his mouth. His body begins to tremble and his muscles twitch involuntarily. He sways backward and falls to the ground, and after a short time appears to be in a swoon. He finally composes himself, goes to his hut and there frets to death.[15]

R. J. W. Burrell, a South African M.D., has witnessed six middle-aged Bantu men who had been cursed to their face.[16] Each was told, "You will die at sunset." Each did. Autopsy failed to show cause of death.

There comes a point at which bizarre anecdotes accumulate such weight that they can no longer be ignored by the scientific community. Hex death is such a phenomenon. While we have as yet no physiological explanation, at least its psychological precursors are clear. A message arrives announcing doom in the form of a curse or prophecy. The victim believes it, and believes he is helpless to do anything about it. He reacts with passivity, depression, and submission. Death follows in a period of hours or days.

This phenomenon is not restricted to South African Bantus, Australian aborigines, and middle-aged American men with domineering mothers. When any serious loss occurs, disease and death may result. G. L. Engel, A. Schmale, W. A. Greene, and their co-workers at the University of Rochester have investigated the consequences of psychological loss on physical disease for the last two decades. In their studies, helplessness seemed to weaken the individual's resistance to physical pathogens that up until then had been warded off. Engel documents 170 cases of sudden death during psychological stress, collected over a six-year period. He classifies the psychological settings of such deaths into eight categories. The first five involve helplessness:

(1) The collapse or death of a loved one

An 88-year-old man, without known heart disease, became upset and excited, wringing his hands upon being told of the sudden death of his daughter. He did not cry but kept asking, "Why has this happened to me?" While talking with his son on the phone he developed acute pulmonary edema and died just as the doctor reached the house.

(2) Acute grief

A 22-year-old girl with malignant paraganglioma had been deteriorating but was still able to take drives with her mother. On one such outing the mother was killed when thrown from the car in an accident; the girl was not injured. Within a few hours she lapsed into coma and died. Necropsy showed widespread metastases but no evidence of trauma.

(3) Threatened loss of a loved one

A 43-year-old man died four hours after his 15-year-old son, faking a kidnap call over the phone, said "If you want to see your son alive, don't call the cops."

(4) Mourning or anniversary of mourning

A particularly poignant case is that of a 70-year-old man who dropped dead during the opening bars of a concert held to mark the fifth anniversary of his wife's death. She was a well-known piano teacher, and he had established a music conservatory in her memory. The concert was being given by conservatory pupils.

(5) Loss of status and self-esteem

A newspaper reporter who had for years stoutly defended the name of a high public official long since dead died suddenly at a banquet commemorating the anniversary of the latter's 101st birthday. One of the invited speakers had stunned the audience by taking the occasion to make charges about the personal life of the official being honored. The reporter rose to his feet in a vigorous defense of the man he so much admired, expressing himself with great feeling and resentment. One account claims that the truth of the charges was publicly acknowledged at the banquet, to which the reporter commented sadly, "In Adam's fall we sinned all." He died a few minutes later.[17]

Additional sudden deaths occurred during danger, on deliverance from danger, and during happy endings. It would be too simple just to say that these people became emotionally overwrought or overexcited. In some cases, particularly those of personal danger, the individual may have "died of fright." In most others not fear, but depression, helplessness, and submission are the dominant moods. The immediate cause of death in Engel's reports is usually heart failure. But, as we have seen, heart failure may be preceded by submission as well as by agitation. Engel provides a few accounts that detail intimately the psychological state of the person at the time of death. From these we can see that helplessness and hopelessness are the pervading emotions.

A 45-year-old man found himself in a totally unbearable situation and felt forced to move to another town. But just as he was ready to make the move difficulties developed in the other town that made the move impossible. In an anguished quandary, he, nonetheless, boarded the train for the new locale. Halfway to his destination, he got out to pace the platform at a station stop. When the conductor called, "All aboard," he felt he could neither go on nor return home; he dropped dead on the spot. He was traveling with a friend, a professional person, with whom he shared his awful dilemma. Necropsy showed myocardial infarction.[18]

A 27-year-old asthmatic woman apparently died of cardiac standstill and did not exhibit asthma either before or during the interview. She had been reluctantly drawn into a discussion of her psychological problems, including the humiliation of a seduction, an illegitimate baby, and a rape attempt by her brother. As she recounted how she had been increasingly rejected by and cut off from her family and had had to quit junior college and take menial jobs only to lose them because of asthmatic attacks, she became increasingly excited, cried, hyperventilated, and finally collapsed unconscious just as she was saying, "Naturally I always lost my job and had no hope anymore to recover. That's why I wanted to die and want to die all the time, because I am no good, no good!"[19]

The Rochester data is not limited to anecdotes. Fifty-one women who had had regular pap-smear cancer checkups were interviewed at length.[20] Each had shown evidence of "suspicious" cells in the cervix, but these were not diagnostic of cervical cancer. The investigator found that 18 of them had experienced significant loss in the last six months, to which they responded with feelings of hopelessness. The others had experienced no such life event. The investigators predicted that the hopeless patients would be predisposed to developing cancer, even though both groups appeared to be equally healthy. Of the 18 who experienced hopelessness, 11 subsequently developed cancer. Of the other 33, only 8 developed cancer.

The death from grief that Flint showed upon Flo's death has been statistically documented in humans. Four thousand five hundred widowers, 55 years of age or older, were identified from British medical records. During the first six months of their bereavement, 213 died.[21] This is 40 percent higher than expected mortality in this age group. After the first six months, death rate returned to normal. Most of the increase probably resulted from cardiac problems.

The sudden deaths of 26 Eastman Kodak workers were intensively investigated.[22] Depression seemed to be the predominating premorbid state. When these depressed people were provoked to anger or anxiety, cardiac death ensued.

Vulnerability to heart attack and reactions to helplessness have been studied by D. S. Krantz and co-workers, using a scale developed by R. H. Rosenman and co-workers.[23] Students were first classified as to whether they exhibited the *coronary-prone behavior pattern*, consisting of a life style that is hard-driving, punctual, competitive, and compulsive. Then they were subjected to either escapable or inescapable noise and tested later in Hiroto's noise shuttle box. Noise was either moderate or loud. Helplessness was observed after inescapable noise of either intensity; but, what is most interesting, coronary-prone people did better than normals when inescapable noise was moderate. When inescapable noise was loud, however, they became more helpless than normal subjects. It seems possible that the combination of a coronary-prone personality and helplessness during high stress may be particularly lethal.

Since I have argued that depression and helplessness are bound up together, it is not surprising to find depression implicated in sudden death. Depression also postpones recovery from various infections.[24] Six hundred army-base employees were given a battery of personality inventories. A few months later an influenza epidemic swept the area. Twenty-six persons came down with the flu; of these, twelve still had flu symptoms three weeks later. These twelve individuals had been among the significantly more depressed six months earlier, when the personality tests were given.

There are methodological difficulties in almost all the studies on death reviewed so far, but even though the data are hardly conclusive at this point, there is one lesson that caution should nevertheless have us draw. Helplessness seems to make people more vulnerable to the pathogens, some deadly, that are always around us. When one of our parents dies (or when our own spouse dies), we must be particularly careful. I suggest complete bi-monthly physical checkups during the first year following the loss. It seems to me wise to adopt this procedure following *any* major life change.[25]

Institutionalized helplessness

Institutional systems are all too often insensitive to their inhabitants' need for control over important events. The usual doctor-patient relationship is not designed to provide the patient with a sense of control. The doctor knows all, and usually tells little; the patient is expected to sit back "patiently" and rely on professional help. While such extreme dependency may be helpful to certain patients in some circumstances, a greater degree of control would help others. Being hospitalized, then stripped of control over even simple things—such as when you wake up and what pajamas you may wear, may promote efficiency, but it does not promote health. This loss of control may further weaken a physically sick person and cause death. R. Schulz and D. Aderman (1974) considered two groups of terminal cancer patients matched for severity of illness. All patients had just been transferred to the terminal ward. One group had been transferred from other hospitals, while the other group had come directly from their homes. Patients who had come from home died sooner. The authors suggest that the sudden break in routine, and the loss of control that occurs in leaving home, produced helplessness and contributed to early death.[26]

H. M. Lefcourt (1973) reports a striking instance of sudden death in an institutional setting:

> This writer witnessed one such case of death due to a loss of will within a psychiatric hospital. A female patient who had remained in a mute state for nearly 10 years was shifted to a different floor of her building along with her floor mates, while her unit was being redecorated. The third floor of this psychiatric unit where the patient in question had been living was known among the patients as the chronic, hopeless floor. In contrast, the first floor was most commonly occupied by patients who held privileges, including the freedom to come and go on the hospital grounds and to the surrounding streets. In short, the first floor was an exit ward from which patients could anticipate discharge fairly rapidly. All patients who were temporarily moved from the third floor were given medical examinations prior to the move, and the patient in question was judged to be in excellent medical health though still mute and withdrawn. Shortly after moving to the first floor, this chronic psychiatric patient surprised the ward staff by becoming socially responsive such that within a two-week period she ceased being mute and was actually becoming gregarious. As fate would have it, the redecoration of the third-floor unit was

soon completed and all previous residents were returned to it. Within a week after she had been returned to the "hopeless" unit, this patient, who like the legendary Snow White had been aroused from a living torpor, collapsed and died. The subsequent autopsy revealed no pathology of note, and it was whimsically suggested at the time that the patient had died of despair.

Institutionalized patients, whether in terminal cancer wards, leukemic children's wards, or old-age homes, should be given maximum control over all aspects of their daily lives: choice of omelets or scrambled eggs for breakfast, blue or red curtains, going to the movies on Wednesdays or Thursdays, whether they wake up early or sleep late. If the theory of helplessness set forth here has any validity, these people may live longer, may show more spontaneous remissions, and will certainly be much happier.

There are less benign institutions that promote helplessness and produce psychogenic death. Foremost among these are prisons, particularly concentration camps and POW camps. Major Kushner's extraordinary experience documents this. Similarly, the death rate of American prisoners in Japanese prison camps cannot wholly be attributed to physical causes. Four thousand of thirty thousand American POW's died within the first few months of imprisonment during the Philippine campaign. J. E. Nardini (1952) reports:

The members of this group found themselves suddenly deprived of name, rank, identity, justice, and any claim to be treated as human beings. Although physical disease and the shortages of food, water, and medicine were at their highest during this period, emotional shock and reactive depression played a great part in individual inability to cope with physical symptoms and disease, and undoubtedly contributed much to the massive death rate.[27]

What made for survival under these conditions? Most prominent among the factors that Nardini believed promoted survival were "strong motivation for life with persistent exertion of will."

The psychosomatic effects of exertion of will—active control over outcomes—and the will to live cannot be overestimated. Of all psychosomatic variables, this one may be the most powerful. When a prisoner gives up, death may soon follow. Bruno Bettelheim describes those peculiar inmates, the "Muselmänner," who rapidly gave up and died without apparent physical cause in the Nazi concentration camps:

> Prisoners who came to believe the repeated statements of the guards—that there was no hope for them, that they would never leave the camp except as a corpse—who came to feel that their environment was one over which they could exercise no influence whatsoever, these prisoners were in a literal sense, walking corpses. In the camps they were called "moslems" (Muselmänner) because of what was erroneously viewed as a fatalistic surrender to the environment, as Mohammedans are supposed to blandly accept their fate.
>
> . . . they were people who were so deprived of affect, self-esteem, and every form of stimulation, so totally exhausted, both physically and emotionally, that they had given the environment total power over them.[28]

Shortly after the beginning of captivity, these men stopped eating, sat mute and motionless in corners, and expired.

Death from helplessness in old age

If a person or animal is in a marginal physical state, weakened by malnutrition or heart disease, a sense of control can mean the difference between living and dying. There is one aspect of the human condition that invariably entails physical weakening—growing old. The aged are most susceptible to loss of control, particularly in American society; no group, neither blacks, Indians, nor Mexican-Americans, are in as helpless a state as our aged. The mediocre life span of Americans, relative to other prosperous nations, may be a testimony not to mediocre medical care, but to the way we treat our aged psychologically. We force them to retire at 65, we place them in old age homes. We ignore our grandparents, we shunt them aside—we are a nation that deprives old persons of control over the most meaningful events in their lives. We kill them.[29]

N. A. Ferrari (1962) has written an unnoticed, but very important, doctoral dissertation on perceived freedom of choice in an old age home. Her main interest was in attitude change in the home, but in the course of writing the dissertation she produced a major finding on survival. Fifty-five females, over 65 years old and with an average age of 82, applied for admission to an old age home in the Midwest. Ferrari asked them upon admission how much freedom of choice they had felt in moving to the home, how many other possibilities had been open to them, and how much pressure their relatives had applied to them to enter the home. Of the 17 women who said they had no alternative but to move to the home, 8 died after four weeks in residence and 16 were dead in ten weeks. Apparently, only one person of the 38 who saw an alternative died in the initial period. These deaths were called "unexpected" by the staff. Another sample of 40 merely applied for admission, but never became residents because they died. Of the 22 whose family made application for them, 19 were dead within one month after the application was received. Of the 18 who applied for themselves, only 4 had died by the end of the month.

It is possible that these data are confounded by different levels of physical health in the various groups—the sicker you are, the more your relatives will try to put you out of sight. It's hard to tell from the original dissertation. On the other hand, the results may directly reflect the lethal effect of helplessness on old people. To my mind, this study should have been a trumpet call to action, or at least further research, but it fell on deaf ears.

D. R. Aleksandrowicz observed the lethal psychogenic effects on geriatric patients of a fire in their ward. No one was injured by the blaze, but the ward was so damaged that the patients were moved out for several weeks until repairs were completed. Within a month of the fire, 5 of the 40 patients were dead; 3 more died in the next two months. This 20-

percent death rate was substantially greater than the 7.5-percent rate of the preceding three months. These deaths again were largely "unexpected." Here is a typical case:

> A 76-year-old former horse trader, gambler, and adventurer had been admitted to the hospital in 1957 in a state of severe emaciation and with signs of taboparesis. His physical condition improved with treatment, but he remained confined to a chair or to a walker. He also had a chronic urinary infection, which proved resistant to treatment. His peevish, complaining attitude, constant demands, competition with and provocation of other patients, and cunning attempts to test the personnel made him a management problem. At the same time, several members of the team had a certain liking for this unusual patient. He showed strong, though ambivalent, attachment to the nurse, the charge aide, and the physician. It was possible to handle him only by a well-coordinated, rigid system of privileges and controls.
>
> After the fire, this patient was transferred to the neurological ward where his former special privileges (such as providing him with cartons of milk at certain hours each day) and controls could not be maintained. The patient appeared dejected and sad. He did not express his bitter anger as usual and usually answered when addressed. Two weeks after the fire, he was found dead and the diagnosis was probably myocardial infarction. Autopsy was not performed.
>
> Although the patient had been undernourished and feeble, there was nothing to indicate a critical condition and his death came as a complete surprise. Death was classified as "unexpected."[30]

I suggest that such deaths no longer be seen as unexpected. We should expect that when we remove the vestiges of control over the environment of an already physically weakened human being, we may well kill him. Mandatory retirement is a case in point. The same logic that precludes not hiring blacks and women should apply to firing a person simply because his 65th birthday has arrived. Not only is it discriminatory because individual merit is not taken into account, but it may also be lethal—deprive a man of work and you may remove his most meaningful source of instrumental control.

Infant death and anaclitic depression

Like the aged, infants probably can perceive how helpless they are. R. Spitz (1946) first reported the phenomenon of anaclitic depression or hospitalism. As mentioned in the last chapter (p. 145), two conditions produced it: If infants were raised with minimal stimulation in foundling homes, they became torpid and unresponsive. Alternatively, when infants between six and eighteen months of age were separated from their mothers in prisons, depression also developed.[31] Of the 91 children showing hospitalism in a foundling home, 34 died over the next two years. Death was caused by respiratory infections, measles, and intestinal disorders. It is unlikely that the physical conditions of the home were sufficiently bad to produce a 40-percent death rate. But what does lack of stimulation and separation from mother mean to an infant at the age when he is developing instrumental control? Helplessness. By now we should not be surprised to see its consequence in increased susceptibility to death.

CONCLUSION

I apologize (although not too heartily) to the academic reader for the impressionistic nature of the argument in this chapter. What I have adduced is a weight of anecdotes and several experimental studies, only a few of them particularly well-designed or executed. But perhaps the importance of the problem is extenuating. If sudden death from helplessness is a fact, it is a fact of such importance as to deserve a brief, appealing to research scientists to work seriously on it. I hope that I have made a persuasive case for controlled investigation in this field.

A variety of species—from cockroaches to wild rats, from chickens to chimpanzees, from infant to aged humans— seem to show death from helplessness: In the course of such deaths an individual loses control over matters important to him. Behaviorally he reacts with depression, passivity, and submission. Subjectively, he feels helpless and hopeless. Consequently, unexpected death ensues.

What causes these deaths? A wide range of terminal physical conditions occur: heart failure, asthma, pneumonia, cancer, infection, malnutrition. No single physical cause has been assigned, but slowing of the heart is implicated. Medical investigators have suggested vagal inhibition of heart action, the diving reflex, and parasympathetic hyperactivity as possible causes, among others.[32] I am not expert enough to evaluate these hypotheses, but I suspect that no one physical substratum will be found. The absence of physical uniformity, however, should not blind us to the reality of the phenomenon or to its regular psychological cause, the only single cause we can specify at this stage of our knowledge: helplessness, the perception of uncontrollability.

Assigning only a psychological cause does not necessarily consign a phenomenon to a metaphysical or parapsychological status. Death from helplessness is real enough. Understanding its psychological basis may allow us to prevent some of these deaths by building instrumental control into the lives of those who are vulnerable.

This has, I suppose, been said before. But no statement of it moves me more than Dylan Thomas':

> *Do not go gentle into that good night,*
> *Old age should burn and rave at close of day;*
> *Rage, rage against the dying of the light.*
> . . .
> *And you, my father, there on the sad height,*
> *Curse, bless, me now with your fierce tears, I pray.*
> *Do not go gentle into that good night.*
> *Rage, rage against the dying of the light.*

NOTES

CHAPTER ONE

1. *New York Times*, Travel Section, January 30 and February 19, 1972.
2. Wintrob (1972).

CHAPTER TWO

1. See Irwin (1971) and Teitelbaum (1964) for elaboration of the relationship between voluntariness and instrumental, or outcome-sensitive, behavior.
2. There is a fascinating and growing literature on the question of exactly which responses are voluntary in this sense. The list appears to be ever expanding, since there is reason to believe that heart rate, urinary flow, and brain alpha waves (among others), can be brought under voluntary control by special training procedures. See Miller (1969) for a review. These data may

blur the ordinary distinction between *voluntary* and *involuntary*, but for my definition, whether any response is voluntary is merely a matter of whether it can be modified by reward and punishment.

3. Humphreys (1939a, b, c) and Skinner (1938).
4. The pigeon gets grain only if he refrains from key pecking. There is an academic controversy about whether it is really possible for an organism not to respond. After all, the argument goes, organisms are always doing something, even if you don't observe it, and this something will be reinforced. While such a position might be defensible a priori, the evidence I shall discuss throughout the book is wholly incompatible with it.
5. The acute reader may wonder why I have bothered to add the thirty-second temporal constraint throughout the example. Couldn't I have just used button pressing and failure to button press? The reason is that, strictly speaking, button pressing is an instantaneous event, but failure to press is not. In order to have $p(O/R)$ and $p(O/\overline{R})$ (the x- and y-axes of the response contingency space) take up the same amount of time, R becomes the occurrence of any response within thrity seconds, and $\overline{R}$ becomes the lack of any R during the thirty seconds. Schoenfeld, Cole, Lang, and Mankoff (1973) employ this procedure extensively. The conceptual framework proposed in this chapter also generalizes to instances without temporal restraints, and the interested reader should consult Seligman, Maier, and Solomon (1971) for the details of the deduction, or Gibbon, Berryman, and Thompson (1974) for a formal discussion of the response contingency space.
6. Seligman and Hager (1972).
7. Staddon and Simmelhag (1971). Also see Staddon (1974) for species-specific analysis of helplessness.

CHAPTER THREE

1. Overmier and Seligman (1967), Seligman and Maier (1967).
2. Overmier (1968), Overmier and Seligman (1967), Seligman and Groves (1970), Seligman and Maier (1967), Seligman, Maier, and Geer (1968).
3. Maier (1970), Maier, Albin, and Testa (1973), Seligman and Beagley (1974), Seligman and Maier (1967). It should be men-

tioned that Church (1964) has argued against the use of the yoked group as a control group for instrumental learning. This argument is not relevant to experiments on helplessness in which the yoked group is the experimental group, and the other groups are control groups.

4. Seligman and Maier (1967).

5. See, for example, the readings in the volume edited by Seligman and Hager (1972).

6. Thomas and Balter (1974). See also Masserman (1943, 1971), Seward and Humphrey (1967), and Zielinski and Soltysik (1964) for other reports of inescapable shock causing debilitation in cats.

7. Padilla, Padilla, Ketterer, and Giacalone (1970). See Bintz (1971), Behrend and Bitterman (1963), Frumkin and Brookshire (1969), and Padilla (1973) for related goldfish data.

8. Maier, Seligman, and Solomon (1969) and Seligman et al. (1971) have reviewed this complicated literature; the interested reader is referred there for further details. See also Anderson, Cole, and McVaugh (1968), DeToledo and Black (1967), Dinsmoor and Campbell (1956a, b), Looney and Cohen (1972), Mullin and Mogenson (1963), and Weiss, Krieckhaus, and Conte (1968) for representative studies.

9. Maier et al. (1973), Seligman and Beagley (1974), Seligman, Rosellini, and Kozak (1974b). In passing it should be mentioned that mice [Braud, Wepman, and Russo (1969)] and even the lowly cockroach [Horridge (1962)] also may show response deficits following inescapable shock.

10. Hiroto (1974), Hiroto and Seligman (1974), Krantz, Glass, and Snyder (1974). For other learned-helplessness experiments on man showing similar results, see Fosco and Geer (1971), Miller and Seligman (1974a), Racinskas (1971), Roth and Kubal (1974), and Thornton and Jacobs (1971).

11. See James (1963), Lefcourt (1966), and Rotter (1966) for the actual personality tests and reviews of the large and controversial literature concerning them.

12. Braud et al. (1969). See also McCulloch and Bruner (1939) for similar findings on the rat; also for, apparently, the earliest helplessness study in the literature.

13. Rosellini and Seligman (1974), A. Amsel (1974, personal communication).

14. See Amsel, Rashotte, and MacKinnon (1966) for a summary of the frustration findings using rats.

15. Brookshire, Littman, and Stewart (1961) gave 30-day-old rats inescapable shock and merely handled a control group. One hundred days later, as adults, the rats were tested in an alleyway that had food at one end. When the rats were only slightly hungry, helpless rats actually performed better than controls. At moderate levels of hunger the groups ran to food with equal success. When hunger became traumatic (96-hour food deprivation), the handled rats continued to run down the alleyway, but the preshocked rats gave up and just sat passively in the start box.

16. Maier, Anderson, and Lieberman (1972). See Powell and Creer (1969) for similar results. See Anderson and Paden (1966) for further evidence of transfer between aversive events.

17. Hiroto and Seligman (1974). See also Miller and Seligman (1974b) for a replication and extension to depression.

18. Hiroto and Seligman (1974).

19. Maier (1949) has used this procedure extensively with rats. Its debilitating consequences for rats will be discussed in Chapter 7.

20. Hiroto and Seligman (1974).

21. Seligman, Meyer, and Testa (unpublished data). See also Hulse (1974).

22. Engberg, Hansen, Welker, and Thomas (1973)—the published version—was entitled "Acquisition of keypecking via autoshaping as a function of prior experience: 'Learned laziness?' " See Gamzu and Williams (1971) for similar pigeon results, as well as Gamzu, Williams, and Schwartz (1973) and Welker, Hansen, Engberg, and Thomas (1973), who engage in a spirited controversy about the explanation of these results.

23. Kurlander, Miller, and Seligman (1974).

24. Miller and Seligman (1974b).

25. Hiroto and Seligman (1974).

26. Thomas, Freeman, Svinicki, Burr, and Lyons (1970).

27. Wallace (1956a).

28. Overmier (1968), Overmier and Seligman (1967), Seligman and Groves (1970).

29. Seligman et al. (1974b). These rats were reared from birth in cages and, like dogs that are cage-reared (p. 58), do not show a time course. Being reared in a cage sharply restricts the op-

portunity for immunization with controllable events.

30. Brady, Porter, Conrad, and Mason (1958). This study is discussed at greater length in Chapter Six, p. 117.

31. Sines, Cleeland, and Adkins (1963).

32. Weiss (1968, 1971a, b, c). See also Moot, Cebulla, and Crabtree (1970) and Chapter Six for more about ulcers, anxiety, and unpredictability.

33. See Brimer and Kamin (1963), Lindner (1968), Desiderato and Newman (1971), and Payne (1972) for an ongoing controversy concerning this data.

34. Hokanson, DeGood, Forrest, and Brittain (1971). See Averill and Rosenn (1972), Bandler, Madaras, and Bem (1968), Corah and Boffa (1970), and Elliot (1969) for related studies of humans, using various other measures of anxiety. This is a complex and inconsistent literature; it is reviewed in different lights by Averill (1973) and Binik and Seligman (1974).

35. Pavlov (1927, 1928).

36. Liddell, James, and Anderson (1934).

CHAPTER FOUR

1. There is considerable convergence of opinion and evidence within the present generation of learning theorists that organisms can learn and store information about the contingencies within this response contingency space, including the crucial 45° line: Catania (1971), Church (1969), Gibbon et al. (1974), Maier et al. (1969), Porefsky (1970), Premack (1965), Rescorla (1967, 1968), Seligman et al. (1971), Wagner (1969), Watson (1967), and Weiss (1968, 1971a).

2. For attempts to spell out in detail the relationship between the contingency information and its cognitive representation, the interested reader should consult Kelley (1967) and Weiner, Frieze, Kukla, Reed, Rest, and Rosenbaum (1971) for an attribution-theory point of view; Irwin (1971) and Seligman and Johnston (1973) for a cognitive-learning-theory point of view; and Lazarus (1966) and Stotland (1969).

3. See also Langer (1974) for a set of experiments on factors that produce the illusion of control. She finds that people feel the illusion of control in chance-determined games when their op-

ponents appear incompetent, when they get to choose which lottery ticket they want, and when they spend more time in the game.

4. It should also be mentioned that innately elicited struggling is another source of responding in a traumatic situation, but it is the waxing and waning of *voluntary* responses that is our concern here. This is not to deny that innate responses can be transformed into voluntary responses [Schwartz and Williams (1972)].

5. Solomon (1948) reviewed the extensive literature on work, and found that, except under extreme conditions, lowering the amount of effort is not an effective reinforcer.

6. See Irwin (1971) and Seligman and Johnston (1973) for operationally defined response-outcome expectations.

7. Thornton and Jacobs (1971).

8. Hiroto and Seligman (1974), Mackintosh (1973), Maier (1949), Mellgren and Ost (1972), Miller and Seligman (1974a), Thomas et al. (1970).

9. See Bowlby (1973), Hinde, Spencer-Booth, and Bruce (1966), Kaufman and Rosenblum (1967), and Sackett (1970) for the details of the protest-despair sequence. See also Selye (1956) for a very general version of this sequence.

10. Solomon and Corbit (1974) have theorized that emotions can antagonize each other just as the colors red and green antagonize each other in the visual system. On such a view it is possible that fear and depression are opponent processes: With repeated experience of an uncontrollable event that produces fear, depression builds during fear. The presence of depression inhibits fear and keeps it within tolerable limits. As soon as the event is removed, fear is also removed; but the opponent process of depression, which is slower to dissipate, remains.

11. Not all play and exercise of competence can be viewed as arising from a drive to avoid the aversive states of fear and depression, since play and exploration often occur when the organism appears to be relaxed, and they can be inhibited by the presence of fear [White (1959)]. On the other hand, it must be noted that when free play or exploration is constrained or forcibly stopped, aversive states such as crying or struggling ensue.

12. The favorite food of dogs in Philadelphia, Pennsylvania and Ithaca, New York. Salami courtesy of Kelly and Cohen's, Philadelphia.

13. See Seligman et al. (1968). See also Black (1958), Maier (1949), and Tolman and Gleitman (1948) for related data on "putting-through" as a training technique. See Seligman et al. (1974b) for the details of the cure in rats.

14. Seligman and Maier (1967). See Seligman et al. (1974b) for the analogous immunization procedures and results with rats.

15. Seligman and Groves (1970).

16. Lessac and Solomon (1969).

17. See Anderson et al. (1968), Bracewell and Black (1974), Gamzu et al. (1973), Hineline (1973), Maier et al. (1969), Miller and Weiss (1969), Staddon (1974), Weiss, Stone, and Harrell (1970), and Weiss, Glazer, and Pohorecky (1974) for criticisms and alternate accounts of helplessness.

18. *Freezing* is a rough label for a class of behaviors exhibited by rats when they are afraid: they grip the grid bars tightly with their paws, hunch up, and shiver. Much has been made of the fact that rats freeze when they are afraid, and it has been claimed that learned helplessness is nothing more than freezing [Anisman and Waller (1973)]. For example, strong shock, which causes more freezing in rats than weak shock, produces more interference with shuttle avoidance [Anisman and Waller (1972)]; and scopolamine, a drug that reduces freezing, makes rats better avoiders [Anisman (1973)]. Such evidence is not very relevant to helplessness, however. I do not deny that there exist many ways to interfere with escape or avoidance responding—cutting off an animal's legs, for example. Inducing freezing is another way. But the fact that freezing interferes with escape from shock does not imply that inescapable shock interferes with escape *by means of* freezing, any more than it implies that inescapable shock interferes with escape by cutting the animal's legs off. Furthermore, dogs do not freeze, people who receive unsolvable discrimination problems do not freeze, and rats who receive noncontingent food do not freeze; yet these conditions all produce helplessness. Finally, there is one question that the freezing theorists have failed to take seriously: Why does inescapable shock, but not escapable shock, produce freezing in rats? Any answer would probably imply that the rat has learned that shock is inescapable, and this is at the heart of our theory of helplessness.

19. Maier et al. (1973), Seligman and Beagley (1974). The data of

Maier and Testa (1974) on FR1 delay, partial reinforcement, and clarification of the FR2 contingency are not easily accounted for by any view that invokes only performance, and not learning deficits.

20. Miller and Weiss (1969) and Weiss et al. (1970, 1974) have so speculated.
21. See Maier and Gleitman (1967) and Underwood (1948) for studies of its effects on man and animals.
22. Miller and Weiss (1969), Weiss (1968, 1970, 1971a, b, c), Weiss et al. (1970, 1974).
23. Abramson and Seligman (1974).
24. See Stein (1964) for the elaboration of the theory.
25. Thomas and Balter (1974).
26. Abramson and Seligman (1974).

CHAPTER FIVE

1. Williams, Friedman, and Secunda (1970).
2. See Carney, Roth, and Garside (1965), Kiloh and Garside (1963), Mendels (1970), and Schuyler (1975) for discussion of the dichotomy.
3. For example, if the mother is a depressive and the father is an alcoholic, the offspring may well become a depressive [see Winokur (1973)]. Incidentally, it has been claimed that alcoholism in males is the masculine equivalent of depression in females.
4. For an important exception, see Wolpe (1967), who discusses criteria for asserting correspondence between animal and human neuroses.
5. See Wittgenstein (1953), paragraphs 66–77, for a general statement of the argument that words from ordinary English like "game" or "depression" do not have necessary features.
6. Grinker, Miller, Sabshin, Nunn, and Nunnally (1961).
7. Beck (1967, p. 28).
8. See Friedman (1964), Martin and Rees (1966), and Shapiro and Nelson (1955) for representative studies. Seligman, Klein, and Miller (1974a) present a review of the literature.
9. See Lewinsohn and Libet (1972).
10. See Payne (1961) and Walton, White, Black, and Young (1959) for representative studies.

11. Lewinsohn (1974).
12. See Beck's (1967) book for the most complete and systematic picture available of the minds of depressed people.
13. Miller and Seligman (1973, 1974a, b), Miller, Seligman, and Kurlander (1974).
14. Miller et al. (1974).
15. David Klein, Ellen Fencil-Morse, and I (1975) have found parallel results using unsolvable discrimination problems instead of inescapable noise. Furthermore, we found that if the depressed person who received unsolvable problems was led to attribute his failure to the difficulty of the problem, rather than his own incompetence, anagram solution improved. Klein (1975) has also demonstrated that depressed people given no pretreatment failed to escape noise just like nondepressed people who had experienced inescapable noise.
16. Wallace (1956b).
17. See Kraines (1957), Lundquist (1945), and Paskind (1929, 1930) for discussion of the role of time in depression.
18. See, for example, Szasz (1963). While I generally find myself in agreement with Szasz on the wrongs of involuntary commitment, I disagree with him about suicide.
19. See Abraham (1911, 1916), Freud (1917), Jacobson (1971), Klein (1968), and Rado (1928) for representative formulations of the psychoanalytic theory of depression.
20. Beck and Hurvich (1959) and Beck and Ward (1961).
21. Suomi and Harlow (1972). See also Akiskal and McKinney (1973) for an overview of the relationship of the primate separation studies to human depression.
22. Schildkraut (1965). See also Akiskal and McKinney (1973) for a review of recent biogenic anime data and an attempt to integrate this with behavioral data. They conclude that present evidence does not allow us to pinpoint any one biogenic anime responsible for depression.
23. See Cole (1964), Davis (1965), and Klerman and Cole (1965) for findings on the effectiveness of these agents in depression.
24. Redmond, Maas, Kling, and DeKirmenjian (1971) and Abramson and Seligman (1974).
25. Janowsky, El-Yousef, Davis, Hubbard, and Sekerke (1972).
26. Weiss (1968, 1971a, b, c).
27. See the factor analytic study of Grinker et al. (1961) on the subjective phenomena of depression.

28. See Paykel, Myers, Dienelt, Klerman, Lindenthal, and Pepper (1969) for a well-controlled study of the life events that precede depression.
29. Copyright 1969 by the American Medical Association.
30. Ferster (1966, 1973), Kaufman and Rosenblum (1967), Lewinsohn (1974), Liberman and Raskin (1971), and McKinney and Bunney (1969).
31. Response decrements following acquisition are produced by this procedure in the appetitive case [e.g. Rescorla and Skucy (1969)] and in the aversive case [e.g. Kadden (1973)].
32. Carder and Berkowitz (1970), Jensen (1963), Neuringer (1969), Singh (1970), and Stolz and Lott (1964).
33. Watson (1971).
34. Dorworth (1971).
35. Bibring (1953, p. 43).
36. See also Dorworth (1973) and Ellis (1962).
37. Copyright 1969 by the American Medical Association.
38. Taulbee and Wright (1971).
39. Fagan (1974), Lazarus (1968).
40. Beck, Seligman, Binik, Schuyler, and Brill (unpublished data).
41. Klein (1975) found that success at solving discrimination problems completely broke up symptoms produced by inescapable noise, as well as symptoms of naturally occurring depression. Nondepressed students who had first received inescapable noise, as well as depressed students, were given a series of solvable discrimination problems as therapy. Unlike untreated controls, they later escaped noise rapidly and believed their skilled actions to be correlated with success and failure. To my knowledge, this is the very first well-controlled laboratory study of therapy for depression, and it shows that the same procedures that alleviate learned helplessness also alleviate depression.
42. This is an extensive, contradictory, and complex literature. See Beck, Sethi, and Tuthill (1963) and Birtchnell (1970a, b, c, d) for representative positive findings. But see Granville-Grossman (1967) for a negative view.

CHAPTER SIX

1. See Wittgenstein (1953), paragraphs 66–77.
2. See Seligman (1968), Seligman and Binik (1974), and Seligman et al. (1971) for a complete statement of this hypothesis.

3. It has become clear in the past decade that animals in Pavlovian conditioning experiments learn not only that a stimulus predicts a US (excitation) but also learn that a stimulus paired with the absence of the US predicts no US. Pavlov (1927) called this *differential inhibition*. See, for example, Boakes and Halliday (1972), Bolles (1970), Denny (1971), Maier et al. (1969), and Rescorla (1967). Stimuli paired with the absence of shock (i.e., safety signals) can inhibit shock-avoidance behavior [see Rescorla and LoLordo (1965)] and can serve as positive reinforcers [see Weisman and Litner (1969)].

4. Azrin (1956), Brimer and Kamin (1963), Byrum and Jackson (1971), Davis and McIntire (1969), Imada and Soga (1971), Seligman (1968), Seligman and Meyer (1970), Shimoff, Schoenfeld, and Snapper (1969), and Weiss and Strongman (1969).

5. Averill and Rosenn (1972), Geer (1968), Glass and Singer (1972), Glass, Snyder, and Singer (1974), and Price and Geer (1972). See also Badia and Culbertson (1970) and Paré and Livingston (1973) for other dependent variables that reflect anxiety during unpredictable trauma.

6. Brady (1958), Brady et al. (1958), Porter, Brady, Conrad, Mason, Galambos, and Rioch (1958).

7. Sines et al. (1963).

8. Weiss (1968, 1970, 1971a, b, c).

9. Caul, Buchanan and Hays (1972), Mezinskis, Gliner, and Shemberg (1971), Price (1970), Seligman (1968), Seligman and Meyer (1970), Weiss (1970).

10. Badia and Culbertson (1970) present evidence that strongly supports this: rats constantly held a bar during unpredictable shock, but released it when safety signals occurred.

11. Rats: Lockard (1963, 1965). Men: Badia, Suter, and Lewis (1967), Jones, Bentler, and Petry (1966), Lanzetta and Driscoll (1966), Pervin (1963). But see Averill and Rosenn (1972) and Furedy and Doob (1971, 1972) for contrary results.

12. Badia and Culbertson went on to test between the safety-signal hypothesis and another explanation of the preference for signalled shock, the *preparatory response* hypothesis. This hypothesis claims that when events are predictable the subject can make an instrumental response during the signal that modifies the intensity of the US. [Proposed by Perkins (1955). See Seligman et al. (1971), and Seligman and Binik (1974) for a more complete discussion of the evidence separating these two hypotheses.]

The preparatory response allegedly renders aversive US's less painful, while it renders appetitive US's more pleasurable. For example, the subject might brace himself for a shock, making it hurt less, or salivate before signalled food, making it taste better. The main virtues of the preparatory-response hypothesis are: (1) it is sometimes reported that the US itself feels less intense when it is signalled [Hare and Petrusic (1967)], and that the GSR to the shock itself is lower when shock is signalled [Kimmel (1965), Lykken (1962), Kimmel and Pennypacker (1962), and Morrow (1966); but see Seligman et al. (1971) for a different explanation]; (2) signalled positive events are preferred to unsignalled ones [e.g., Cantor and LoLordo (1970) and Prokasy (1956); but see Hershisher and Trapold (1971) and Seligman et al. for a different account]. The safety-signal hypothesis does not account directly for either of these sets of data. It should be noted that there is no logical incompatibility between the safety-signal and preparatory-response hypotheses; both could be true: an animal could both be in chronic fear during unpredictable shock, and it could also prepare itself for shock during a signal. The preparatory-response hypothesis, like the safety-signal hypothesis, directly predicts preference for predictable aversive events. Unlike the safety-signal hypothesis, however, it needs a major additional assumption to account for more fear occuring in unpredictable shock. Somewhat more overall fear might occur when shock is unpredictable because the shock feels more intense; it is hardly likely, however, that preparatory response could render predictable shock much less aversive than unpredictable shock: rats prefer predictable shock four times as long and three times as intense as unpredictable shock [Badia, Culbertson and Harsh (1973)]. It would be an extremely effective yet unobserved [Perkins, Seymann, Levis, and Spencer (1966)] preparatory response that had such a potent effect. Furthermore, the preparatory-response hypothesis does not account for the uniform time distribution of anxiety observed using CER and GSR measures.

Badia and Culbertson were able to tease these two hypotheses apart by running three extinction procedures. In the first, pressing the bar no longer changed the schedule, so that the rat remained in the unsignalled condition no matter what he did. All rats stopped pressing. In the second, and most intriguing, bar pressing produced the stimulus (light off) that had been correlated with signalled shock, but now unsignalled shock occurred. Here the rats are in the presence of the safety signal but cannot prepare themselves for shock, since the tone does not occur. This procedure plays off the power of the safety signal against the power of the preparatory response. All rats still showed a strong preference for the erstwhile safety signal, even without the tone. This preference cannot be due to a preparatory response since such responses were precluded by the absence of the tone. In the third extinction procedure, a bar press produced shock preceded by a tone, but did not turn the light off. Here the safety signal (light off) did not appear, but shocks were preceded by the danger stimulus. Again preparatory responses are played off against safety signals, since the rats can now prepare themselves during the tone if they press the bar, but they get no safety signal. The rats do not press the bar. So producing a safety signal is necessary (extinction 3) and sufficient (extinction 2) for preference, and having the opportunity to make a preparatory response is neither necessary (extinction 2) nor sufficient (extinction 3).

13. Badia, McBane, Suter, and Lewis (1966), Badia et al. (1967), Cook and Barnes (1964), D'Amato and Gumenik (1960).
14. I am grateful to Yitzchak M. Binik for his help on this and the following sections of this chapter.
15. See also Staub, Tursky, and Schwartz (1971).
16. See Lazarus (1966) for a discussion of the role of perception of control in threatening situations. Lazarus reviews studies suggesting that when a subject is threatened, he makes two appraisals of the threat. His first appraisal is "How dangerous is the threat?" His second appraisal is "What can I do about it?"
17. See also Bowers (1968), Corah and Boffa (1970), and Houston (1972) for similar beneficial results of perceived control.
18. Geer, Davison, and Gatchel (1970).
19. See also Champion (1950).
20. See Wolpe and Lazarus (1969) for details of this therapy.
21. See Davison (1966), Goldfried (1971), Jacobs and Wolpin (1971), and Wilkins (1971) for details of such criticism.
22. Masters and Johnson (1966).

CHAPTER SEVEN

1. Watson (1924), p. 104.
2. Seligman and Hager (1972).

3. See Lipsitt, Kaye, and Bosack (1966) and Sameroff (1968, 1971).
4. Siqueland (1968) and Siqueland and Lipsitt (1968).
5. Watson (1967) argues that contingency analysis does not effectively begin until after the first two or three months of life.
6. Watson (1971). See also Hunt and Uzgiris (1964), Rovee and Rovee (1969), and Vietze, Watson, and Dorman (1973). Piaget also has a construct similar to the contingency analysis of the dance of development. At its most primitive stage, it is called *efficacy*, a dim sense that the infant's actions change the external world. As the infant grows, efficacy matures into *psychological causality*, or the awareness of causing one's own acts [Flavell (1963), pp. 142-147].
7. Hein and Held (1967), Held (1965), Held and Bauer (1967), Held and Bossom (1961), Held and Hein (1963).
8. See also Bowlby (1969, 1973) and Goldfarb (1945). These observations have been cogently criticized on methodological grounds [Pinneau (1955) and Casler (1961)], but none of the critics maintain that institutional rearing is good for children.
9. See Hinde et al. (1966), Kaufman (1973), and Kaufman and Rosenblum (1967a, b) for related descriptions of primate infants separated from their mothers.
10. Harlow and Zimmerman (1959).
11. Redmond, Maas, DeKirmenjian, and Schlemmer (1973).
12. Rapaport and Seligman (1974).
13. Thompson (1957). See also Denenberg and Rosenberg (1967), Denenberg and Whimbey (1963), Gauron (1966), Joffe (1965), Ressler and Anderson (1973a, b), and Thompson, Watson, and Charlesworth (1962) for related findings.
14. Raymond Miles at the University of Colorado and Hardy Wilcoxon at George Peabody College have designed such environments for infant rats and monkeys.
15. Kozol (1967).
16. Harlow (1949) performed the first of many discriminative learning-set experiments.
17. Levine (1966) has elaborated this "win-stay, lose-shift" theory of learning set.
18. Rozin, Poritsky, and Sotsky (1971).
19. See also Higgins (1968) on the deleterious effects of inconsistent socialization.
20. Banfield (1958), p. 109.

21. The literature on crowding is controversial. Following Calhoun's (1962) initial findings on social breakdown among rats when crowded, statistical attempts have been made to determine the relation of crowding to social breakdown among humans. Once poverty, race, and lack of education are controlled, population density seems not to be correlated with social pathology [Freedman, Klevansky, and Erlich (1971)]. Variables finergrained than number of persons per acre, however, such as number of persons per room, may be better indications of degree of uncontrollability [Galle, Gove, and McPherson (1972)].
22. Goeckner, Greenough, and Mead (1973).
23. Miller and Seligman (1974b).
24. Jensen (1973).
25. E.g., Brinton (1965).
26. See Ryan (1967) on the therapeutic nature of social action among the poor.

CHAPTER EIGHT

1. Richter (1957).
2. Thomas and Balter (1974) and Janowsky et al. (1972).
3. Galef and Seligman (unpublished data, 1967).
4. Such deaths have been experimentally observed in a creature as "lowly" as the cockroach. Cockroaches have clear dominance hierarchies. A subordinate cockroach approaching a dominant cockroach drops his antennae on the ground. This "salaaming" posture will usually bring the attack of a dominant cockroach to a halt. When repeatedly aggressed against by dominants, however, subordinate cockroaches die [Ewing (1967)]. Characteristically, there is no sign of external damage, and the physiological mechanism of death remains unknown. But such repeated defeat may produce helplessness, with death the consequence.
5. See Ratner (1967) for a review.
6. Maser and Gallup (1974).
7. See American Petroleum Institute, *Operation rescue* for instructions on how to wash oil-coated birds.
8. Romanes (1886) reports anecdotes of sudden death in elephants and other species when a mate is killed—death from a broken heart.

9. See Mathis (1964).

10. *Washington Post*, December 9, 1973.

11. Personal communication.

12. Scarf (1973). Copyright 1973 by the New York Times Company. Reprinted by permission. Goodall reported that this sudden death of chimpanzees younger than five years had now been seen five times when the mother died (Psychosomatic Society meeting, Philadelphia, April 1974).

13. Mathis (1964) reports this case.

14. Cannon (1942). See also Wintrob (1973).

15. Cannon (1942) as quoted by Richter (1957). Reproduced by permission of the American Anthropology Association.

16. Burrell (1963).

17. Engel (1971).

18. From Saul (1966), quoted by Engel.

19. From Bauer (1957), quoted by Engel.

20. Schmale and Iker (1966).

21. Parkes, Benjamin, and Fitzgerald (1969). See also Rahe and Lind (1971) for a study of the amount of life change preceding heart attacks.

22. Greene, Goldstein, and Moss (1972).

23. Rosenman, Friedman, Straus, Wurm, Kositchek, Hahn, and Werthessen (1964) and Rosenman, Friedman, Straus, Wurm, Jenkins, and Messinger (1966). Krantz et al. (1974).

24. Imboden, Cantor, and Cluff (1961).

25. See Rahe (1969) for information regarding life change and susceptibility to a variety of physical illnesses.

26. See also Davies, Quinlan, McKegney, and Kimbel (1973), Kubler-Ross (1969), and Stavraky, Buck, Lott, and Wanklin (1968) for assessments of the role of psychological factors in death from cancer.

27. See also Strassman, Thaler, and Schein (1956) for helpless deaths among American prisoners in the Korean War. See also the striking description in Zimbardo, Haney, Banks, and Jaffe (1974) of the helplessness-inducing effects of imprisonment on volunteer college students.

28. Bettelheim (1960).

29. See Kastenbaum and Schaberg (1971) for a discussion of will to live and survival in the aged. See also Weisman and Kastenbaum (1968).

30. Aleksandrowicz (1961). Reprinted with permission from the *Bulletin of the Menninger Clinic.* Vol. 25, pp. 23–32. Copyright 1961 by The Menninger Foundation.
31. See Bowlby (1969, 1973), Kaufman and Rosenblum (1967a, b), and Suomi and Harlow (1972) for related results and discussion.
32. See Cannon (1942), Engel (1971), Richter (1957), and Wolf (1967) for physiological speculations.

BIBLIOGRAPHY

Abraham, K. The first pregenital stage of the libido (1916). In *Selected papers on psychoanalysis*. New York: Basic Books, 1960. Pp. 243–279.

———. Notes on the psychoanalytic investigation and treatment of manic-depressive insanity and allied conditions (1911). In *Selected papers on psychoanalysis*. New York: Basic Books, 1960. Pp. 137–156.

Abramson, L. and Seligman, M. E. P. The effects of AMPT on learned helplessness in the rat. Submitted, 1974.

Akiskal, H. S. and McKinney, W. T. Depressive disorders: Toward a unified hypothesis. *Science,* 1973, *182,* 20–28.

Aleksandrowicz, D. R. Fire and its aftermath on a geriatric ward. *Bulletin of the Menninger Clinic,* 1961, *25,* 23–32.

American Petroleum Institute. *Operation rescue: Cleaning and care of oiled water fowl.* Washington, 1972.

Amsel, A., Rashotte, N. E., and MacKinnon, J. R. Partial reinforcement effects within subject and between subjects. *Psychological Monographs,* 1966, *80* (20, whole number 628).

Anderson, D. C. and Paden, P. Passive avoidance response learning as a function of prior tumbling trauma. *Psychonomic Science,* 1966, *4,* 129–130.

Anderson, D. C., Cole, J., and McVaugh, W. Variations in unsignaled inescapable preshock as determinants of responses to punishment. *Journal of Comparative and Physiological Psychology,* 1968, *65* (Monogr. Suppl. 1–17).

Anderson, L. T. and Ressler, R. H. Response to a conditioned aversive event in mice as a function of frequency of premating maternal shock. *Developmental Psychobiology,* 1973, *6,* 113–121.

Anisman, H. Effects of pretraining compatible and incompatible responses on subsequent one-way and shuttle-avoidance performance in rats. *Journal of Comparative Physiological Psychology,* 1973, *82,* 95–104.

Anisman, H. and Waller, T. G. Facilitative and disruptive effect of prior exposure to shock on subsequent avoidance performance. *Journal of Comparative Physiological Psychology,* 1972, *78,* 113–122.

———. Effects of inescapable shock on subsequent avoidance performance: Role of response repertoire changes. *Behavioral Biology,* 1973, *9,* 331–335.

Averill, J. R. Personal control over aversive stimuli and its relationship to stress. *Psychological Bulletin,* 1973, *80,* 286–303.

Averill, J. R. and Rosenn, M. Vigilant and nonvigilant coping strategies and psychophysiological stress reactions during the anticipation of electric shock. *Journal of Personality and Social Psychology,* 1972, *23,* 123–141.

Azrin, N. H. Some effects of two intermittent schedules of immediate and non-immediate punishment. *Journal of Psychology,* 1956, *42,* 3–21.

Badia, P. and Culbertson, S. Behavioral effects of signalled vs. unsignalled shock during escape training in the rat. *Journal of Comparative and Physiological Psychology,* 1970, *72* (2), 216–222.

———. The relative aversiveness of signalled vs. unsignalled escapable and inescapable shock. *Journal of the Experimental Analysis of Behavior,* 1972, *17,* 463–471.

Badia, P., McBane, B., Suter, S., and Lewis, P. Preference behavior in an immediate versus variably delayed shock situation with and without a warning signal. *Journal of Experimental Psychology,* 1966, *72,* 847–852.

Badia, P., Suter, S., and Lewis, P. Preference for warned shock: Information and/or preparation. *Psychological Reports*, 1967, *20*, 271–274.

Badia, P., Culbertson, S., and Harsh, J. Choice of longer or stronger signalled shock over shorter or weaker unsignalled shock. *Journal of the Experimental Analysis of Behavior*, 1973, *19*, 25–33.

Bainbridge, P. L. Learning in the rat: Effect of early experience with an unsolvable problem. *Journal of Comparative and Physiological Psychology*, 1973, *82*, 301–307.

Bandler, R. J., Jr., Madaras, G. R., and Bem, D. J. Self-observation as a source of pain perception. *Journal of Personality and Social Psychology*, 1968, *9*, 205–209.

Banfield, E. C. *The moral basis of a backward society.* New York: The Free Press, 1958.

Bauer, J. Sudden, unexpected death. *Postgraduate Medicine*, 1957, *22*, A34–A45.

Beck, A. T. *Depression: Clinical, experimental, and theoretical aspects.* New York: Hoeber, 1967.

——. Cognitive therapy: Nature and relation to behavior therapy. *Behavior Therapy*, 1970, *1*, 184–200.

——. Cognition, affect, and psychopathology. *Archives of General Psychiatry*, 1971, *24*, 495–500.

Beck, A. T. and Hurvich, M. S. Psychological correlates of depression. 1. Frequency of "masochistic" dream content in a private practice sample. *Psychosomatic Medicine*, 1959, *21*, 50–55.

Beck, A. T. and Ward, C. H. Dreams of depressed patients: Characteristic themes in manifest content. *Archives of General Psychiatry*, 1961, *5*, 462–467.

Beck, A. T., Sethi, B., and Tuthill, R. W. Childhood bereavement and adult depression. *Archieves of General Psychiatry*, 1963, *9*, 295–302.

Behrend, E. R. and Bitterman, M. E. Sidman avoidance in the fish. *Journal of the Experimental Analysis of Behavior*, 1963, *13*, 229–242.

Bettelheim, B. *The informed heart—autonomy in a mass age.* New York: Free Press, 1960.

Bibring, E. The mechanism of depression. In P. Greenacre (Ed.), *Affective disorders.* New York: International Universities Press, 1953. Pp. 13–48.

Binik, Y. and Seligman, M. E. P. Controllability and stress. Unpublished manuscript, 1974.

Bintz, J. Between- and within-subject effect of shock intensity on avoidance in goldfish (*Carassius auratus*). *Journal of Comparative and Physiological Psychology*, 1971, *75*, 92–97.

Birtchnell, J. Depression in relation to early and recent parent death. *British Journal of Psychiatry*, 1970a, *116*, 299–306.

———. Early parent death and mental illness. *British Journal of Psychiatry*, 1970b, *116*, 281–287.

———. Recent parent death and mental illness. *British Journal of Psychiatry*, 1970c, *116*, 287–289.

———. The relationship between attempted suicide, depression and parent death. *British Journal of Psychiatry*, 1970d, *116*, 307–313.

Black, A. H. The extinction of avoidance responses under curare. *Journal of Comparative and Physiological Psychology*, 1958, *51*, 519–524.

Boakes, R. A. and Halliday, M. S. (Eds.). *Inhibition and learning*. New York: Academic Press, 1972.

Bolles, R. C. Species-specific defense reactions in avoidance learning. *Psychological Review*, 1970, 77, 32–48.

Bowers, K. S. Pain, anxiety, and perceived control. *Journal of Consulting and Clinical Psychology*, 1968, *32*, 596–602.

Bowlby, J. *Attachment*, vol. 1. New York: Basic Books, 1969.

———. *Attachment and loss*, vol. 2, *Separation; Anxiety and anger*. New York: Basic Books, 1973.

Bracewell, R. J. and Black, A. H. The effects of restraint and noncontingent pre-shock on subsequent escape learning in the rat. *Learning and Motivation*, 1974, *5*, 53–69.

Brady, J. P. Comments on methohexitone-aided systematic desensitization. *Behavior Research and Therapy*, 1967, *5*, 259–260.

Brady, J. V. Ulcers in "executive" monkeys. *Scientific American*, 1958, *199*, 95–100.

Brady, J. V., Porter, R. W., Conrad, D. G., and Mason, J. W. Avoidance behavior and the development of gastroduodenal ulcers. *Journal of the Experimental Analysis of Behavior*, 1958, *1*, 69–72.

Braud, W., Wepman, B., and Russo, D. Task and species generality of the "helplessness" phenomenon. *Psychonomic Science*, 1969, *16*, 154–155.

Brimer, C. J. and Kamin, L. J. Disinhibition, habituation, sensitzation and the conditioned emotional response. *Journal of Comparative and Physiological Psychology*, 1963, *56*, 508–516.

Brinton, C. C. *The anatomy of revolution*. New York: Prentice-Hall, 1952.

Bronfenbrenner, U. Psychological costs of quality and equality in education. In V. L. Allan (Ed.), *Psychological factors in poverty*. Chicago: Markham, 1970.

Brookshire, K. H., Littman, R. A., and Stewart, C. N. Residua of shock-trauma in the white rat: A three factor theory. *Psychological Monographs*, 1961, *75*, no. 10 (whole no. 514).

Burgess, E. P. The modification of depressive behaviors. In R. D. Rubin and C. M. Franks (Eds.), *Advances in behavior therapy*. New York: Academic Press, 1968. Pp. 193–199.

Burrell, R. J. W. The possible bearing of curse death and other factors in Bantu culture on the etiology of myocardial infarction. In T. N. James and J. W. Keyes (Eds.), *The etiology of myocardial infarction*. Boston, Mass.: Little, Brown and Co., 1963. Pp. 95–97.

Byrum, R. P. and Jackson, D. E. Response availability and second-order conditioned suppression. *Psychonomic Science*, 1971, *23*, 106–108.

Calhoun, J. B. Population density and social pathology. *Scientific American*, 1962, *206*, 139–148.

Cannon, W. B. "Voodoo" death. *American Anthropologist*, 1942, *44*, 169–181.

———. "Voodoo" death. *Psychosomatic Medicine*, 1957, *19*, 182–190.

Cantor, M. B. and LoLordo, V. M. Rats prefer signalled reinforcing brain stimulation to unsignalled ESB. *Journal of Comparative and Physiological Psychology*, 1970, *71*, 183–191.

Carder, B. and Berkowitz, K. Rats' preference for earned in comparison with free food. *Science*, 1970, *167*, 1273–1274.

Carney, M. W. P., Roth, M., and Garside, R. F. The diagnosis of depressive syndromes and the prediction of E. C. T. response. *British Journal of Psychiatry*, 1965, *111*, 659–674.

Casler, L. Maternal deprivation: A critical review of the literature. *Monographs of the Society for Research in Child Development*, 1961, *26*, 1–64.

Catania, A. C. Elicitation, reinforcement, and stimulus control. In

R. Glaser (Ed.), *The nature of reinforcement*. New York: Academic Press, 1971. Pp. 196–220.

Caul, W. F., Buchanan, D. C., and Hayes, R. C. Effects of unpredictability of shock on incidence of gastric lesions and heart rate in immobilized rats. *Physiology and Behavior*, 1972, 8(4), 669–672.

Champion, R. A. Studies of experimentally induced disturbance. *Australian Journal of Psychology*, 1950, 2, 90–99.

Church, R. M. Systematic effect of random error in the yoked control design. *Psychological Bulletin*, 1964, 62, 122–131.

Church, R. M. Response suppression. In B. A. Campbell and R. M. Church (Eds.), *Punishment and aversive behavior*. New York: Appleton-Century-Crofts, 1969. Pp. 111–156.

Clark, K. A. *Youth in the ghetto: A study of the consequences of powerlessness and a blueprint for change*. New York: Haryou, 1964.

Cole, J. O. Therapeutic efficacy of antidepressant drugs. *Journal of the American Medical Association*, 1964, 190, 448–455.

Cook, J. and Barnes, L. W. Choice of delay of inevitable shock. *Journal of Abnormal and Social Psychology*, 1964, 68, 669–672.

Cook, L. and Seligman, M. E. P. Learned helplessness, depression, and apparent horizon. Unpublished manuscript, 1974.

Coopersmith, S. *The antecedents of self esteem*. San Francisco: W. H. Freeman, 1967.

Corah, N. L. and Boffa, J. Perceived control, self-observation, and response to aversive stimulation. *Journal of Personality and Social Psychology*, 1970, 16, 1–4.

D'Amato, M. R. and Gumenik, W. E. Some effects of immediate versus randomly delayed shock on an instrumental response and cognitive processes. *Journal of Abnormal and Social Psychology*, 1960, 60, 64–67.

Davies, R. K., Quinlan, D. M., McKegney, F. P., and Kimbel, C. P. Organic factors in psychological adjustment in advanced cancer patients. *Psychosomatic Medicine*, 1973, 35, 464–471.

Davis, H. and McIntire, R. W. Conditioned suppression under positive, negative, and no contingency between conditioned and unconditioned stimuli. *Journal of the Experimental Analysis of Behavior*, 1969, 12, 633–640.

Davis, J. Efficacy of tranquilizing and antidepressant drugs. *Archives of General Psychiatry*, 1965, 13, 552–572.

Davison, G. C. Anxiety under total curarization: Implications for the role of muscular relaxation in the desensitization of neurotic fears. *Journal of Nervous and Mental Diseases*, 1966, *143*, 443–448.

———. Systematic desensitization as a counter-conditioning process. *Journal of Abnormal Psychology*, 1968, *73*, 91–99.

Denenberg, V. H. and Rosenberg, K. M. Nongenetic transmission of information. *Nature*, 1967, *216*, 549-550.

Denenberg, V. H. and Whimbey, A. E. Behavior of adult rats is modified by the experiences their mothers had as infants. *Science*, 1963, *142*, 1192–1193.

Denny, M. R. Relaxation theory and experiments. In F. R. Brush (Ed.), *Aversive conditioning and learning*. New York: Academic Press, 1971. Pp. 235–295.

Desiderato, O. and Newman, A. Conditioned suppression produced in rats by tones paired with escapable or inescapable shock. *Journal of Comparative and Physiological Psychology*, 1971, *77*, 427–435.

De Toledo, L. and Black, A. H. Effects of preshock on subsequent avoidance conditioning. *Journal of Comparative and Physiological Psychology*, 1967, *63*, 493–499.

Deutsch, M. Minority group and class status as related to social and personality factors in scholastic achievement. *Monograph of the Society for Applied Anthropology*, 1960, *2*, 1–32.

Dinsmoor, J. A. Pulse duration and food deprivation in escape from shock training. *Psychological Reports*, 1958, *4*, 531–534.

Dinsmoor, J. A. and Campbell, S. L. Escape-from-shock training following exposure to inescapable shock. *Psychological Reports*, 1956a, *2*, 43–49.

———. Level of current and time between sessions as factors in adaptation to shock. *Psychological Reports*, 1956b, *2*, 441–444.

Dorworth, T. R. The effect of electroconvulsive shock on "helplessness" in dogs. Unpublished doctoral dissertation, University of Minnesota, 1971.

———. Learned helplessness and RET. *Rational Living*, 1973, *3*, 27–30.

Dweck, C. S. The role of expectations and attributions in the alleviation of learned helplessness. Unpublished doctoral dissertation, Yale University, 1972.

Dweck, C. S. and Reppucci, N. D. Learned helplessness and reinforcement responsibility in children. *Journal of Personality and Social Psychology*, 1973, *25*, 109–116.

Ekman, P. and Friesen, W. V. Non-verbal behavior in psychopathology. In R. J. Friedman and M. M. Katz (Eds.), *The psychology of depression: Contemporary theory and research*. Washington: Winston-Wiley, 1974.

Elliot, R. Tonic heart rate: Experiments on the effects of collative variables lead to an hypothesis about its motivational significance. *Journal of Personality and Social Psychology*, 1969, *12*, 211–228.

Ellis, A. *Reason and emotion in psychotherapy*. New York: Lyle Stuart, 1962.

Engberg, L. A., Hansen, G., Welker, R. L., and Thomas, D. R. Acquisition of key-pecking via autoshaping as a function of prior experience: "Learned laziness?" *Science*, 1973, *178*, 1002–1004.

Engel, G. L. Sudden and rapid death during psychological stress, folklore or folkwisdom? *Annals of Internal Medicine*, 1971, *74*, 771–782.

Estes, W. K. and Skinner, B. F. Some quantitative properties of anxiety. *Journal of Experimental Psychology*, 1941, *29*, 390–400.

Ewing, L. S. Fighting and death from stress in the cockroach. *Science*, 1967, *155*, 1035–1036.

Fagan, M. M. The efficacy of group psychotherapy and group assertive training in alleviating depression. Unpublished master's essay, John Carroll University, 1974.

Ferrari, N. A. Institutionalization and attitude change in an aged population: A field study and dissidence theory. Unpublished doctoral dissertation, Western Reserve University, 1962.

Ferster, C. B. Animal behavior and mental illness. *Psychological Record*, 1966, *16*, 345–356.

————. A functional analysis of depression. *American Psychologist*, 1973, *28*, 857–870.

Fisher, S. Depressive affect and perception of up-down. *Journal of Psychiatric Research*, 1964, *2*, 201–208.

Flavell, J. H. *The developmental psychology of Jean Piaget*. Princeton: Van Nostrand, 1963.

Fosco, E. and Geer, J. Effects of gaining control over aversive stimuli after differing amounts of no control. *Psychological Reports*, 1971, *29*, 1153–1154.

Freedman, J., Klevansky, S. and Erlich, P. The effect of crowding on human task performance. *Journal of Applied Social Psychology*, 1971, *1*, 7–25.

Freedman, J., Levy, A., Buchanan, R. and Price, J. Crowding and human aggressiveness. *Journal of Experimental Social Psychology*, 1972, *18*, 528–548.

Freud, S. Mourning and melancholia (1917). In *Collected works*. London: Hogarth Press. Pp. 243–258.

Friedman, A. S. Minimal effects of severe depression on cognitive functioning. *Journal of Abnormal and Social Psychology*, 1964, *69*, 237–243.

Frumkin, K. and Brookshire, K. H. Conditioned fear training and later avoidance learning in goldfish. *Psychonomic Science*, 1969, *16*, 159–160.

Furedy, J. J. and Doob, A. N. Autonomic responses and verbal reports in further tests of the preparatory-adaptive-response interpretation of reinforcement. *Journal of Experimental Psychology*, 1971, *89*, 258–264.

———. Signalling unmodifiable shock limits on human informational cognitive control. *Journal of Personality and Social Psychology*, 1972, *21*, 111–115.

Galle, O. R., Gove, W. R., and McPherson, J. M. Population density in pathology: What are the relations for man? *Science*, 1972, *176*, 23–30.

Gamzu, E. and Williams, D. A. Classical conditioning of a complex skeletal response. *Science*, 1971, *171*, 923–925.

Gamzu, E., Williams, D. A., and Schwartz, B. Pitfalls of organismic concepts: "Learned laziness?" *Science*, 1973, *101*, 367–368.

Gauron, E. F. Effects of mother's shock traumatization in infancy upon offspring behavior. *Journal of Genetic Psychology*, 1966, *108*, 221–224.

Geer, J. A test of the classical conditioning model of emotion: The use of non-painful aversive stimuli as UCSs in a conditioning procedure. *Journal of Personality and Social Psychology*, 1968, *10*, 148–156.

Geer, J. and Maisel, E. Evaluating the effects of the prediction-control confound. *Journal of Personality and Social Psychology*, 1972, *23*, 314–319.

Geer, J., Davison, G. C., and Gatchel, R. I. Reduction of stress in humans through nonveridical perceived control of aversive stimulation. *Journal of Personality and Social Psychology*, 1970, *16*, 731–738.

Gellhorn, E. Interruption of behavior, inescapable shock, and experimental neurosis: A neurophysiologic analysis. *Conditional Reflex*, 1967, *2*, 285–293.

Gibbon, J. Contingency spaces and random controls in classical and instrumental conditioning. Paper presented at meeting of the Eastern Psychological Association, Atlantic City, April 1970.

Gibbon, J., Berryman, R., and Thompson, R. L. Contingency spaces and measures in classical and instrumental conditioning. *Journal of the Experimental Analysis of Behavior*, 1974, *21*, 585–605.

Ginsberg, H. J. Controlled vs. noncontrolled termination of the immobility reaction in domestic fowl (*Gallus gallus*): Parallels with the learned helplessness phenomenon. Unpublished manuscript, 1974.

Glass, D. C. and Singer, J. E. *Urban stress: Experiments on noise and social stressors*. New York: Academic Press, 1972.

Glass, D. C., Snyder, M. L., and Singer, J. E. Periodic and aperiodic noise: The safety signal hypothesis and noise aftereffects. *Psychonomic Science*, 1974, in press.

Goeckner, D. J., Greenough, W. T., and Mead, W. R. Deficits in learning tasks following chronic overcrowding in rats. *Journal of Personality and Social Psychology*, 1973, *28*, 256–261.

Goldfarb, W. Psychological privation in infancy and subsequent adjustment. *American Journal of Orthopsychiatry*, 1945, *15*, 247–255.

Goldfried, M. R. Systematic desensitization as training in self control. *Journal of Consulting and Clinical Psychology*, 1971, *37*, 228–234.

Granville-Grossman, K. L. The early environment in affective disorders. In A. Coppen and A. Walk (Eds.), *Recent developments in affective disorders: A symposium*. Special publication No. 2, *British Journal of Psychiatry*, 1967. Pp. 65–79.

Greene, W. A., Goldstein, S., and Moss, A. J. Psychosocial aspects of sudden death. *Archives of Internal Medicine*, 1972, *129*, 725–731.

Grinker, R., Miller, J., Sabshin, M., Nunn, R., and Nunnally, J. *The phenomena of depression*. New York: Hoeber, 1961.

Gurin, G. and Gurin, P. Expectancy theory in the study of poverty. *Journal of Social Issues*, 1970, *26*, 83–104.

Hannum, R. D., Rosellini, R., and Seligman, M. E. P. Development of learned helplessness in the rat. Submitted, 1974.

Hare, R. D. and Petrusic, W. M. Subjective intensity of electric shock as a function of delay in administration. Paper read at meeting of Western Psychological Association, San Francisco, May 1967.

Harlow, H. F. The formation of learning sets. *Psychological Review*, 1949, *56*, 51–65.

———. The heterosexual affectional system in monkeys. *American Psychologist*, 1962, *17*, 1–9.

Harlow, H. F. and Zimmerman, R. R. Affectional responses in the infant monkey. *Science*, 1959, *130*, 421–432.

Hearst, E. Stress induced breakdown of an appetitive discrimination. *Journal of the Experimental Analysis of Behavior*, 1965, *8*, 135–146.

Hein, A. and Held, R. Dissociation of the visual placing response into elicited and guided components. *Science*, 1967, *158*, 390–392.

Held, R. Plasticity in sensory-motor systems. *Scientific American*, 1965, *213*, 84–94.

Held, R. and Bauer, J. A. Visually guided reaching in infant monkeys after restricted rearing. *Science*, 1967, *155*, 718–720.

Held, R. and Bossom, J. Neonatal deprivation and adult rearrangement: Complimentary techniques for analyzing plastic sensory-motor coordinations. *Journal of Comparative and Physiological Psychology*, 1961, *54*, 33–37.

Held, R. and Hein, A. Movement produced stimulation in the development of visually guided behavior. *Journal of Comparative and Physiological Psychology*, 1963, *56*, 872–876.

Hershisher, D. and Trapold, M. A. Preference for unsignalled over signalled direct reinforcement in the rat. *Journal of Comparative and Physiological Psychology*, 1971, *77*, 323–332.

Higgins, J. Inconsistent socialization. *Psychological Reports*, 1968, *23*, 303–336.

Hinde, R. A., Spencer-Booth, Y., and Bruce, M. Effects of six day maternal deprivation on rhesus monkey infants. *Nature*, 1966, *210*, 1021–1023.

Hineline, P. N. Varied approaches to aversion: A review of "Aversive conditioning and learning." *Journal of Experimental Analysis of Behavior*, 1973, *19*, 531–540.

Hiroto, D. S. Locus of control and learned helplessness. *Journal of Experimental Psychology,* 1974, *102,* 187–193.

Hiroto, D. S. and Seligman, M. E. P. Generality of learned helplessness in man. *Journal of Personality and Social Psychology,* 1974, in press.

Hofer, M. A. Cardiac and respiratory function during sudden prolonged immobility in wild rodents. *Psychosomatic Medicine,* 1970, *32,* 633–647.

Hokanson, J. E., DeGood, D. E., Forrest, M. S., and Brittain, T. M. Availability of avoidance behaviors in modulating vascular-stress responses. *Journal of Personality and Social Psychology,* 1971, *19,* 60–68.

Horridge, G. A. Learning of leg position by headless insects. *Nature,* 1962, *193,* 697–698.

Houston, B. K. Control over stress, locus of control, and response to stress. *Journal of Personality and Social Psychology,* 1972, *21,* 249–255.

Hulse, S. H. Patterned reinforcement. In G. H. Bower and J. T. Spence (Eds.), *The Psychology of learning and motivation,* vol. 7. New York: Academic Press, 1974.

Humphreys, L. G. Aquisition and extinction of verbal expectations in a situation analogous to conditioning. *Journal of Experimental Psychology,* 1939a, *25,* 294–301.

———. Generalization as a function of method of reinforcement. *Journal of Experimental Psychology,* 1939b, *25,* 361–372.

———. The effect of random alternation of reinforcement on the aquisition and extinction of conditioned eyelid reactions. *Journal of Experimental Psychology,* 1939c, *25,* 141–158.

Hunt, J. McV. and Uzgiris, I. C. Cathexis for recognitive familiarity: An exploratory study. Paper presented at the convention of the American Psychological Association, Los Angeles, September 1964.

Imada, H. and Soga, M. The CER and BEL as a function of the predictability and escapability of an electric shock. *Japanese Psychological Research,* 1971, *13,* 116–123.

Imboden, J. B., Cantor, A., and Cluff, L. E. Convalescence from influenza: The study of the psychological and clinical determinants. *Archives of Internal Medicine,* 1961, *108,* 393–399.

Irwin, F. W. *Intentional behavior and motivation: A cognitive theory.* Philadelphia: Lippincott, 1971.

Jacobs, A. and Wolpin, M. A second look at systematic desensitization. In A. Jacobs and L. B. Sachs (Eds.), *The psychology of private events*. New York: Academic Press, 1971. Pp. 77–108.

Jacobson, E. *Depression: Comparative studies of normal, neurotic, and psychotic conditions*. New York: International Universities Press, 1971.

James, W. H. *DeKalb survey tests: Student opinion survey from I-E*, I. DeKalb, Ill.: Author, 1963.

Janowsky, D. S., El-Yousef, M. K., Davis, J. M., Hubbard, B., and Sekerke, H. J. Cholinergic reversal of manic symptoms. *Lancet*, 1972, *1*, 1236–1237.

Jensen, A. R. How much can we boost I.Q. and scholastic achievement? *Harvard Educational Review*, 1969, *39*, 1–123.

————. *Educability and group differences*. New York: Harper and Row, 1973.

Jensen, G. D. Preference for bar-pressing over "free loading" as a function of the number of rewarded presses. *Journal of Experimental Psychology*, 1963, *65*, 451–454.

Joffe, J. M. Genotype and prenatal and premating stress interact to affect adult behavior in rats. *Science*, 1965, *150*, 1844–1845.

Joffe, J. M., Rawson, R. A., and Mulick, J. A. Control of their environment reduces emotionality in rats. *Science*, 1973, *180*, 1383–1384.

Jones, A., Bentler, P. M., and Petry, G. The reduction of uncertainty concerning future pain. *Journal of Abnormal Psychology*, 1966, *71*, 87–94.

Kadden, R. M. Facilitation and suppression of responding under temporally defined schedules of negative reinforcement. *Journal of Experimental Analysis of Behavior*, 1973, *19*, 469–480.

Kahn, N. W. The effect of severe defeat at various age levels on the aggressive behavior of mice. *Journal of Genetic Psychology*, 1951, *79*, 117–130.

Kastenbaum, R. and Schaberg, B. K. Hope and survival in the caring environment. In F. C. Jeffers and E. Palmore (Eds.), *Prediction of life span*. New York: Heath, 1971. Pp. 249–271.

Kaufman, I. C. Mother-infant separation in monkeys: An experimental model. In J. P. Scott and E. Senay (Eds.), *Separation and depression: clinical and research aspects*. Washington: American Association for the Advancement of Science, 1973.

Kaufman, I. C. and Rosenblum, L. A. Depression in infant monkeys separated from their mothers. *Science*, 1967a, *155*, 1030–1031.

———. The reaction to separation in infant monkeys: Anaclitic depression and conservation-withdrawal. *Psychosomatic Medicine*, 1967b, *29*, 648–675.

Kavanau, J. L. Behavior of captive white-footed mice. *Science*, 1967, *155*, 1523–1539.

Kelley, H. H. Attribution theory in social psychology. In David Levine (Ed.), *Nebraska symposium on motivation*. Lincoln: University of Nebraska Press, 1967. Pp. 192–238.

———. *Causal schemata and the attribution process*. Morristown, N. J.: General Learning Press, 1972.

Kemler, D. and Shepp, B. The learning and transfer of dimensional relevance and irrelevance in children. *Journal of Experimental Psychology*, 1971, *90*, 120–127.

Kiloh, L. G. and Garside, R. F. The independence of neurotic depression and endogenous depression. *British Journal of Psychiatry*, 1963, *109*, 451–463.

Kimmel, H. D. Instrumental inhibitory factors in classical conditioning. In W. Prokasy (Ed.), *Classical conditioning*. New York: Appleton, 1965. Pp. 148–171.

Kimmel, H. D. and Pennypacker, H. Conditioned diminution of the unconditioned response as a function of the numbers of reinforcements. *Journal of Experimental Psychology*, 1962, *64*, 20–23.

Klein, D. Alleviation of depression and learned helplessness in man. Unpublished doctoral dissertation, University of Pennsylvania, 1975.

Klein, D., Fencil-Morse, E., and Seligman, M. E. P. Depression, learned helplessness, and the attribution of failure. Submitted, 1975.

Klein, M. A contribution to the psychogenesis of manic-depressive states. In W. Gaylin (Ed.), *The Meaning of Despair*. New York: Science House, 1968.

Klerman, G. L. and Cole, J. O. Clinical pharmacology of imipramine and related antidepressant compounds. *Pharmacological Review*, 1965, *17*, 101–141.

Knapp, R. K., Kause, R. H., and Perkins, C. C., Jr. Immediate vs.

delayed shock in T-maze performance. *Journal of Experimental Psychology*, 1959, *58*, 357–362.

Kozol, J. *Death at an early age.* Boston: Houghton-Mifflin, 1967.

Kraines, S. H. *Mental depressions and their treatment.* New York: Macmillan, 1957.

Krantz, D. S., Glass, D. C., and Snyder, M. L. Helplessness, stress level, and the coronary prone behavior pattern. *Journal of Experimental Social Psychology*, 1974, in press.

Kubler-Ross, E. *On death and dying.* New York: Macmillan, 1969.

Kurlander, H., Miller, W., and Seligman, M. E. P., Learned helplessness, depression, and prisoner's dilemma. Submitted, 1974.

Lang, P. J. The mechanics of desensitization and the laboratory study of human fear. In. C. M. Franks (Ed.), *Behavior therapy: Appraisal and status.* New York: McGraw-Hill, 1969. Pp. 160–191.

Langer, E. J. The illusion of control. Unpublished doctoral dissertation, Yale University, 1974.

Lanzetta, J. T. and Driscoll, J. M. Preference for information about an uncertain but unavoidable outcome. *Journal of Personality and Social Psychology*, 1966, *3*, 96–102.

Lazarus, A. A. Learning theory and the treatment of depression. *Behavior Research and Therapy*, 1968, *6*, 83–89.

Lazarus, R. S. *Psychological stress and the coping process.* New York: McGraw-Hill, 1966.

Lefcourt, H. M. Internal versus external control of reinforcement: A review. *Psychological Bulletin*, 1966, *65*, 206–220.

———. The function of the illusions of control and freedom. *American Psychologist*, 1973, *28*, 417–425.

Lessac, M. and Solomon, R. L. Effects of early isolation on the later adaptive behavior of beagles: A methodological demonstration. *Developmental Psychology*, 1969, *1*, 14–25.

Levine, M. Cue neutralization: The effects of random reinforcements upon discrimination learning. *Journal of Experimental Psychology*, 1962, *63*, 438–443.

———. Hypothesis behavior by humans during discrimination learning. *Journal of Experimental Psychology*, 1966, *71*, 331–338.

Lewinsohn, P. A behavioral approach to depression. In R. J. Friedman and M. N. Katz (Eds.), *The psychology of depression: Contemporary theory and research.* Washington: Winston-Wiley, 1974.

Lewinsohn, P. and Libet, J. Pleasant events, activity schedules, and depressions. *Journal of Abnormal Psychology*, 1972, *79*, 291–295.

Liberman, R. P. and Raskin, D. E. Depression: A behavioral formulation. *Archives of General Psychiatry*, 1971, *24*, 515–523.

Lichtenberg, P. A definition and analysis of depression. *Archives of Neurology and Psychiatry*, 1957, *77*, 519–527.

Liddell, H. S. *Emotional hazards in animals and man.* Springfield, Illinois: The Free Press of Glencoe, 1953.

Liddell, H. S., James, W. T., and Anderson, O. D. The comparative physiology of the conditioned motor reflex: Based on experiments with the pig, dog, sheep, goat and rabbit. *Comparative Psychology Monograph*, 1934, *11*, 89.

Lindner, M. Hereditary and environmental influences upon resistance to stress. Unpublished doctoral dissertation, University of Pennsylvania, 1968.

Lipsitt, L. P., Kaye, E. H., and Bosack, T. N. Enhancement of neonatal sucking through reinforcement. *Journal of Experimental Child Psychology*, 1966, *4*, 163–168.

Lockard, J. S. Choice of a warning signal or no warning signal in an unavoidable shock situation. *Journal of Comparative and Physiological Psychology*, 1963, *56*, 526–530.

———. Choice of a warning signal or none in several unavoidable-shock situations. *Psychonomic Science*, 1965, *3*, 5–6.

Looney, T. A. and Cohen, P. S. Retardation of jump-up escape responding in rats pretreated with different frequencies of noncontingent electric shock. *Journal of Comparative and Physiological Psychology*, 1972, *78*, 317–322.

Lundholm, H. Reaction time as an indicator of emotional disturbances in manic-depressive psychoses. *Journal of Abnormal Psychology*, 1922, *17*, 292–318.

Lundquist, G. Prognosis and course in manic-depressive psychosis; a follow-up study of 319 first admissions. *Acta Psychiatrica et Neurologica*, Copenhagen, 1945, *35*, 95.

Lykken, D. Preception in the rat: Autonomic response to shock as a function of length of warning interval. *Science*, 1962, *137*, 665–666.

MacKintosh, N. J. Stimulus selection: learning to ignore stimuli that predict no change in reinforcement. In R. A. Hinde and J.

Stevenson-Hinde (Eds.), *Constraints on learning*. New York: Academic Press, 1973. Pp. 75–100.

Maier, N. R. F. *Frustration*. Ann Arbor: University of Michigan Press, 1949.

Maier, S. F. Failure to escape traumatic shock: Incompatible skeletal motor responses or learned helplessness? *Learning and Motivation*, 1970, *1*, 157–170.

Maier, S. F., and Gleitman, H. Proactive interference in rats. *Psychonomic Science*, 1967, *36*, 1–12.

Maier, S. F. and Testa, T. Failure to learn to escape by rats previously exposed to inescapable shock is partly produced by associative interference. *Journal of Comparative and Physiological Psychology*, 1974, in press.

Maier, S. F., Seligman, M. E. P., and Solomon, R. L. Pavlovian fear conditioning and learned helplessness. In B. A. Campbell and R. M. Church (Eds.), *Punishment*. New York: Appleton-Century-Crofts, 1969. Pp. 299–343.

Maier, S. F., Anderson, C., and Lieberman, D. A. Influence of control of shock on subsequent shock-elicited aggression. *Journal of Comparative and Physiological Psychology*, 1972, *81*, 94–100.

Maier, S. F. Albin, R. W., and Testa, T. J. Failure to learn to escape in rats previously exposed to inescapable shock depends on the nature of the escape response. *Journal of Comparative and Physiological Psychology*, 1973, *85*, 581–592.

Martin, I. and Rees, L. Reaction times and somatic reactivity in depressed patients. *Journal of Psychosomatic Research*, 1966, *9*, 375–382.

Maser, J. D. and Gallup, G. G. Tonic immobility in chickens: Catalepsy potentiation by uncontrollable shock and alleviation by imipramine. *Psychosomatic Medicine*, 1974, *36*, 199–205.

Masserman, J. H. *Behavior and neurosis*. Chicago: University of Chicago Press, 1943.

———. The principle of uncertainty in neurotigenesis. In H. D. Kimmel (Ed.), *Experimental psychopathology*. New York: Academic Press, 1971. Pp. 13–32.

Masters, V. H. and Johnson, V. E. *Human sexual response*. London: Churchill, 1966.

Mathis, J. L. A sophisticated version of voodoo death: Report of a case. *Psychosomatic Medicine*, 1964, *26*, 104–107.

McCulloch, T. L. and Bruner, J. S. The effect of electric shock upon subsequent learning in the rat. *Journal of Psychology*, 1939, 7, 333–336.

McKinney, W. T. and Bunney, W. E., Jr. Animal model of depression. *Archives of General Psychiatry*, 1969, 21, 240–248.

Melges, F. T. and Bowlby, J. Types of hopelessness in psychopathological process. *Archives of General Psychiatry*, 1969, 20, 690–699.

Mellgren, R. L. and Ost, J. W. P. Discriminative stimulus preexposure and learning of an operant discrimination in the rat. *Journal of Comparative and Physiological Psychology*, 1971, 77, 179–187.

Mendels, J. Depression: The distinction between symptom and syndrome. *British Journal of Psychiatry*, 1968, 114, 1549–1554.

———. *Concepts of depression.* New York: Wiley, 1970.

Mezinskis, J., Gliner, J., and Shemberg, K. Somatic response as a function of no signal, random signal, or signalled shock with variable or constant durations of shock. *Psychonomic Science*, 1971, 25, 271–272.

Miller, N. E. Learning of visceral and glandular responses. *Science*, 1969, 163, 434–445.

Miller, N. E. and Weiss, J. M. Effects of somatic or visceral responses to punishment. In B. A. Campbell and R. M. Church (Ed.), *Punishment and aversive behavior.* New York: Appleton-Century-Crofts, 1969. Pp. 343–372.

Miller, W. and Seligman, M. E. P. Depression and the perception of reinforcement. *Journal of Abnormal Psychology*, 1973, 82, 62–73.

———. Depression, learned helplessness and the perception of reinforcement. Submitted, 1974a.

———. Depression and learned helplessness in man. *Journal of Abnormal Psychology*, 1974b, in press.

Miller, W., Seligman, M. E. P., and Kurlander, H. Learned helplessness, depression, and anxiety. Submitted, 1974.

Moot, S. A., Cebulla, R. P., and Crabtree, J. M. Instrumental control and ulceration in rats. *Journal of Comparative and Physiological Psychology*, 1970, 71, 405–410.

Morrow, M. C. Recovery of conditioned UCR diminution following extinction. *Journal of Experimental Psychology*, 1966, 71, 884–888.

Mowrer, O. H. and Viek, P. An experimental analogue of fear from a sense of helplessness. *Journal of Abnormal and Social Psychology*, 1948, *43*, 193–200.

Mullin, A. D. and Mogenson, G. J. Effects of fear conditioning on avoidance learning. *Psychological Reports*, 1963, *13*, 707–710.

Murphy, L. B. Infants' play and cognitive development. In M. W. Piers (Ed.), *Play and development*. New York: Norton, 1972. Pp. 119–126.

Nardini, J. E. Survival factors in the American prisoners of war of the Japanese. *The American Journal of Psychiatry*, 1952, *109*, 241–247.

Neuringer, A. Animals respond for food in the presence of free food. *Science*, 1969, *166*, 399–401.

———. Pigeons respond to produce periods in which rewards are independent of responding. *Journal of the Experimental Analysis of Behavior*, 1970, *19*, 39–54.

O'Brien, R. A. Positive and negative sets in two choice discrimination learning by children. Unpublished master's thesis, University of Illinois, Champaign-Urbana, 1967.

Overmier, J. B. Interference with avoidance behavior: Failure to avoid traumatic shock. *Journal of Experimental Psychology*, 1968, *78*, 340–343.

Overmier, J. B. and Seligman, M. E. P. Effects of inescapable shock upon subsequent escape and avoidance learning. *Journal of Comparative and Physiological Psychology*, 1967, *63*, 23–33.

Padilla, A. M. Effects of prior and interpolated shock exposures on subsequent avoidance learning by goldfish. *Psychological Reports*, 1973, *32*, 451–456.

Padilla, A. M., Padilla, C., Ketterer, T., and Giacalone, D. Inescapable shocks and subsequent avoidance conditioning in goldfish (*Carrasius auratus*). *Psychonomic Science*, 1970, *20*, 295–296.

Paré, W. P. and Livingston, A. Shock predictability and gastric secretion in chronically gastric fistulated rats. *Physiology and Behavior*, 1973, *11*, 521–526.

Parkes, M. C., Benjamin, B., and Fitzgerald, R. G. Broken heart: A statistical study of increased mortality among widowers. *British Medical Journal*, 1969, *1*, 740–743.

Paskind, H. A. Brief attacks of manic-depressive depression. *Archives of Neurology and Psychiatry*, 1929, *22*, 123–134.

———. Manic-depressive psychosis in private practice: Length of attack and length of interval. *Archives of Neurology and Psychiatry*, 1930, *23*, 789–794.

Pavlov, I. P. *Conditioned reflexes*. New York: Dover, 1927.

———. *Lectures on conditional reflexes: The higher nervous activity (behaviour) of animals*, vol. 1, trans. H. Gant. London: Lawrence and Wishart, 1928.

———. *Conditioned reflexes and psychiatry*. New York: International Publishers, 1941.

Paykel, E. S., Myers, J. K., Dienelt, M. N., Klerman, G. L., Lindenthal, J. J., and Pepper, M. N. Life events and depression: A controlled study. *Archives of General Psychiatry*, 1969, *21*, 753–760.

Payne, R. J. Alterations of Sidman avoidance baselines by CSs paired with avoidable or unavoidable shock. *Psychological Reports*, 1972, *31*, 291–294.

Payne, R. W. Cognitive abnormalities. In H. J. Eysenck (Ed.), *Handbook of abnormal psychology*. New York: Basic Books, 1961. Pp. 193–261.

Perkins, C. C. The stimulus conditions which follow learned responses. *Psychological Review*, 1955, *62*, 341–348.

Perkins, C. C., Seymann, R., Levis, D. J., and Spencer, R. Factors affecting preference for signal-shock over shock-signal. *Journal of Experimental Psychology*, 1966, *72*, 190–196.

Pervin, L. A. The need to predict and control under conditions of threat. *Journal of Personality*, 1963, *31*, 570–585.

Pettigrew, T. F. *A profile of the Negro American*. Princeton, N. J.: Van Nostrand, 1964.

Pinneau, S. The infantile disorders of hospitalism and anaclitic depression. *Psychological Bulletin*, 1955, *52*, 429–452.

Porefsky, R. Noncontingency detection and its effects. Paper presented at meeting of Eastern Psychological Association, Atlantic City, April 1970.

Porter, R. W., Brady, J. V., Conrad, D., Mason, J. W., Galambos, R., and Rioch, D. Some experimental observations on gastrointestinal lesions in behaviorally conditioned monkeys. *Psychosomatic Medicine*, 1958, *20*, 379–394.

Powell, D. A. and Creer, T. L. Interaction of developmental and environmental variables in shock-elicited aggression. *Journal of Comparative and Physiological Psychology*, 1969, *69*, 219–225.

Premack, D. Reinforcement theory. In M. Jones (Ed.), *Nebraska symposium on motivation*. Lincoln: University of Nebraska Press, 1965. Pp. 123–180.

Price, K. P. The pathological effects in rats of predictable and unpredictable shock. Unpublished bachelor's thesis, Brandeis University, 1970.

Price, K. P. and Geer, J. H. Predictable and unpredictable aversive events: Evidence for the safety signal hypothesis. *Psychonomic Science*, 1972, *26*, 215–216.

Prokasy, W. F. The acquisition of observing responses in the absence of differential external reinforcement. *Journal of Comparative and Physiological Psychology*, 1956, *49*, 131–134.

Racinskas, J. R. Maladaptive consequences of loss or lack of control over aversive events. Unpublished doctoral dissertation, Waterloo University, Ontario, Canada, 1971.

Rado, S. The problem of melancholia. *International Journal of Psychoanalysis*, 1928, *9*, 420–438.

Rahe, R. H. Life crisis and health change. In Philip R. A. May and J. R. Wittenborn (Eds.), *Psychotropic drug response: Advances in prediction*. Springfield, Illinois: Charles C. Thomas, 1969. Pp. 92–125.

Rahe, R. H. and Lind, E. Psychosocial factors and sudden cardiac death: A pilot study. *Journal of Psychosomatic Research*, 1971, *15*, 19–24.

Rapaport, P. and Seligman, M. E. P. Uncontrollable trauma: Transmission of fear from mother to offspring. 1974.

Ratner, S. C. Comparative aspects of hypnosis. In J. Gordon (Ed.), *Handbook of clinical and experimental hypnosis*. New York: Macmillan, 1967, Pp. 550–587.

Redmond, D. E., Maas, J. W., Kling, D., and DeKirmenjian, H. Changes in primate social behavior after treatment with alpha-methyl-para-tyrosine. *Psychosomatic Medicine*, 1971, *33*, 97–113.

Redmond, D. E., Maas, J. W., DeKirmenjian, H., and Schlemmer, R. F. Changes in social behavior in monkeys after inescapable shock. *Psychosomatic Medicine*, 1973, *35*, 448–449.

Reed, J. L. Comments on the use of methohexitone sodium as a means of inducing relaxation. *Behavior Research and Therapy,* 1966, 4, 323.

Renner, K. E. and Houlihan, J. Conditions affecting the relative aversiveness of immediate and delayed punishment. *Journal of Experimental Psychology,* 1969, *81,* 411–420.

Rescorla, R. A. Pavlovian conditioning and its proper control procedures. *Psychological Review,* 1967, *74,* 71–79.

———. Probability of shock in the presence and absence of the CS in fear conditioning: *Journal of Comparative and Physiological Psychology,* 1968, *66,* 1–5.

Rescorla, R. A. and LoLordo, V. M. Inhibition of avoidance behavior. *Journal of Comparative and Physiological Psychology,* 1965, *59,* 406–410.

Rescorla, R. A. and Skucy, J. Effect of response independent reinforcers during extinction. *Journal of Comparative and Physiological Psychology,* 1969, *67,* 381–389.

Ressler, R. H. and Anderson, L. T. Avoidance conditioning in mice as a function of their mothers' training. *Developmental Psychobiology,* 1973a, *6,* 97–103.

———. Avoidance conditioning in mice as a function of their mothers' exposure to shock. *Developmental Psychobiology,* 1973b, *6,* 105–111.

Richter, C. P. On the phenomenon of sudden death in animals and man. *Psychosomatic Medicine,* 1957, *19,* 191–198.

———. The phenomenon of unexplained sudden death in animals and man. In W. H. Gant (Ed.), *Physiological basis of psychiatry.* Springfield, Illinois: Charles C. Thomas, 1958. Pp. 148–171.

Rodin, J. Crowding, perceived choice and response to controllable and uncontrollable outcomes. *Journal of Experimental Social Psychology,* 1974, in press.

Romanes, G. J. *Animal intelligence* (4th edition). London: Kegan Paul, Trench, 1886.

Rosellini, R. and Seligman, M. E. P. Learned helplessness and escape from frustration. *Journal of Experimental Psychology: Animal Behavior Processes,* 1974, in press.

Rosenman, R. H., Friedman, M., Straus, R., Wurm, M. Kositchek, R., Hahn, W., and Werthessen, N. T. Predictive study of coronary heart disease: The western collaborative group study. *Journal of the American Medical Association,* 1964, *189,* 15–26.

Rosenman, R. H., Friedman, M., Straus, R., Wurm, M., Jenkins, C. D., and Messinger, H. B. Coronary heart disease in the western collaborative group study: A follow-up of two years. *Journal of the American Medical Association*, 1966, *196*, 130–136.

Roth, S. The effects of experimentally induced expectancies of control: Facilitation of controlling behavior or learned helplessness? Unpublished doctoral dissertation, Northwestern University, 1973.

Roth, S. and Bootzin, R. R. Effects of experimentally induced expectancies of external control: An investigation of learned helplessness. *Journal of Personality and Social Psychology*, 1974, *29*, 253–264.

Roth, S. and Kubal, L. The effects of noncontingent reinforcement on tasks of differing importance: Facilitation and learned helplessness effects. Submitted, 1974.

Rotter, J. B. Generalized expectancies for internal vs. external control of reinforcements. *Psychological Monographs*, 1966, *80*(whole no. 609).

Rovee, K. H. and Rovee, D. T. Conjugate reinforcement of infant exploratory behavior. *Journal of Experimental Child Psychology*, 1969, *8*, 33–39.

Rozin, P., Poritsky, S., and Sotsky, R. American children with reading problems can easily learn to read English represented by Chinese characters. *Science*, 1971, *171*, 1264–1267.

Ryan, W. Preventive services in the social context: Power, pathology, and prevention. In B. C. Bloom and D. P. Buck (Eds.), *Proceedings of mental health institute*. Salt Lake City, 1967.

Sackett, G. P. Innate mechanisms, rearing conditions, and a theory of early experience effects in primates. In N. R. Jones (Ed.), *Miami symposium on prediction of behavior: Early experience*. Coral Gables: University of Miami Press, 1970. Pp. 11–53.

Sameroff, A. J. The components of sucking in the human newborn. *Journal of Experimental Child Psychology*, 1968, *6*, 607–623.

———. Can conditioned responses be established in the newborn infant: 1971? *Developmental Psychology*, 1971, *5*, 411–442.

Saul, I. J. Sudden death at impasse. *Psychoanalytic Forum*, 1966, *1*, 88–89.

Scarf, M. Goodall and chimpanzees at Yale. *New York Times Magazine*, Feb. 18, 1973.

Schildkraut, J. J. The catecholamine hypothesis of affective disorders: A review of supporting evidence. *American Journal of Psychiatry*, 1965, *112*, 509–522.

Schmale, A. and Iker, H. The psychological setting of uterine cervical cancer. *Annals of the New York Academy of Sciences*, 1966, *125*, 807–813.

Schoenfeld, W. N., Cole, B. K., Lang, J., and Mankoff, R. "Contingency" in behavior theory. In F. J. McGuigan and D. B. Lumsden (Eds.), *Contemporary approaches to conditioning and learning*. Washington: Winston-Wiley, 1973. Pp. 151–172.

Schulz, R. and Aderman, D. Effect of residential change on the temporal distance to death of terminal cancer patients. *Omega: Journal of Death and Dying*, 1973, 2, 157–162.

Schuyler, D. *The depressive spectrum*. New York: Jason Aronson, 1975.

Schwartz, B. and Williams, D. R. Two different kinds of key peck in the pigeon: Some properties of responses maintained by negative and positive response-reinforcer contingencies. *Journal of the Experimental Analysis of Behavior*, 1972, *18*, 201–216.

Scott, J. P. and Senay, E. C. *Separation and depression: Clinical and research aspects*. Washington: American Association for the Advancement of Science, 1973.

Seligman, M. E. P. Chronic fear produced by unpredictable shock. *Journal of Comparative and Physiological Psychology*, 1968, *66*, 402–411.

———. Control group and conditioning: A comment on operationism. *Psychological Review*, 1969, *76*, 484–491.

Seligman, M. E. P. and Beagley, G. Learned helplessness in the rat. *Journal of Comparative and Physiological Psychology*, 1974, in press.

Seligman, M. E. P. and Binik, Y. The safety signal hypothesis. Submitted, 1974.

Seligman, M. E. P. and Groves, D. Non-transient learned helplessness. *Psychonomic Science*, 1970, *19*, 191–192.

Seligman, M. E. P. and Hager, J. L. (Eds.). *Biological boundaries of learning*. New York: Appleton-Century-Crofts, 1972.

Seligman, M. E. P. and Johnston, J. C. In F. J. McGuigan and D. B. Lumsden (Eds.), *Contemporary approaches to conditioning and learning*. Washington: Winston-Wiley, 1973. Pp. 69–110.

Seligman, M. E. P., and Maier, S. F. Failure to escape traumatic shock. *Journal of Experimental Psychology*, 1967, 74, 1–9.

Seligman, M. E. P. and Meyer, B. Chronic fear and ulcers as a function of the unpredictability of safety. *Journal of Comparative and Physiological Psychology*, 1970, 73, 202–207.

Seligman, M. E. P., Maier, S. F., and Geer, J. The alleviation of learned helplessness in the dog. *Journal of Abnormal and Social Psychology*, 1968, 73, 256–262.

Seligman, M. E. P., Meyer, B., and Testa, T. Appetitive helplessness: Noncontingent reinforcement retards instrumental learning. Unpublished manuscript, University of Pennsylvania, 1971a.

Seligman, M. E. P., Maier, S. F., and Solomon, R. L. Unpredictable and uncontrollable aversive events. In F. R. Brush (Ed.), *Aversive conditioning and learning*. New York: Academic Press, 1971b. Pp. 347–400.

Seligman, M. E. P., Klein, D. C., and Miller, W. Depression. In H. Leitenberg (Ed.), *Handbook of behavior therapy*. Englewood Cliffs, N.J.: Prentice-Hall, 1974a, in press.

Seligman, M. E. P., Rosellini, R. A., and Kozak, M. Learned helplessness in the rat: Reversibility, time course, and immunization. *Journal of Comparative and Physiological Psychology*, 1974b, in press.

Selye, H. *The stress of life.* New York: McGraw-Hill, 1956.

Seward, J. and Humphrey, G. L. Avoidance learning as a function of pretraining in the cat. *Journal of Comparative and Physiological Psychology*, 1967, 63, 338–341.

Shapiro, M. B. and Nelson, E. H. An investigation of the nature of cognitive impairment in co-operative psychiatric patients. *British Journal of Medical Psychology*, 1955, 28, 239–256.

Shimoff, E. H., Schoenfeld, W. N., and Snapper, A. G. Effects of CS presence and duration on suppression of positively reinforced responding in the rat. *Psychological Reports*, 1971, 25, 111–114.

Sidowski, J. B. Psychopathological consequences of induced social helplessness during infancy. In H. D. Kimmel (Ed.), *Experimental psychopathology: Recent research and theory*. New York: Academic Press, 1971. Pp. 231–248.

Sines, J. O., Cleeland, C., and Adkins, J. The behavior of normal and stomach lesion susceptible rats in several learning situations. *Journal of Genetic Psychology*, 1963, 102, 91–94.

Singh, D. Preference for bar pressing to obtain reward over free-loading in rats and children. *Journal of Comparative and Physiological Psychology*, 1970, *73*, 320–327.

Siqueland, E. R. Reinforcement patterns and extinction in human newborns. *Journal of Experimental Child Psychology*, 1968, *6*, 431–432.

Siqueland, E. R. and Lipsitt, L. P. Conditioned head turning behavior in newborns. *Journal of Experimental Child Psychology*, 1966, *3*, 356–376.

Skinner, B. F. "Superstition" in the pigeon. *Journal of Experimental Psychology*, 1948, *38*, 168–172.

————. *The behavior of organisms.* New York: Appleton-Century-Crofts, 1938.

Solomon, R. L. The influence of work on behavior. *Psychological Bulletin*, 1948, *45*, 1–40.

Solomon, R. L. and Corbit, J. D. An opponent-process theory of motivation: I. Temporal dynamics of affect. *Psychological Review*, 1974, *81*, 119–145.

Sowell, T. *Black education: Myths and tragedies.* New York: McKay, 1972.

Spitz, R. Anaclitic depression. *The Psychoanalytic Study of the Child*, 1946, *2*, 313–342.

Staddon, J. E. R. Maladaptive behavior and the concept of linkage. Unpublished manuscript, Duke University, Durham, N.C., 1974.

Staddon, J. E. R. and Simmelhag, V. L. The "superstition" experiment: A reexamination of its implications for the principles of adaptive behavior. *Psychological Review*, 1971, *78*, 3–43.

Staub, E., Tursky, B., and Schwartz, G. E. Self-control and predictability: Their effects on reactions to aversive stimulation. *Journal of Personality and Social Psychology*, 1971, *18*, 157–162.

Stavraky, K. M., Buck, C. N., Lott, J. S., and Wanklin, J. Psychological factors in the outcome of human cancer. *Journal of Psychosomatic Research*, 1968, *12*, 251–259.

Stein, L. Reciprocal action of reward and punishment mechanisms. In R. G. Heath (Ed.), *The role of pleasure in behavior.* New York: Hoeber Medical Division, Harper and Row, 1964. Pp. 113–139.

Steiner, S. S., Beer, B., and Shaffer, M. M. Escape from self produced rates of brain stimulation. *Science*, 1969, *163*, 90–91.

Stolz, S. B. and Lott, D. F. Establishment in rats of a persistent response producing a net loss of reinforcement. *Journal of Comparative and Physiological Psychology*, 1964, *57*, 147–149.

Stotland, E. *The psychology of hope.* San Francisco: Jossey-Bass, 1969.

Stotland, E. and Blumenthal, A. The reduction of anxiety as a result of the expectation of making a choice. *Canadian Journal of Psychology*, 1964, *18*, 139–145.

Strassman, H. D., Thaler, M., and Schein, E. H. A prisoner of war syndrome: Apathy as a reaction to severe stress. *American Journal of Psychiatry*, 1956, *112*, 998–1003.

Stroebel, C. F. Biologic rhythm correlates of disturbed behavior in the rhesus monkey. *Bibliotheca Primatologica*, 1969, *9*, 91–105.

Suomi, S. J. and Harlow, H. F. Depressive behavior in young monkeys subjected to vertical chamber confinement. *Journal of Comparative and Physiological Psychology*, 1972, *80*, 11–18.

Szasz, T. S. *Law, liberty, and psychiatry.* Englewood Cliffs, N.J.: Prentice-Hall, 1963.

Taulbee, E. S. and Wright, H. W. A psycho-social-behavioral model for therapeutic intervention. In C. D. Spielberger (Ed.), *Current topics in clinical and community psychology*, III. New York: Academic Press, 1971. Pp. 92–125.

Teitelbaum, P. Appetite. *Proceedings of the American Philosophical Society*, 1964, *108*, 464–472.

Thomas, D. R., Freeman, F., Svinicki, J. G., Burr, D. E., and Lyons, J. Effects of extradimensional training on stimulus generalization. *Journal of Experimental Psychology*, 1970, *83*, 1–22.

Thomas, E. and Balter, A. Learned helplessness: Amelioration of symptoms by cholinergic blockade of the septum. Submitted, 1974.

Thompson, W. R. Influence of prenatal maternal anxiety on emotionality in young rats. *Science*, 1957, *125*, 698–699.

Thompson, W. R., Watson, J., and Charlesworth, W. R. The effects of prenatal maternal stress on offspring behavior in rats. *Psychological Monographs*, 1962, 76(whole number 557).

Thorndike, E. L. *Animal intelligence: An experimental study of the associative processes in animals.* New York: Columbia University Press, 1898.

Thornton, J. W. and Jacobs, P. D. Learned helplessness in human subjects. *Journal of Experimental Psychology*, 1971, *87*, 369–372.

Tolman, E. C. and Gleitman, H. Studies in learning and motivation: I. Equal reinforcements in both end-boxes, followed by shock in one end-box. *Journal of Experimental Psychology*, 1949, *39*, 810–819.

Underwood, B. J. Retroactive and proactive inhibition after five and forty-eight hours. *Journal of Experimental Psychology*, 1948, *38*, 29–38.

Vietze, P., Watson, J. S., and Dorman, L. Extended infant learning: A comparison of two responses and two visual reinforcers. Paper presented at the meeting of the Society for Research and Child Development, Philadelphia, April 1973.

Wagner, A. R. Stimulus selection and a "modified continuity theory." In G. H. Bower and J. T. Spence (Eds.), *The psychology of learning and motivation*, Vol. 3. New York: Academic Press, 1969. Pp. 1–41.

Wallace, A. F. C. Mazeway disintegration: The individual's perception of socio-cultural disorganization. *Human Organization*, 1956a, *16*, 23–27.

————. *Tornado in Worchester: An exploratory study of individual and community behavior in an extreme situation.* Washington: National Academy of Sciences—National Research Council, Publication 392, Disaster Study No. 3, 1956b.

Walton, D., White, J. G., Black, D. A. and Young, A. J. The modified word-learning test: A cross-validation study. *British Journal of Medical Psychology*, 1959, *32*, 213–220.

Wapner, S., Werner, H., and Kraus, D. M. The effect of success and failure on space localization. *Journal of Personality*, 1957, *25*, 752–756.

Watson, J. B. *Behaviorism.* Chicago: University of Chicago Press, 1924.

Watson, J. S. Memory and "contingency analysis" in infant learning. *Merrill-Palmer Quarterly*, 1967, *13*, 55–76.

————. Cognitive perceptual development in infancy: Setting for the Seventies. *Merrill-Palmer Quarterly*, 1971, *17*, 139–152.

Watson, J. S. and Ramey, C. G. Reactions to response-contingent stimulation in early infancy. *Merrill-Palmer Quarterly*, 1972, *18*, 219–228.

Weiner, B., Frieze, I., Kukla, A., Reed, L., Rest, S., and Rosenbaum, R. M. *Perceiving the causes of success and failure.* Morristown, N.J.: General Learning Press, 1971.

Weisman, A. D. and Kastenbaum, R. The psychological autopsy: A study of the terminal phase of life. *Community Mental Health Journal,* Monograph No. 4. New York: Behavioral Publications, 1968.

Weisman, R. G. and Litner, J. S. Positive conditioned reinforcement and avoidance behavior in rats. *Journal of Comparative and Physiological Psychology,* 1969, 68, 597–603.

Weiss, J. M. Effects of coping response on stress. *Journal of Comparative and Physiological Psychology,* 1968, 65, 251–260.

———. Somatic effects of predictable and unpredictable shock. *Psychosomatic Medicine,* 1970, 32, 397–409.

———. Effects of coping behavior in different warning signal conditions on stress pathology in rats. *Journal of Comparative and Physiological Psychology,* 1971a, 77, 1–13.

———. Effects of punishing the coping response (conflict) on stress pathology in rats. *Journal of Comparative and Physiological Psychology,* 1971b, 77, 14–21.

———. Effects of coping behavior with and without a feedback signal on stress pathology in rats. *Journal of Comparative and Physiological Psychology,* 1971c, 77, 22–30.

Weiss, J. M., Krieckhaus, E. E., and Conte, R. Effects of fear conditioning on subsequent avoidance behavior. *Journal of Comparative and Physiological Psychology,* 1968, 65, 413–421.

Weiss, J. M., Stone, E. A., and Harrell, N. Coping behavior and brain norepinephrine in rats. *Journal of Comparative and Physiological Psychology,* 1970, 72, 153–160.

Weiss, J. M., Glazer, H., and Pohorecky, L. Coping behavior and neurochemical changes in rats. Paper presented at the Kittay Scientific Foundation Conference, New York, March 1974.

Weiss, K. M. and Strongman, K. T. Shock-induced response bursts and suppression. *Psychonomic Science,* 1969, 15, 238–240.

Welker, R. L., Hansen, G., Engberg, L. A., and Thomas, D. R. Reply to Gamzu, Williams, and Schwartz. *Science,* 1973, 181, 368–369.

White, B. L. *Human infants: Experience and psychological development*. Englewood Cliffs, New Jersey: Prentice-Hall, 1971.

White, R. W. Motivation reconsidered: The concept of competence. *Psychological Review*, 1959, *66*, 297–333.

Wilkins, W. Desensitization: Social and cognitive factors underlying the effectiveness of Wolpe's procedure. *Psychological Bulletin*, 1971, *76*, 311–317.

Williams, T. A., Friedman, R. J., and Secunda, S. K. *Special report: The depressive illnesses*. Washington: National Institute of Mental Health, November 1970.

Winokur, G. The types of affective disorders. *Journal of Nervous and Mental Disease*, 1973, *156*, 82–96.

Wintrob, R. M. Hexes, roots, snake eggs? MD vs. occult. *Medical Opinion*, 1972, *1*, No. 7, 54–57.

Wittgenstein, L. *Philosophical investigations*. New York: Macmillan, 1953.

Wolf, S. The bradycardia of the dive reflex—a possible mechanism of sudden death. *Conditional Reflex*, 1967, 2, 192–200.

Wolpe, J. Parallels between animal and human neuroses. In J. Zubin and H. Hunt (Eds.), *Comparative Psychopathology*, New York: Grune and Stratton, 1967. Pp. 305–313.

Wolpe, J. and Lazarus, A. A. *The practice of behavior therapy*. New York: Pergamon, 1969.

Zielinski, K. and Soltysik, S. The effect of pretraining on the acquisition and extinction of the avoidance reflex. *Acta Biologicae Experimentalis*, 1964, 24, 73–87.

Zimbardo, P. G., Haney, C., Banks, W. C., and Jaffe, D. The psychology of imprisonment: Privation, power, and pathology. *Scientific American*, 1974, in press.

NAME INDEX

SUBJECT INDEX

Childhood loss and prevention of
  depression and learned helplessness, 104f
Cholinergic activity of the septum, 70
Cognitions
  of helplessness, 95
  plasticity of, 136f
Cognitive deficits in helplessness,
  52f
Cognitive disturbance, 51
Cognitive representation of a
  contingency, 47f
Cognitive theory of helplessness
  and norepinephrine depletion,
  71f
  versus learned freezing, 64f
Competence, 55
Competing motor response, 62ff
Competitiveness
  lack of in depression, 90
  and uncontrollable rewards, 35f
Conditioned emotional response as an
  index of fear, 114
Conditioning, classical
  and helplessness, 12
  and learning theory, 12
  and response-independent reinforce-
    ment, 19
  and species-specific responses, 19
  and superstitious instrumental
    learning, 20
  and unpredictability, 108ff
Contingency, 11
  analysis, 139ff
  learning, 16
Continuous reinforcement, 13
Controllability, 12, 17
  in childhood and adolescence, 151
  in the classroom, 153
  examples of, 9f
  experience with over trauma, 57ff
  and fear reduction, 54
  institutionalization of, 183ff
  loss of in reactive depression, 94
  and maternal conflicts, 146f

perception of, 31, 101, 131, 137ff
  and persistence at problem solving,
    48
  prior expectations of, 60f
  and response initiation, 49f
  uncertainty of in fear induction,
    53ff
  in voluntary relaxation, 130f
Coping response
  and fear and frustration, 55
  in phobias, 131
  and unpredictability and ulcers,
    120f
Coronary-prone behavior pattern, 180f
Counterconditioning of fear, 129
Crowding, 161ff

Dance of development, 137
Death, 166ff
  by curse, 5, 176f
  feint, 171ff
  from helplessness, 175, 184ff
  of infants, 187
  of loved ones, 178
  parasympathetic, 170
  psychogenic, 176f
  sympathetic, 170
  and tonic immobility, 172
  see also Sudden death
Delayed reinforcement, 52
Depression, 1
  anaclitic, 143f, 187
  biochemical basis of, 91f
  bipolar endogenous, 78
  from crowding, 161ff
  cure of, 100f
  and death from cardiac failure,
    179ff
  and dreams, 89
  drug therapy for, 91f
  endogenous, 78f
  etiology of, 93, 98f
  fear displaced by, 54
  Freudian view of, 89
  graded-task treatment of, 101ff
  individual case histories of, 75f

induced by uncontrollable trauma,
53ff
intellectual deficits caused by, 83
and IQ, 83f
lack of aggression in, 89f
lack of competitiveness in, 90
and learned helplessness, summarized, 106
loss of libido and appetite in, 91
manic, 78
negative cognitive set of, 84f
and noncontingent positive events,
98f
and paralysis of the will, 83
pessimism in, 86
persistence in and cure of, 102f
physiological basis for, 91f
precipitating events of, 93f
prevalence of, 78
prevention of, 104f
in prisoners of war, 183f
and psychomotor retardation, 83
reactive, 78, 93
resistance to, summarized, 99
self-devised remedies for, 103
social deficits of, 84
success as cause of, 98f
success therapy for, 87f
suicidal, 2
symptoms of, 77, 82f, 92f
therapy for, 91f, 105f
unipolar endogenous, 78
and vulnerability to disease, 181f
and vulnerability to heart attack,
180
Developmental studies of uncontrollability, 58f, 148ff
Differential reinforcement of other
behavior (DRO), 15
Directive therapy, 56f
Disaster syndrome, 40
Drive
to avoid helplessness, 55
to master events in the environment, 55
to resist compulsion in wild
animals, 55

Ego strength, 151, 159f
Electroconvulsive shock, 99, 103
Emergency death, 170
Emotion, plasticity of, 136
Emotional disturbance in helpless-
ness, 40ff, 53ff
Emotional exhaustion, biochemical
view of, 67
Emotionality, heightened, and unpre-
dictability and ulcers, 120f
Endogenous depression, 78
and belief in helplessness, 94
treatment of, 79
Endogenous-reactive continuum, 94
Environmentalism, 135
Escape-avoidance learning, 22f
Etiology of depression
control of reinforcers in, 96ff
extinction in, 95f
and learned helplessness, 93
loss of reinforcers in, 89, 95f
Executive monkey, 41f, 117f
Expectations of control, 48f, 60f
Expectations of success
in depression, 86
in learned helplessness, 38
Externality, 30
Extinction, 13, 95f

Failure
in childhood, 4f
in the classroom, attribution of, 157
inexperience with, 105
maternal transmission of, 148f
and positive feedback, 4f
symbols of, 4f
Fear, 53, 55, 112
chronic, 122f
as a coping response, 55
counterconditioning of, 129
in hopeless situations, 55
as motivator, 55
trauma-induced, 55
and unpredictability, 114
Fear states, indicators of, 114

Insight-oriented therapy, 100f
Institutional care of infants, 143ff
Institutionalized helplessness, 181ff
Intellectual deficits caused by depression, 83
Interference with responding, 52
Intermittent reinforcement, 14
  of other behavior, 16
Internality, 30
IQ, 83f, 163f

Laboratory phobias, 79
Learned freezing versus cognitive deficit, 64f
Learned helplessness, 23, 28f
  characteristics of, 6
  and depression summarized, 106
  etiology of, 93
  and expectancy of success, 38
  as a model of depression, 79ff
  negative cognitive set of, 37f
  physiological symptoms of, 82
  prevention of, 104f
  symptoms of, 82
  therapy for, 105f
  time course of, 40f
  see also Helplessness
Learned laziness, 35
Learning
  artifacts of, 19
  contingency, 16
  instrumental, 12
  magic-moment, 14, 16, 18
  one-trial, 155
  theory of, 12f
  win-stay, lose-shift, 155
Learning set, 154
Limits on helplessness, 59ff
Locus of control, 30
Loss
  of appetite in learned helplessness, 82
  childhood, and prevention of learned helplessness, 104f

of libido and appetite in depression, 91
of self-esteem, sudden death from, 178
of status, sudden death from, 178

Magic-moment learning, 14, 16, 18
Manic depression, 78
Mastery of events in environment, 55, 104
Maternal communication of helplessness, 148f
Maternal deprivation, 143f
  and autistic behavior in monkeys, 145
  and enrichment of control, 146
  and surrogate mother, 145
Mesmerism, 171ff
Methohexitone, 130
Monoamine oxidase (MAO) inhibitor, 91
Morasmus, 143f
Motivation
  development of, 134, 150
  fear and frustration as, 55
  plasticity of, 136
Motivational deficits, 23ff
  and adaptation to trauma, 66
  time course of, 40
  from uncontrollable trauma, 22
Motivational disturbance and expectation of control, 49f

Negative cognitive set, 1, 37f
  in depression, 84ff
  as a symptom of learned helplessness, 82
Neurosis, experimental, 43f, 79
Noise, uncontrollable, 31
Noncontingent positive events in depression, 98f
Norepinephrine depletion, 67, 69, 71f
  and cholinergic activity in depression, 91

species-specific, 19

Response contingency space, 16

Response-outcome contingencies,
14ff, 139
and cognitive integration, 17f
and what can be learned, 39

Response-outcome dependence, 17

Response-outcome independence, 13,
16
proactive interference by, 51

Response initiation
debilitation of as a result of uncontrollability, 34
and expectation of controllability,
49f
fear-elicited, 55

Revolution, 165

Safety-signal hypothesis, 112ff, 115

Secondary gain, 102

Secondary impotence, 132

Self-administration of aversive
stimulation, 125ff

Self-appraisal. See Negative cognitive
set

Sensitization, objections to, 67

Separation
as cause of death, 174f, 187
from mother, 54, 144

Septal stimulation, 28
as cause of helplessness, 70
passivity and lethargy caused by, 70

Shock-elicited aggression, 32

Social deficits
produced experimentally, 90f
as symptoms of depression, 84

Species-specific responses, 19

"Spoiled brat" design, 35

Status loss and sudden death, 178

Success
as cause of depression, 98f
therapeutic effects of in depression,
87f
perception of in helplessness, 37ff

unbroken, as cause of helplessness,
158f

Sudden death, 5, 171ff
developmental studies of, 171
and helplessness, 59, 169f
and major life changes, 181
precipitating factors of, 178
psychosomatic, 5
of wild animals in captivity, 173f
see also Death

Superstition experiments, 18

Superstitious instrumental learning,
20, 63f

Symbols of failure, 4f

Sympathetic death, 170

Systematic desensitization, 127, 129ff

Tachycardia, 170

Time course
of depression, 68, 88f
of helplessness, 40f, 60, 82

Tonic immobility
and death, 172
in helplessness, 171ff
and uncontrollability, 171f

Transfer of helplessness, 31ff

Trauma
fear and frustration induced by, 54f
reduction of, 64
of separation, 54

Triadic design, 25

Tricyclics as antidepressants, 91

Tuscaloosa plan, 101

Ulcers and unpredictability, 116ff,
120f

Uncontrollability, 9, 16
and breakdown of appetitive discrimination, 42f
components of, 11
depletion of norepinephrine by, 69
developmental studies of, 58f, 148ff
emotional effects of, 28
examples of, 10
frustration due to followed by

Uncontrollability (*continued*)
    helplessness, 54
  and hopelessness, 59
  and involuntary relaxation, 130f
  and loss of appetite, 42
  and motivational disturbance, 49f
  neurological effects of, 68f
  of noise, 31
  physiological consequences of, 68f
  and poverty, 159
  of reward, 34f
  symptoms of not studied in
    depression, 92
  and tonic immobility, 171f
  vulnerability to illness and death
    caused by 181ff

Uncontrollable rewards and competitiveness, 35f

Uncontrollable trauma
  and depression, 53
  and motivational deficits, 22

Unpredictability, 108ff
  and anxiety, 3, 107
  and fear, 114
  and level of active responding, 119ff
  and classical conditioning, 108ff
  and separation anxiety, 151ff
  and stomach ulcers, 116ff

Unsolvable followed by solvable
  problems, 54

Unteachable children, 4f, 153f
  use of Chinese characters by, 4f,
    156

Voluntary responding, 11, 13
  Aristotelian view of, 50
  Galilean view of, 50

Voodoo death, 176f

Vulnerability to helplessness,
  developmental, 58f

"Welfare state" of pigeons, 35